Fresh Heart for a New Day

Finding Joy for Your Journey

Paul Walterman

Copyright:
ISBN: 1497533694
ISBN 13: 9781497533691
Library of Congress Control Number: 2014906409
CreateSpace Independent Publishing Platform
North Charleston, South Carolina

Introduction

Sometimes we just need to stop.

And not just to smell the roses. There are other reasons to occasionally hit the pause button, even if only for a couple of minutes.

We typically move too fast to see some of God's greatest work taking place all around us. The noise in our lives keeps us from hearing God's still small voice. In today's world of 'fast and faster', 'loud and louder', we need to slow down to match his unhurried pace and quiet directions.

Fresh Heart For a New Day is a compilation of 365 devotions, written over the last ten years. A lot has happened during those years. There have been interstate moves, additional grandchildren added to the mix, the marriage of our oldest grandson and a myriad of insignificant happenings with very significant meanings.

Hopefully, some of those meanings come through on these pages.

It won't take you long to realize that this isn't a normal 'devotional book.' It's a bit eclectic in its make-up. A typical day's reading won't be typical. You'll be left with a challenge ... or a prod to move ahead spiritually ... or a new way of looking at an old truth.

I worry that as we mine God's Word for words to live by and for truth to anchor our souls in a turbulent era, we often leave valuable nuggets under the soil. Think of a Fresh Heart devotional as a spiritual 'metal detector' to help you get more of God's Word into your life in a practical way.

And as you move from day to day ... always insist on and experience joy for your journey!

January 1

Mercy For a New Year

"But there's one other thing I remember, and remembering,
I keep a grip on hope: God's loyal love couldn't have run
out, his merciful love couldn't have dried up. They're
created new every morning. How great your faithfulness!"
(Lamentations 3:21-23 The Message)

I see a lot more sunrises in the winter than I do any other time
of year. And it's not because my sleep patterns change. It has everything to do with the fact that this time of year the sun hangs
around Southern California a lot more than it hangs around
Seattle.

But even given the romantic theme of the setting sun, I'm
kind of partial to the rising sun. Every one reminds me of a very
comforting Biblical principle…that God commits Himself to being merciful to us every new day.

It's like getting a renewed gift subscription to Mercy
Magazine in every day's mail. Like receiving a personal invitation to a new screening of "God's Amazing Mercy" every evening. Like finding love notes from God in your sock drawer…
in the kitchen cupboard where you keep your coffee cups…like
turning on your car radio every morning to God, in his an-
nouncer voice, saying, "Here I am again and have I got wonderful things planned for you!"

And so this New Year becomes another milestone for each
of us. It becomes the capstone on another 365 days of God's
continuing mercy. The truth of the matter is, God's first response is to deal with us in mercy…it's built into his very nature.
We, however, keep blinking in surprise when it overtakes us
every day.

It's going to be a wonderful year because we have an absolutely wonderful Father!

Happy (mercy-filled) New Year! Enjoy joy.

January 2
The Doorway

We've just stepped through the transitional door from last year into this new one. How did you take that step?

Was it with cautious skepticism because of a less-than ideal ending year? Or did you hit the door running…almost knocking it off its hinges in your enthusiasm to see what the coming year holds? Did you approach the door slowly with head turned back nostalgically, not wanting to let go of what was a very special season of your life?

The actual day of January 1st is not magical in any sense. It will be remarkably like the previous day except, depending on where you live, with two or three additional minutes of daylight to spend. So while the day isn't particularly unusual, its place on your calendars makes it special. It represents both an end and a beginning … at the same time. And for some, that creates unique pressures and many times, very distinctive opportunities.

A lot of years ago I wrote the following phrase in the front of my Bible… "This too shall pass." It's a great reminder to me of the cycles of life. There are times when the 'tide is in' and other times when the 'tide is out.' At the moment I may be riding high. Everything I touch turns, if not to gold, at least to satisfaction. And at other times, the bottom is somewhere far above me and I literally 'can't get no satisfaction.' Knowing that either end of the spectrum is transitory somehow helps me see with more clarity.

The Apostle Paul said it well: *"…for I have learned how to get along happily whether I have much or little. I know how to live on almost nothing or with everything. I have learned the secret of living in every situation, whether it is with a full stomach or empty, with plenty or little. For I can do everything with the help of Christ who gives me the strength I need." Philippians 4:11-13 New Living Translation*

Sometimes it takes as much of God's grace and help to get down off the mountain, as it does to climb up out of a deep valley. My need of his presence does not diminish when things are going well.

So as I begin this new year, there's not much about it I know in advance. But I've got a companion in Jesus who has given me a history that produces faith and excitement about the future. I am ready for anything *"…with the help of Christ who gives me the strength I need."*

January 3
New Things

The first time I wasn't in church on New Year's Eve was the first year Joanie and I were married. We said good bye to the old and rang in the new eating pizza with another couple. It was appropriate to be eating because the high point of the New Year's Eve "Watch Night" service was always the incredible potluck that the Scandinavians were famous for.

But now I'm older and can eat pickled herring and sliced ham on hard rolls any time I desire. New Year's eve is now just another way to measure my passage through life and give myself time to reflect and consider just how quickly that passage is happening.

So as I sit here the first week of the new year, am I concerned about the standard resolutions? Am I hung up on my weight? Do I need a new and dynamic attitude to get me through the coming year? Are there more things I'd like to have in my garage?

Not really.

But I am concerned about several 'new' things that could make a huge difference in my life and in the lives of those I come in contact with. For instance, this verse is big on my list of desires for the coming year: *"And I will give you a new heart with new and right desires, and I will put a new spirit in you. I will take out your stony heart of sin and give you a new, obedient heart."* Ezekiel 36:26 *New Living Translation* This year I want to want what God wants. Period. I long for a soft heart, easily touched by the needs of others and easily molded by the Potter.

Another 'new' is found in Psalms. *"He has given me a new song to sing, a hymn of praise to our God. Many will see what he has done and be astounded. They will put their trust in the Lord."* Psalm 40:3 *New Living Translation* Some songs get old quick. I no longer get a blessing out of the twelve verses of "Nobody Knows The Trouble I've Seen." It leaves me feeling cold and empty. So this week and this whole year I'm learning a brand new song … one that pre-Christians will relate to. It's a song about the awesome relationship I have with the Father, with verses depicting his immense love, his mercy and ability and desire to be patient with us. It's a song I won't necessarily sing, but will live out.

I will sing this song even if I don't believe anyone is listening because it will bubble up from deep within me at all times. And just imagine the sound and the impact if we all joined in and spread this 'new song' to every corner of our culture!

Go with joy on your journey.

January 4

Giving Up Control

This is an ode to the 'control freak' spirit that lives quietly in some of us and boisterously in others.

No one likes to be out of control, but the matter has more to do with losing control of the circumstances and decisions of our lives than it does with our lives falling apart. And one of the major things some of us seek to take command over, is the issue of timing. Shortly before Jesus left earth for heaven following his resurrection, his disciples excitedly asked Him, *"Master, are you going to restore the kingdom to Israel now? Is this the time?"* Acts 1:6 *The Message*

Good question, but for some the inquiry smacks of a desire to be 'in the know' to retain a certain knowledge superiority over others. Plus we feel more secure if we think we know exactly what is coming down the pike. So imagine the dismay these followers of Jesus must have felt when He responded *"You don't get to know the time. Timing is the Father's business." Acts 1:7 The Message*

If you would like to know what's ahead in the coming year, join the club. If you long to control not only the circumstances of your life, but the chronological order in which you'd like them to occur (or not occur, in many cases) you are not alone. But to any follower of Jesus… to anyone serious about his Lordship in his life…the fact that timing is in God's hands is both threatening to our sense of independence, but also, one of the most comforting of all the aspects of God's love in our lives.

Begin the process of giving God absolute right to order your steps throughout this year. And having made the decision, be prepared to keep making it…daily if necessary, until the evidence begins piling up. In time you will see wonderful examples of his way making sense…of his plan besting yours… of his timing saving you time, energy, sorrow and confusion. As the song says, 'when you can't trace his hand, trust his heart.'

Allow God to give you an incredible year and enjoy the journey.

January 5
Not Exactly

"Did you take the prescription as I instructed? "Not exactly. I was feeling better the second day so threw the rest away."

"Did you fill out the application precisely as I told you to?" "Not exactly. I didn't think some of the information asked for was important."

"Did you read all the instructions before attempting to put the swing set together?" "Not exactly. Maybe that's why I have so many pieces left over!"

We don't always comply with the directives given us in life. And even when we do it's often not done 'exactly' as requested. Spiritually this short-circuits much of what God is attempting to do for us and through us.

I am seriously impressed with some of my Bible heroes. Take Noah ... whose instructions were specific, but made little sense. *"So Noah did everything exactly as God had commanded him." Genesis 6:22 New Living Translation* Out of absolute obedience came the salvation of the planet!

Peter and Andrew's successful life mission began when they 'immediately' responded to Jesus' command to leave their careers behind. Joseph received divine instructions via angels and obeyed at the moment and without question.

The start of a brand new year would be an excellent time to purpose in our hearts that our obedience to the King would be total and prompt. No more 'selective hearing' and compromised obedience. No more second-guessing ... no more holding back until we understand how it will all work out. No more "Listen, Lord, for your servant speaketh", but a lot more "Speak Lord, for your servant heareth!"

May you follow obediently and quickly this year and then experience more joy for your journey than you thought possible!

January 6
Let Him

The more I study God's Word and reflect back on His interaction with me over the years, the more sure I am that He does have good plans in mind for me ... plans that will give me both a future and a hope.

From the earliest pages of Scripture we are introduced to a God who has thought a lot about our future and has every intention of bringing it successfully to pass. In Genesis He offers a lifestyle of fulfilling activity and divine relationship. After sin ruins those plans, He offers a fresh start.

He has a beautiful land as an inheritance for his people. He has victory after victory available as they take that land. He promises his permanent presence and the use of his might against all enemies. It's all there ... the exquisite intentions and the power and plan to accomplish every bit of it.

And that's what makes reading the second half of the Old Testament so frustrating. God is always saying, "I wanted to ... but you wouldn't!" At times you can almost hear the catch in His voice and see a tear coursing down His cheek as He speaks through His prophets about the consequences of failing to let Him be a good God to His people.

God has wonderful gifts to lavish on you this year. **Let Him!** He has places He would like to take you. **Let Him!** He has victories over your enemies and addictions and failures He wants to give you. **Let Him!**

♦ This isn't the year to run away, but to draw close.
♦ This isn't the year to let go, but to hang on.
♦ This isn't the year to wither, but to bloom.
♦ This isn't the year to surrender, but to stand.
♦ This isn't the year to question, but to trust.

You've never been better positioned for God to take you to your personal 'Promised Land' and to astound you with his powerful plans. This year don't fight Him ... let Him!

> *"Take delight in the Lord, and he will give you your heart's desires. Psalm 37:4 New Living Translation*

May you enjoy much joy on your journey!

January 7
The Violinist

I heard the story of a world famous violinist playing to an over-flow crowd in a large American city concert hall. He finished his first song to thunderous applause and to the utter amazement of everyone in attendance … broke his violin over the back of a chair. The audience gasped.

Everyone knew that he played on an incredibly rare and costly Stradivarius that was worth more than the average person could conceive. In fact, the violin and not the violinist were prominently featured in all the news stories about the concert. That morning, for instance, one newspaper even ran a close up picture of this almost priceless instrument.

When the crowd had quieted he told them he had gone to a local pawn shop that morning and had picked up a violin for $30, then put new strings on it. It was that relic with which he had opened his concert.

"I just wanted you to know," he explained "that the violinist is more important than the violin." Point made.

We live in a culture that makes much of the violin. It's the education, the charisma, the money, the entrepreneurial skill. But to any of us who have walked with God for any length of time and have the humility to admit it … it's the Violinist who makes it all happen. At least the stuff that's the most important and that will last the longest.

So go ahead and put some new strings on your old violin and throw a little polish on it. But never forget that without the Violinist drawing his bow over your life and producing the music, there's nothing happening.

"We carry this precious Message around in the unadorned clay pots of our ordinary lives. That's to prevent anyone from confusing God's incomparable power with us." II Corinthians 4:7 The Message

January 8

Goodness and Grace

In "The Sound of Music," one of Hollywood's most memorable movies, there is a romantic scene in a moonlit gazebo when Julie Andrews, playing Maria, makes a heart-stopping discovery. The man she has grown to love reveals that he also loves her. As she dances in his arms and the violins soar, she sings a song of searching her memory bank for a clue as to what has brought her this incredible gift of love.

Her assumption? She must have been something good to have caused favor.

And so it is that when God delivers a wonderful blessing in our lives, we immediately begin combing the archives of our memories for some indication of what we had done to deserve it. But God's goodness in our lives is not meant to produce angst, frantic recollections or apologies. It's meant to produce gratitude.

Vainly attempting to locate the justification for the display of God's good hand in our lives is pointless. If any of us got what we deserved it certainly wouldn't be a 'blessing.' Eugene Peterson's Message says it this way: *"Immense in mercy and with an incredible love, he embraced us. He took our sin dead lives and made us alive in Christ. He did all this on his own, with no help from us! Then He picked us up and set us down in highest heaven in company with Jesus, our Messiah. Now God has us where he wants us, with all the time in this world and the next to shower grace and kindness upon us in Christ Jesus." Ephesians 2:4-6 The Message*

A lot of us have a difficult time understanding how something insanely wonderful could ever evolve from something we can't remember doing. And that's just it … it didn't! It all comes from the loving heart of our Heavenly Father. Celebrate that and quit trying to find something in your sorry past that set you up for such a lavish display of love. You won't find it. Be insanely joyful over this incredibly good news!

*"Every desirable and beneficial gift comes out of heaven.
The gifts are rivers of light cascading down from the Father
of Light. There is nothing deceitful in God, nothing two-
faced, nothing fickle. He brought us to life using the true
Word, showing us off as the crown of all his creatures."
James 1:17,18 The Message*

January 9

Lotsa People Syndrome

It's called the 'Lotsa People Syndrome'

It means we feel so much better when we're surrounded and backed up by a huge crowd. If our viewpoint is supported by the majority we feel more confident defending it. If our path is applauded by the masses we assume we're headed in the right direction. If our actions parallel those of the hoards, then consensus eggs us on.

But God seldom works with the majority. Democracy isn't the pervading operating system of his Kingdom. It operates on eternals laws …tested principles and the unwavering obedience of its adherents. What makes it work is God's utter trustworthiness and the integrity of every Word He utters. He can be trusted. As Jonathan told his armor bearer: *"…nothing can hinder the Lord. He can win a battle whether he has many warriors or only a few!"* I Samuel 14:6 New Living Translation

So don't feel sorry for poor Gideon with his 300 when he could have had 32,000 to go up against the Midianites. His was a promised victory that wasn't dependent on strength of numbers. Don't waste any sympathy on little boy David facing an adversary twice his height and three times his weight. He was fighting a prepared battle with the outcome already determined by God.

And don't feel bad for yourself when the enemy comes in like a flood and you can't seem to locate your life jacket. Just remember that underneath you are the Everlasting Arms of the One who has never lost a battle. Simply smile at the enemy knowing that once again he has picked on somebody who has a strong Defender.

Lotsa people? Don't need them!

January 10
The Good and the Bad

As we move along in life we encounter things so horrific … so difficult … so discouraging … that had we known they were coming we'd have gotten off the bus at the previous stop.

Other serendipitous delights so overwhelmed us with joy that we may not have gotten anything else done in life just reveling in the fact that they were coming. A case in point … had I known that being married to Joanie was going to bring such pleasure and satisfaction to my life, I probably would have opted to elope at 14!

The Shepherd Boy's words in Psalm 139: 15,16 come to mind here. *"You watched me as I was being formed in utter seclusion, as I was woven together in the dark of the womb. You saw me before I was born. Every day of my life was recorded in your book. Every moment was laid out before a single day had passed." New Living Translation*

When you lay this passage alongside the words of Jeremiah 29:11 some thing wonderful emerges. This prophet wrote God's heart when He told his people, *"For I know the plans I have for you … they are plans for good and not for disaster, to give you a future and a hope."*

So we come away with the realization that all the stuff that comes into our lives has already been previewed by God and fits into the scope of His overarching desire to give us a hopeful future. That means the good, the bad and the truly ugly. God redeems it all for his ultimate purpose.

How can God possibly take 'everything', knowing that it includes some really bad stuff and turn it into something beautiful and valuable? I haven't got a clue.

But neither do I understand how an ugly caterpillar is able to seclude itself briefly and reappear as a majestic Monarch butterfly. But it does.

January 11

Sticks Into Trees

"Faith is the confidence that what we hope for will actually happen;
it gives us assurance about things we cannot see."
Hebrews 11:1 New Living Translation

I love being around 'glass half-full' people ... who see through obstacles and the obvious to what isn't presently available to our five senses. I love people who believe in God, themselves and others. They are a rare breed in today's cynical environment.

My good friend Brad is one of these optimists. He encouraged me to buy 9 sticks a year ago. Of course, to get someone to buy them they were labeled 'fruit trees' by the nursery. To this purchase we continued on ... in faith ... and invested in an underground watering system. Then came the three hundred feet of trenching through cement-like desert soil. Finally we added fencing around each stick so the rabbits wouldn't eat the bark off of it.

And then we waited ... Brad with barely contained excitement; me with carefully concealed apprehension and a bit of suspicion over what to expect.

That was then. Now the trees are proudly displaying a variety of blossoms in all their glory.

The sticks turned into trees whose blossoms promise a fruitful and delicious future. But I needed someone who had been there and done that to convince me that there really was life and fruit in those sticks.

For me, it's been a lesson in faith and believing. Brad has proven to be trustworthy. I'd buy more sticks that turn into trees at his suggestion. My Heavenly Father is even more worthy of my trust and confidence. Daily I'm called upon to believe, not what is readily confirmed by what I see and hear and feel … but on a far more stable platform … the words of Almighty God.

I desire God to reveal his will, his intentions and his abilities to me through his Word. And then I want, more than anything else, the ability to agree with Him regardless of competing viewpoints.

There was fruit in those spindly sticks that I didn't see. I want to be able to not only see the fruit, but enjoy the fruit of those 'God-gifts' that aren't here yet … but are coming!

January 12
Heartbreak Hill

Starting at about mile sixteen of the Boston Marathon, runners encounter the first of four small hills called the 'Newton Hills'. If a competitor in this historic race emotionally and physically 'hits the wall' it will generally come at the fourth hill … appropriately named "Heartbreak Hill."

Nobody wins the Boston Marathon who quits at "Heartbreak Hill".

With a vertical rise of only 88 feet it shouldn't be that big a deal. But a combination of things make this hill difficult. First, it's at the point in the race where the racer's muscle store of glycogen is likely to be depleted. Second, immediately preceding this hill has been a nice long stretch of downhill running. The hard part is behind us we are tempted to think. And third, the mind and body scream out "Oh no ... another hill. Are they ever going to end?

Boston marathoners aren't the only ones familiar with "Heartbreak Hill". Every life has them. They tax the strength and resolve of the bravest and strongest.

- ♦ when you hear only the doctor's voice and God hasn't said a thing in a long, long time ... you're there!
- ♦ when you paid your last house payment a year ago and there's absolutely no way you'll ever catch up ... you're there!
- ♦ when the only news coming from any source in your life is bad news ... you're there!
- ♦ When an old destructive bondage returns to your life after a period of freedom and you can't break it ... you're there!
- ♦ when quitting is the only option that comes to mind ... you're there!

This is when 'keeping the faith' is vital, but also the time when we feel like we have no more faith to keep. The floodwaters have covered every recognizable landmark and we're paddling to keep the water under us – not in us.

The Apostle Paul was a "Heartbreak Hill" veteran. He finished his race because he never quit on that incline! His counsel? *"Be prepared. You're up against far more than you can handle on your own. Take all the help you can get, every weapon God has issued so that when it's all over but the shouting you'll still be on your feet."* Ephesians 6:12,13 The Message

Remember ... you've come too far to quit now. Up ahead is the finish line and the One who stands ready to commend you for faithfulness, valor and perseverance is the same One who runs this race by your side. So look around for help. Stay in the Word. Enlist prayer partners. Don't seclude yourself from fellow believers. This is your race to win!

January 13
Only One God

Hear, O Israel: The Lord our God, the Lord is one. Love the Lord your God with all your heart and with all your soul and with all your strength.

These commandments that I give you today are to be upon your hearts. Impress them on your children. Talk about them when you sit at home and when you walk along the road, when you lie down and when you get up. Tie them as symbols on your hands and bind them on your foreheads. Write them on the doorframes of your houses and on your gates. Deuteronomy 6:4-9 NIV

God worked hard to turn his people Israel from multi-theism to mono-theism. He revealed Himself to them in so many ways, all of which pointed to his supremacy. Other nations had multiple gods, but not Israel. "The Lord our God, the Lord is one!"

May I be so bold as to say that God's people today, the Body of Christ, still struggles with the same issue. It's not that we don't believe it theologically … but at times don't live it out practically.

We worship our work. It becomes all consuming. We worship our week-ends. They often end up providing us with little in the way of 'Sabbath rest.' We worship our entertainment. It disquiets our hearts, making true communion with the Father almost an impossibility. We worship our future security. The 501K has eliminated our need to trust. We even at times, worship our religion. The rituals become a tawdry, cheap imitation of life-satisfying relationships.

So once again the command to worship God as the only god in our lives needs to become our greatest heart hunger. Our kids deserve to know a God like this – One who takes preeminence over everything else in life. They need to be impressed by the God of their parents. The breathtaking attributes of God ... his omniscience, his omnipotence, his omnipresence ... alongside his mercy, justice, compassion and patience must be discussed at home, in the car, before bedtime and during breakfast.

Failing this, our faith becomes little more than an ongoing competition between the multiple gods who attempt to give our life meaning, and the One True God who is the only One who can.

May you have joy on your journey!

January 14

Brought Out To Be Taken In

So Moses said to the people, "This is a day to remember forever—the day you left Egypt, the place of your slavery. Today the Lord has brought you out by the power of his mighty hand. Exodus 13:3 New Living Translation

Take possession of the land and settle in it, because I have given it to you to occupy. Numbers 33:53 New Living Translation

Here at Fresh Heart Ministries having 'joy for your journey' is important to us. But comprehending the 'purpose of your journey' is even more vital.

When God miraculously brought Israel out of Egypt only part of his plan was fulfilled at that point. He *brought them out* in order to *take them in* to his promise for their future. Leaving slavery was just the introduction to his ultimate blessings in their lives.

And so it is with us. As Christians we too have been '*brought out by the power of his mighty hand.*' Our escape is no less miraculous. Those who once owned us and controlled our lives can no longer be seen in our rear view mirror. But the release is only the beginning.

In 1978 Phil Johnson wrote a song that was later recorded by the Imperials. The chorus said this:

> *He didn't bring us this far to leave us; He didn't teach us to swim to let us drown; He didn't build His home in us to move away; He didn't lift us up to let us down*

Ultimately our 'promised land' will be heaven. But there are many other 'waypoints' in life that are God-intended destinations along the way. And they are just as important in the scheme of things as our ultimate port of call.

See today as a vital part of God's intentions for your tomorrow. Don't minimize the substance of that which lies between being 'brought out' and being 'taken in.' There is eternal value to each step in your journey. God has big and wonderful plans for your life and they are in effect in you right at the moment. Enjoy the journey, but learn to appreciate God's purpose in it. And be joyful!

January 15
Great!

I loved asking my three year old grandson how he was doing.

"Great" he would respond enthusiastically. It was his standard answer no matter what was going on in his little world. He may have misplaced his favorite toy car, just learned that he'd have to take an early nap or pinched his finger in the doorway. Yet he was always "Great"!

His grandpa Paul is a lot like that in his thinking. It isn't mind over matter, nor is it just my emotional make-up. It is more than my predisposition that tips me in the direction of the positive.

I have had many decades to observe the goodness and faithfulness of God at work in my life and in the world around me. Doom and gloom? Predictions of disaster? The possibilities of failure and disappointment? Sure, they're all there. But stronger far than any of them singly or taken together is the unbelievable goodness of God at work on my behalf.

Who can fault the Apostle Paul's logic when he asks, *"He who did not spare his own Son, but gave him up for us all – how will he not also, along with him, graciously give us all things?"* Romans 8:32 NIV

So when we're asked how we're doing and we respond with "Great", our answer may have more to do with our confidence in God than a factual report on the immediate circumstances. We live by faith, not by sight … and although we'd rather see the victory than wait in faith for it to come, the experience grows our faith if we allow it to.

So what testimony will you share with your world today? Are you still waiting for all the reports to come in? Are you withholding a verdict until you see it all lining up as you wish it to? Or is your confidence in what has been promised, even though it isn't currently discernable?

> *"Now faith is being sure of what we hope for and certain of what we do not see." Hebrews 11:1 NIV*

January 16

Second String

There is a drive in many to lead.

They want to sit 'first chair' … to be picked first for the team … to stand out as the one to follow or emulate. They want clear air in front of them, not the taillights of someone else's life.

We look up to these people. We are pulled along by their strong management and vision. These entrepreneurs spawn books, get the television interviews, speak and people listen. Percentage wise, there are not that many who fit into this principal position. And this devotional really isn't about them.

The truth is, these frontrunners can't get the job done by themselves. Occasionally they fail or fall or both. And when the dust settles a truth is made apparent ... leaders are not leaders if not being followed. As John Maxwell has said for years, "If you thinketh yourself a leader and no one followeth, you are simply taking a walk!"

Let's hear it for the 'second string'! If you were an archer in the Middle Ages you never left home without a second string for your bow, in case the first string broke in the middle of a battle. The 'second string' could mean the difference between victory and defeat ... between living and dying. It was that crucial.

One of my heroes from Scripture is Andrew (Simon Peter's brother). As a matter of fact, he is rarely named without us being told that he is Simon Peter's brother. As a 'second stringer' living in the enormous shadow of a superstar, Andrew played his part with grace and aplomb. Without jealousy or striving he used his life and his gifts to further the work and purposes of God.

It seems like every time we visit Andrew (Simon Peter's brother) he is bringing people to Jesus. We find him bringing some Greeks to meet Jesus. He is the one who brought the little boy with the lunch that ultimately fed 5,000 plus. And truth be known, there would never have been 'first chair' Peter if Andrew (his brother) hadn't introduced him to Jesus.

So celebrate your role and play it extraordinarily well. If you sit first chair, do it with humility as well as skill. But if your part reads "Second Trumpet" as mine did in school, play it with all the gusto and exuberance you can.

Your second part may just save the day and tip the tide of the battle!

> *"The body we're talking about is Christ's body of chosen people. Each of us finds our meaning and function as a part of his body. But as a chopped-off finger or cut-off toe we wouldn't amount to much, would we? So since we find ourselves fashioned into all these excellently formed and marvelously functioning parts in Christ's body, let's just go ahead and be what we were made to be, without enviously or pridefully comparing ourselves with each other, or trying to be something we aren't." Romans 12:4,5 The Message*

January 17
He's Still Awesome

> *"By the word of the LORD the heavens were made, And all the host of them by the breath of His mouth. He gathers the waters of the sea together as a heap; He lays up the deep in storehouses." (Psalm 33:6-7, NKJV)*

Does God still awe us?

Are we more impressed with what He made than in the fact that He made it? In a time when we 'supersize' everything from French fries to our homes, does God come across as 'down-sized' and uninspiring?

Like that once new car that now languishes at the curb, do we need an atomizer to bring back that 'new God' smell? Sitting in church do we yawn through "How Great Thou Art" (… when I in awesome wonder …)? Does friendship with this God still send a shiver down our spine with its breathtaking possibilities?

Almost everything in our world tends to minimize God while exalting everything else. It's why the average person seldom thinks about Him. But we're not average, because this God is our Father. We're intimately related and his life touches every area of ours.

So … if the thrill is gone, it's not because He's become less awesome. We've become less aware.

So live in his Word, watch for evidence of his work, listen for his voice. He is still the God whose voice breaks the cedars (Psalm 29:5), whose work is worth reporting (Psalm 64:9), and whose word is astonishing (Mark 10:24).

Stridently fight the trend of worshiping a less-than-awesome God. His presence can't be duplicated by a can of air freshener or an old Sunday School lesson!

May you find joy for your journey!

January 18
Time Zones

Time zones!

Standing in the pre-dawn darkness of the Hawaiian Islands I place a call to Florida. "Good afternoon" comes the reply! The six hour time difference is difficult to comprehend. And then there are the calls to me at 3:30 a.m. from friends on the East Coast who wonder why I'm not up yet.

Time has a way of weaving both sense and nonsense into our lives. There is never enough *time*. We had a wonderful *time*. *Times* are definitely changing. If I get the *time* I'll do such and so. And occasionally, but not often, we have *time* on our hands.

Time both enriches and enrages us. It has the capability of ruining our lives with pressure or blessing us with grand memories of what took place during it. But the day is coming when time shall be no more. The Book of Revelations talks about a coming period when there will no longer be any night. That in itself would powerfully effect the commodity of time. But beyond that an even stronger definer of time will be dealt with.

There will be no more death!

And with no more death time will be meaningless…because we'll have all there is of it. Literally! So, while operating under the dictates of time…while adhering to its demanding schedules…I look forward to the end of its tyranny. When Jesus returns (and He certainly will), He will follow a script described in First Corinthians fifteen by Eugene Peterson in The Message: *"But let me tell you something wonderful, a mystery I'll probably never fully understand. We're not all going to die – but we are all going to be changed. You hear a blast to end all blasts from a trumpet, and in the time that you look up and blink your eyes – it's over. On signal from that trumpet from heaven, the dead will be up and out of their graves, beyond the reach of death, never to die again. At the same moment and in the same way, we'll all be changed. Then the saying will come true: Death swallowed by triumphant Life! Who got the last word, oh, Death? Oh, Death, who's afraid of you now?" I Corinthians 15:51, 52, 54-55 The Message.*

I still have some time to tell others that when we all run out of time, there is an incredible eternity of indescribable happiness for those who live life listening for that trumpet blast.

Be joyful!

January 19
Stuff

"You have let go of the commands of God and are holding on to human traditions." Mark 7:8 NIV

In the context of living a simpler lifestyle, I was once told that the best thing that could happen to me would be for my garage to burn to the ground.

I gasped and gaped. I cringed and sweated. And then I sneered. Get rid of my garage? Why that's where I keep my 'stuff.' That's preposterous.

Yet I'd be embarrassed for you to see the stuff in my garage, not because it's bad stuff, but because it's largely unnecessary. There's the large family-sized tent that has been used once in the last 20 years. And since it's about half the size of Rhode Island, it's almost comical thinking about my wife and I now using it. Especially out in the woods! And then there are several pieces of wood-working equipment that I had intended to use in making useful artifacts my children and grandchildren would cherish. But my lack of operating knowledge and my fear of going to heaven fingerless have kept them largely unused. You get the picture.

We're now preparing to move to another state. This is helping me sort through some of the stuff of my life. And that's a good thing. I want to be light on my feet...a 'lean mean fighting machine' for God's Kingdom. But that's hard to do while toting thousands of pounds of unnecessary stuff along. So as I've been chucking things and giving things and eyeing things in this 'keep or discard' mode, I've been thinking a lot about spiritual stuff that accumulates in our lives.

There's the box of 'worship-style preferences' that I've been carrying for several decades now. And the cartons filled with all the do's and don'ts that were meaningful and acceptable 35 years ago, but make little sense today. And in another corner, I've collected a ton of traditions that I now realize were never a part of God's requirements in the first place. Stuff...lots of stuff. Stuff that slows me down as I attempt to obey God today. Things that hold me back when I'm challenged to move out and forward.

I don't need a lot of it. And maybe you've been collecting and hauling and storing things yourself. Wouldn't this be a good week to do something about your spiritual 'garage?' Don't burn it down, but perhaps lighten your load and have a garage sale or give it away.

Enjoy joy and freedom from stuff on your journey!

January 20

A Life Review

I moved back to the California high desert after serving here as a youth pastor (among other tasks) from 1968 until 1974. One of the hidden surprises in returning to a past post is that, while *you* haven't aged or changed all that much, those you left behind have! Some of my former teens are now grandparents...

It certainly gives pause for thought and reflection. Did my almost seven years of pastoring those kids leave the results both God and I wanted?

In some of the marriages I performed, the knot wasn't tied very tight. Some who were 'believers' then have slipped into the category of 'doubters' now. And yet, a number of the teens are still on pretty good terms with the God of their youth and I'm happy for that.

How much of both the successes and the failures are my responsibility? No one can know that.

None of us can look back to a perfect, unblemished record. So, when we look back, what are we to look for? Can the results be neatly categorized into two parallel columns labeled "Success" and "Failure?" Not with just the information I have at my disposal. I'm also impeded by my inability to look into hearts. Only God does that well.

When you and I look back at past events in our lives...the good, the bad and the truly ugly...how do we make any sense of it? And what are we looking for? First to come to mind (because we have an 'accuser') are our mistakes and sins. We must repent, grieve them and then leave them in the ocean of God's forgiveness.

Second, we must let God sort out our actions from our intentions. We have all done right and had it misinterpreted. Again, leave it. Third, for much of the good that has come out of our hands and hearts, we must wait for commendation. It will come...Someone is keeping score ... our labor not in vain. We don't need accolades now to keep us going.

Remember more than the past…remember this: He who began the good work in you will complete it to his satisfaction as we allow Him to direct our paths.

> *"Don't just do what you have to do to get by, but work heartily, as Christ's servants doing what God wants you to do. And work with a smile on your face, always keeping in mind that no matter who happens to be giving the orders, you're really serving God. Good work will get you good pay from the Master, regardless of whether you are slave or free." Ephesians 6:6-8 The Message*

January 21

The Blame Game

> *"People ruin their lives by their own foolishness and then are angry at the Lord." Proverbs 19:3 New Living Translation*

It takes unmitigated gall to put God on the defense stand!

- ◆ we sow seeds of unfaithfulness in a relationship, then shake our fist at God when that relationship fails
- ◆ we sow seeds of indifference in our eating habits, then blame God when diagnosed with diabetes or high blood pressure
- ◆ we run right by God-planted 'caution' and 'stop' signs leading up to a decision, then roll our eyes at him when we make the wrong one and it bites us
- ◆ we fail as parents to instruct, guide and set parameters for our children, then question the faithfulness of God when their rebelliousness breaks our hearts
- ◆ we foolishly sow to the wind, then accuse God of bullying when hit by the whirlwind

As we probe the issue of bad things happening to good people we pull God into the matter as the instigator and perpetrator of all the bad and disappointing that happens to us.

- ♦ we carelessly vote into office people with immoral character and greedy intentions, then complain to God about the direction they take us
- ♦ we take scant interest in our children's schooling, then stand aghast at God when their faith is destroyed by secularism
- ♦ we take our spouse for granted, never investing in that primary relationship, then somehow put the blame on God when it dissolves into irrelevance

It's time to 'fess up' … to take responsibility for our own actions or lack thereof. When Adam sinned, he put God on the defense stand. "It's the woman **who you gave to me** that made me mess up," he pouted. But when the prophet confronted King David about his adulterous, murderous actions, David took responsibility saying, "I was wrong." II Samuel 12:13.

Adam lost paradise … David was forgiven and called 'a man after God's heart.'

So let's quit blaming God for the effects of our bad decisions and let him help us make correct ones. Let's stop insinuating that God didn't guide us and start listening carefully for his voice. Let's end our practice of using God as a scapegoat and invite him to be the Friend and Confidante that he wants to be.

May you experience joy for your journey!

January 22

Above The Clouds

Above these clouds, there's a literal 'storm of sunshine.'

I get hyper almost every time it happens. The trip to the airport is under blackened skies unloosing torrents of rain. You board the plane knowing full well that the storm centered over the city and its accompanying low-pressure system will certainly make for bumps in the air. As the airliner races down the runway, the rain-streaked windows begin to clear as the airspeed forces the heavy rain off of the windows. There's a flash of lightening nearby and its presence only adds to the uneasiness the storm has produced in your mind.

> *"If the entire trip is destined to be like it is right now I'd just as soon be back on the ground," you mutter nervously.*

But within minutes you notice a slight difference in the scene out the window. While still stormy, the clouds have lost some of their dark intensity. They seem to have lost a bit of their malevolent intent. As the plane continues to climb the sky brightens noticeably. The air gets smoother as the light begins conquering the darkness outside your window. And then it happens…the aircraft punctures the top of the cloud bank and instantly you are in bright sunlight…sunlight made all the brighter by the darkness you have just escaped. I never fail to respond emotionally to this experience.

As I have become more of an experienced flyer I have learned to anticipate the break into sunshine, even on the trip to the airport. And the spiritual lesson is hard to miss.

For a child of God, regardless of how dark any day or any set of circumstances may be…above it all (in the direction we are heading) there is a literal 'storm of sunshine.' You may not pop out into it precisely when you wish to or think you ought to, but the light is there in spite of any delay. The battle must turn in favor of those who serve Creator. The tempest still must come under the control of the Master of wind and waves. Our story does have a riotously happy ending.

May God give you the ability to cease your 'storm watching' and begin concentrating on the Storm Stopper.

"I exhort you to be of good cheer." Acts 27:22 KJV

January 23

The Speed of Love

"As for me, since I am poor and needy, let the Lord keep me in his thoughts. You are my helper and my savior. O my God, do not delay." Psalm 40:17 New Living Translation

I was a teen when the sound barrier was broken by Chuck Yeager. The speed of sound intrigues me greatly. Knowing a bit about it can help you determine how fast you need to be going to break it at varying altitudes and can also tell you just how far away that last lightning strike was to you.

But then my interest turned to the speed of light. At 186,000 miles per second, that would means 33 round trips between Los Angeles and New York City...all in the space of one short second! And in the time taken to read to this point in the devotional, light would have made that scenic round trip 730 times! But even at that speed, travel through the expanse of God's creation would take a serious bite out of your accrued vacation time.

Want to visit Pluto, one of nine planets orbiting our sun? Take a lunch because it's a six hour trip, even at a speed of 186,000 miles a second. How about visiting our closest star (Proxima Centauri)? That will require about four years and three months years of your life. Travel to the nearest large galaxy (Andromeda) would require time off from work in the amount of 2,200,000 years.

And to get to the most distant parts of our universe...traveling at 186,000 miles per second...would take close to 15 billion years. (And who knows if that really is the most distant, or simply as far as we can detect at the moment?)

Now here's where I'm devotionally challenged this week. Where is God in all of this? Where does He reside? And from where He lives, how long does it take Him to get to me when I need Him? Scripture tells me that He 'inhabits eternity' so I know He lives outside the boxes that we call 'time and space'. So, when my world caves in …when circumstances have stopped the clock in its tracks in my life…when up seems down and everything is turned on its side…and I desperately need God to come quickly…all the equations relating to time, distance and speed become meaningless.

I can't judge his travel time by either sound or light. He comes to me at 'the speed of love.' And the human mind will never be able to grasp that speed! Enjoy the journey.

January 24

Removing The Obstacles

"There were some Greeks in town who had come up to worship at the Feast. They approached Philip, who was from Bethsaida in Galilee: "Sir, we want to see Jesus. Can you help us?" John 12:20,21 The Message

One of the disciples, Philip, was approached by some Greeks (read: Gentile, heathen, unbeliever, etc.) who said to him, "Sir, we would like to meet Jesus."

I am haunted by the strange possibility that religious people can stand in the way of legitimate seekers who are trying to find the Lord. It happened in Matthew the twentieth chapter when the crowd following Jesus attempted to keep two blind men from bringing themselves and their desperate physical needs before the only One who could help them.

It happened again to the mothers of young children who desired an audience with Jesus. "Leave Him alone," they were

told in a rebuke that still makes me shiver. "Don't you know that
the Master doesn't have time for this sort of thing...can't you
see we're busy? We have places to go and important things to do
and dynamic schedules to keep!"

What kind of crowd would tell blind men that Jesus didn't
care? What kind of people would imply that the Master had
more important things to do than to meet needs and alleviate suffering? Who would have the audacity to put Jesus
'off limits' to people with hungry hearts and obvious needs?
Tragically, they were rebuked and rebuffed by the followers
of Jesus! And in the quest to keep their religious agenda going, they overlooked the tender heart of the Master and his
search for the very lost sheep they were attempting to keep at
a distance.

Whenever I 'talk Christian' and live another way, I block
people from getting to Jesus. In those times when 'doing
church' has so occupied my time and stolen all my energy that I
fail to 'be church' and follow the Kingdom's authentic agenda,
I've hidden Jesus from the very people who need Him and want
Him the most.

Today I reaffirm that it's the time between Sundays when I
have the best (and normally the only) chance to give the people
in my world a clear picture of Jesus and provide them an opportunity to approach Him with the deep needs and hungers in
their lives.

Share his life and enjoy the journey.

January 25
Boasting

It was close to 3:00 a.m. on a black, still morning almost 46
years ago. I was spending the night patrolling the campus of
my Bible School with the old Montana-cowboy-turned-night-
watchman, when he had a candid observation about a fellow

classmate of mine. "I'd like to buy him for what he's worth and sell him for what he thinks he's worth" said Pop Sundquist.

The student he referred to perfectly summed up the old adage: A person all wrapped up in himself makes a very small package. He believed he was God's answer to every girl's prayer ... he alone had the insights that would redefine ministry in the 1960s ... we were all very fortunate indeed that God had placed him in our institution. We all knew these things, because he told us so!

There is a strong warning against boasting in Jeremiah 9 and verse 23. It reads: *"This is what the Lord says: Don't let the wise boast in their wisdom, or the powerful boast in their power, or the rich boast in their riches."* And according to Proverbs 8:13, God hates pride and arrogance.

But lest you think you must give up all boasting to please God, watch what transpires in verse 24 of Jeremiah 9. God has just cautioned the wise, the powerful and the rich but then says, *"But those who wish to boast should boast in this alone: that they truly know me and understand that I am the Lord who demonstrates unfailing love and who brings justice and righteousness to the earth, and that I delight in these things. I, the Lord, have spoken!"*

So today, quit flexing your muscles. Stop trumpeting your brilliance. Cease tracking your material assets. Instead, take stock in how well you know God ... really know Him. How well have you figured out his absolute Lordship and submitted to it? And how awed are you at his unfailing love and the justice and righteousness with which He rules this world?

If you begin cracking these codes, you'll have something worth crowing about!

January 26
Stubborn

There seems to be a fine line between persistence and stubbornness. The trick is to know when you're about to cross that line, because on one side of the line people praise you … on the other side they'd like for you to go away.

Being determined and resolute in the face of seemingly insurmountable obstacles is the stuff great biographies are made of. But refusing to yield to reason and to 'flex' accordingly is the stuff great defeats are made of.

Stubbornness grows quickly in people who have an extremely high opinion of themselves and do not value the opinion of anyone else. Ancient Israel had a particularly nasty habit of putting their fingers in their ears when God spoke, but aggressively following the dictates of their evil hearts, succumbing to the Godless culture around them. It was a combination that kept them from inheriting God's best gifts.

Is there a cure for being stubborn? Absolutely. The Bible says, *"Do not be stiff-necked, as your fathers were; submit (yield) to the Lord." II Chronicles 30:8 NIV* The writer of Proverbs makes very clear the end results of both stubbornness and submission: *"When people do not accept divine guidance, they run wild. But whoever obeys the law is joyful." Proverbs 29:18 New Living Translation*

So how are we to know when we've crossed from resolute to reckless? From passionate to obstinate? From determined to detrimental? Sometimes only God knows when we're about to move from our character strengths to our character flaws. And that makes it very important to be sensitive to the Spirit. It's his task to keep the steel in your backbone and not in your head!

May you find joy and discernment on your journey!

January 27

It's Good News For Everyone

"And God has given us this task of reconciling people to him." II Corinthians 5:18 New Living Translation

Evangelism can be explained simply as 'one beggar telling another beggar where to get food.' Of course it's more than that if
you want to get technical about it. It's a whole genre of theology
and we teach it sometimes as if it's rocket science and must only
be undertaken by somebody with a ministerial degree.

In its most elementary form, evangelism is sharing the
relationship we have with Jesus with somebody who does not
yet know him. It's a testimonial based on the experience of our
own life. And like the ex-blind man in the Bible, our testimony
can be as simple as "I used to be blind, but now I see and that
Man did it for me!"

There are times when the 'other beggar' bothers us. He or
she is annoying. They're living a life style that we detest. Their
personality grinds against ours. We have almost nothing in
common. They use foul language. They have nasty habits. They
don't live in our neighborhood. They drive a dirty car with junk
on their dashboard. Their humor is crude and degrading and
they absolutely love stupid reality shows on television.

But Jesus loves them and died for them ... anyway!

Sometimes the work that God wants to do supernaturally in
someone's life is preceded by the supernatural work He must do
in ours first. The Apostle Paul talked about this point two verses before our text above. And here's what he said: *"So we have
stopped evaluating others from a human point of view." II Corinthians
5:16 New Living Translation*

If we only share our story with those just like us, then the
Gospel will be 'good news' to a precious few. Our evaluation
of others must get past the exterior. We must see people as our
Lord does. As lost, lonely, frightened, yearning for freedom,
candidates for a miraculous 'make-over.'

This week, as you move through life and the people in it,
don't evaluate based on what you see and hear and experience,
but on God's assessment. He sees bondage, but also freedom.

He sees a mess, but also a miracle. He sees deep need, but also meeting that need. He sees heartbreak, but also healing.

Never judge a book by its cover, but by the full story it contains. God is at work in our world in the greatest restoration project ever attempted. He'd like your help!

January 28
Two Ears

> *"And the Lord came and called as before, "Samuel! Samuel!" And Samuel replied, 'Speak, your servant is listening.'" I Samuel 3:10 New Living Translation*

I know people who have changed this verse in their lives to read: "Listen, Lord, for your servant is speaking." Now it's not that we can't speak and expect God to listen and respond. There is far too much evidence in Scripture calling us to voice our needs, our praises and our apprehensions to the One who always has an ear attuned to our voices.

However, many of us have mastered the talking part and sadly neglected the listening portion of communication with our Creator. Sometimes we don't want to hear from God … afraid He has instructions we'd rather not follow.

This statement was overheard during a Catholic mass: "I preferred the service in Latin. I like it better when I don't know what they're saying." At some deep level we understand that we're held responsible for knowledge attained. *"When someone has been given much, much will be required in return; and when someone has been entrusted with much, even more will be required." Luke 12:48 New Living Translation*

When God communicates it always looks for a response on our part. We must go … we must submit … we must yield … we must trust. Something that is presently acceptable needs modification or at times elimination. A previous way of thinking must give way to a Kingdom mindset.

This week, remember that there's a reason we have two ears and only one mouth. While true that out of the abundance of the heart the mouth speaks, it's also true that listening to God will put that abundance there to eventually speak wisdom and encouragement to those who lack both.

May you have joy (and listening ears) on your journey!

January 29

Even Though

"Therefore, Lord, **we know** *you will protect the oppressed, preserving them forever from this lying generation,* **even though** *the wicked strut about, and evil is praised throughout the land." Psalm 12:7,8* New Living Translation

There is often a major discrepancy between what we know and what we see. It's what makes living by faith such a different course than living by sight. We must constantly be reminded that reality is seldom what we see, but what is unseen behind the scenes.

The Apostle Paul wrote: *"So we fix our eyes not on what is seen, but on what is unseen. For what is seen is temporary, but what is unseen is eternal."* II Corinthians 4:18 NIV To the natural man this is wild and scary, but the spiritual part of our being thrives in this kind of atmosphere.

So the distance between the 'we know' and the 'even though' in the opening verse above is staggering and wonderful!

We know that God loves us, **even though** the depersonalization of our culture informs us that nobody really cares about us as a person.

We know that all things will turn out for good, **even though** life seems like it's falling apart at the seams and cannot be repaired.

We know that beneath us are the everlasting arms of a caring Father, **even though** it feels remarkably like we're free falling with no bungee cord attached to our ankle.

We know we are never alone, **even though** there are times of loneliness when we're whistling in the dark and not even hearing our own echo.

Today, to what other areas of your life might you apply this simple **we know/even though** formula?

We lift praise to our Heavenly Father that what we see is not always what we get!

January 30
Small Beginnings

I had a relative that was always 'getting in on the ground floor' of opportunities. But they all turned out to be one-story buildings! That's because God wasn't in them. When God is building something we should not be worried about it getting off the ground. Ground floors are starting places.

In the Old Testament, God's angel was attempting to convey to Zechariah the prophet, just how successful a man named Zerrubbabel was going to be in rebuilding God's temple. The angel said, "It's not going to happen by might and power but by God's Spirit." Zacheriah 4:6

And then he told the prophet something we all need to hear and understand. *"The people should not think that small beginnings are unimportant." Zechariah 4:10 The Holy Bible : New Century Version* In a day when "Wow" has been super-sized…when everything is presented as bigger, better, brighter, longer-lasting and beyond amazing… we tend to see small beginnings as just small. We forget that they're beginnings.

When Jesus had thousands of people to feed he began small with a sack lunch from a little boy. When He showed the way into his Kingdom, He began small. He used a child's attitude to point the way. When He wanted to spread the news of his love to every nation on earth, He started small, with just twelve men, including one who didn't make the cut. Historians tell us that every great move of God throughout the centuries can be traced to a solitary kneeling figure…small beginning.

Be very aware that God would love to do something extraordinarily big through your life. But don't be offended if it begins with something small…like just a little faith…just a tiny step of obedience…just the most miniscule glimpse into the future. Don't make the mistake of thinking that small beginnings are unimportant. Every great work of God starts there. Find joy in that.

January 31
Stand

"Therefore put on the full armor of God, so that when the day of evil comes, you may be able to stand your ground, and after you have done everything, to stand." Ephesians 6:13 NIV

Here's the question: What do you do when there's nothing more you can do?

Don't take that question lightly.

Who hasn't been 'living a question with no answer?' Who has never been in a room with no apparent doors or windows … no escape? Who has never faced a test with great resolve and determination only to expend every ounce of energy, every resource and every ounce of hope without a resolution at hand?

Obviously the Apostle Paul had been in battles like this. He had faced defeat head on without the comforting sound of the cavalry mounting a rescue. He had been pushed and pummeled and hemmed in ... had hope trashed ... had options removed one by one until there were none left.

At that point, "after you have done everything" what then? Is it over? To let go of the rope and fall into whatever abyss awaits becomes the only option that comes to our beleaguered hearts and minds.

But wait! There is one more option. The bag isn't entirely empty. There is one instruction left that must be followed. We haven't really done everything until we've taken this last critical step when overwhelmed by disaster.

So with shoulders sagging, hearts questioning, physical impairments screaming, friends misunderstanding and impending doom surrounding us like thick fog we do the only thing left for us to do. "Stand." It may feel like we're doing nothing. But we are. We are waiting for the only One who can really help at this point.

The battle must eventually belong to the Lord. When we reach the end of our resources, we do well to remember the incredible theology in Martin Luther's last line of his hymn "A Mighty Fortress:"

He (God) must win the battle!

Rejoice that you're really not out of options. There still is God!

Beware The Esau Syndrome

"Watch out that no one...becomes careless about God as Esau did: he traded his rights as the oldest son for a single meal." Heb. 12:16 Living Bible

Our current culture not only lives for the 'here and now' but demands it. Nothing is worth waiting for. No pleasure should be put off that can be enjoyed today. Waiting is always a waste of time. Nothing comes to him who waits. It's now, baby…it's all we have. Live life to its fullest and grab for all the gusto you can because you only go around once in life.

Sound familiar? The world we are a part of is driven by this philosophy. But be careful. Because we do only 'go around once in life' be especially careful. The wisdom of God is always directed toward the long term. The temptation will always be there to trade away God's life-long gifts on the altar of short-term appetites.

But good things do come to those who are willing to wait for something significant:

* Simeon and Anna (Luke 2) waited a lifetime and were rewarded by getting to hold the very Son of God in their arms.

* David waits in the wilderness caves and is rewarded with God's blessing and the throne of his own kingdom.

* Israel waits, carrying God's promise in their hearts for decades and is rewarded with a land overflowing with milk, honey and exquisite potential.

* Joseph waits in the dungeon with the memory of his brothers' betrayal, but also with the memory of God's promise to him and is ultimately rewarded with the second highest position in the land.

So…what are you waiting for? Is it significant? Is it God-sized? Does it have eternal implications? The most important things in our life are those spoken of in Habakkuk 2:3 where we read:

> *"But these things I plan won't happen right away. Slowly, steadily, surely, the time approaches when the vision will be fulfilled. If it seems slow, wait patiently, for it will surely take place." New Living Translation*

Lovers and Fighters

How goes your battle? You say you aren't into fighting...you're a lover. Oh, I doubt it. (Not that you're a lover, but that you aren't into fighting!) Consider:

- ♦ It's a battle to stay positive in a negative world
- ♦ It's a battle to stay pure in a polluted world
- ♦ It's a battle to stay sweet in a sour world
- ♦ It's a battle to stay committed in non-committal world
- ♦ It's a battle to stay focused in a distracting world
- ♦ It's a battle to stay honest in a crooked world

Get the picture? Our battles are being fought on a multitude of fronts. And we don't go overseas to fight these battles...we go to work, to school, to the fitness center. We are engaged in battle while we sit in front of our television sets, when we hear a bit of trash talk that would feel so good to pass on, when someone's discouraging word threatens the dream in our heart.

God's Word reminds us of something very important...we don't fight against flesh and blood, against sticks and stones and their modern equivalency. We fight on a different plane, against internal wickedness that comes so easily. We struggle with philosophies that stand diametrically opposed to God's viewpoint. We battle attitudes of racism, materialism and even the idea that everything we need is already within us...we don't need any outside help. That's a lie and it must be fought against every day.

This would be a good day to win a battle or two. And the good news is this: you've been equipped by God to win. Honest! Note the Apostle Paul's words to his protégé Timothy: *"All those prayers are coming together now so you will do this well, fearless in your*

struggle, keeping a firm grip on your faith and on yourself. After all, this is a fight we're in." I Timothy 1:18 (The Message)
Be courageous and joyful on your journey.

February 3
God In The Details

We expect God to show up at the high points of our lives … you know, at our birth, marriage, 50th anniversary and death. After all, with so many people to look after, it is amazing to us that He notices even those occasions.

But the Psalmist said, *"The steps of the godly are directed by the Lord. He delights in every detail of their lives."* Psalm 37:23 New Living Translation God is not only in the details of our lives, but delights in them as well. Pretty awesome news.

He says to the widow in I Kings 17:14 "I'm aware of how much flour and oil is left in your cupboard." In Psalm 23 we find him setting the table for one of his kids. He tells us in Matthew 6 that even our clothes closet with its emptiness or abundance has not escaped his attention. In the same chapter He emphasizes our importance over the birds and yet notices when one of them falls from its nest. God even counts the hairs on our heads, whether curly, straight, colored or about to fall out!

Is it any wonder that in light of this exquisitely detailed care that the Apostle Peter, a man who knew the heart of the Father well, said that we could cast *"…the whole of your care [all your anxieties, all your worries, all your concerns, once and for all] on Him, for He cares for you affectionately and cares about you watchfully."* I Peter 5:7 Amplified Bible.

You don't need to sweat the small stuff, because even there you will find the hand, heart and intentions of a faithful Father.

February 4
It's Not That Hard

I have no idea why some people think that living the Christian life is so tough. If you know how to manage it, it really isn't all that big a challenge. Consider:

- ◆ Humility is relatively easy, as long as you can brag about it to somebody.
- ◆ The new life is not difficult to live if you can keep some of the old life, too.
- ◆ Loving others is really a snap, as long as you hang around great and loving people who love you back.
- ◆ Patience comes easy – just so you don't have to wait for it.
- ◆ Being a giving person isn't much of a challenge, especially if you have a super abundance and won't miss what you give.
- ◆ Living in peace doesn't come hard, as long as you can be stress less and hassle-free.
- ◆ It's extremely easy to forgive as long as no one crosses you or hurts you.
- ◆ Obedience comes easy as well, as long as you aren't asked to do something unusual or particularly difficult.
- ◆ Daily devotions aren't hard to do, as long as they keep making those little boxes with a verse printed on it.
- ◆ Even that 'servanthood' thing can be handled – just as long as you're not treated like one.

On and on it goes ... always looking for an easy way to live a life that God said would be challenging. He promised there'd be dips in the roadway of life with potholes, detours and switchbacks. We still expect an empty freeway.

He says we won't always be well-liked and we still crave affirmation from everyone. He declares that joy comes from giving from the heart, while we look to give from an over-flowing checking account. He says to pray when it's hard and we wait for a perfect environment. He reminds us that we are to regard others as above us, while we are taking notes on where we see ourselves in relation to others.

Remember – this 'looking-for-the-easy-way' brand of living for Christ does not distinguish us from those who aren't interested in discipleship. Pay attention to who it is you're serving; and if it's you, then you're not taking God very seriously!

> *"Calling the crowd to join his disciples, he said, 'Anyone who intends to come with me has to let me lead. You're not in the driver's seat; I am. Don't run from suffering; embrace it. Follow me and I'll show you how.'" Mark 8:34,35 The Message*

February 5
Blurred Pictures

Aside from a fuel stop on my way to Viet Nam in the 70's … this was my first 'feet on the ground' experience in Hawaii. With only one night on Oahu, there wouldn't be much sightseeing.

But I had a cheap camera and a couple of hours to capture the magic of this paradise.

I couldn't wait to get home, have the pictures developed and bring Joanie into the experience. She'd start saving from our food budget for a trip to the islands together and have trouble sleeping at night thinking about it.

And imagine is what she had to do. My pictures had as much appeal as if they had been taken inside a gulag. A couple looked like they had been snapped inside a Costco warehouse. The water was cloudy, the sky a milky white, the sand resembled poorly laid concrete.

Nowhere in my roll of film did the glory of Oahu come through. My pictures didn't make Hawaii somewhere 'she just had to visit.'

The Apostle Paul wrote of this conundrum in the love chapter – I Corinthians 13. He said, *"For now we are looking in a mirror that gives on a dim (blurred) reflection [of reality as in a riddle or enigma], but then [when perfection comes] we shall see in reality and face to face!" verse 12 Amplified Bible*

A lot of life is blurred to us. We are often too close to grasp the full picture. Or we have too few facts available to put 'two and two' together. And heaven fits right into that scenario.

We've had just enough told us that we can in faith label it glorious … but the snapshots I suspect don't do it justice. They don't even come close. There are those who have seen some of its splendor and come back and tried to detail it for us, but even the most powerful recounting can't get the reality to us.

Ah, but one day we will not just visit there, but move there and finally the blurriness will become crystal clear. The veil will be lifted. The presence of our Savior and the eternal glory of that 'unclouded day' will finally be ours to savor.

And there will be no return flight waiting to take us back home … for we will be home!

February 6
Resident to President

Jesus coming into a person's life is a big deal. The very biggest. Winning a $38 million lottery prize is trivial by comparison. That only impacts life. But the personal invitation for Jesus to come in impacts both life and eternity!

However, the role He is given upon entering will tell how much His presence will impact life here and now. If He comes as 'resident' it may not make very much difference, as far as anyone can tell. Oh, we may pick up our spiritual socks from the floor, keep our language under control and work on our selfish traits a bit. But a transformation that shakes our world and the world of those around us will most likely be non-existent.

For a world-rocking, heaven-enhancing, hell bashing thrill of a lifetime experience, Jesus needs the position as 'President' of our lives.

We struggle with this concept because we recognize that we lose control. We can't set the agenda. We must adapt to the flow … His flow. We take our hand off the tiller and run with the wind or against the wind, all depending on the direction He wants to go. And the perceived brilliance of our plans are scrapped as we trust His great heart and relax in His instructions.

Tough? Initially. Hard? Only on our pride. Exciting? You bet!

This week, recognize that those incredible plans He has for you most likely will never materialize if not for His divine intervention. Let go and let God.

Resident or President? With the first you get control, security and eternal life. With the second the control is handed to another and in its place you still get security and eternal life, but also a radical, life-fulfilling journey of exquisite adventure and the potential of impacting your entire world for God's Kingdom.

> *"The LORD says, 'I will guide you along the best pathway for your life. I will advise you and watch over you.'"*
> *Psalm 32:8 New Living Translation*

February 7

Faithful Love In Hard Times

There are a multitude of Scriptures that edify, comfort, challenge and energize me. But there are passages that elicit a "Say, what?" from me when I come across them. They are verses that appear so naturally incorrect or so 'oxymoronic' that they pull me up short.

I came across this interesting one the other morning in my devotional time. It's the story of a young man whose jealous brothers have sold him into Egyptian slavery. Making the best of an already terrible situation, he is now confronted with the lustful intentions of the wife of his master. When she makes advances, he flees (the correct spiritual response) and for his choice and sterling character, he is thrown into prison. This is a bummer of a story so far, right?

Now comes the verse in question from Genesis 39:21: *"But the Lord was with Joseph in the prison and showed him his faithful love." New Living Translation* That's a fact of God's dealing with us that we seldom comprehend ... God's faithful love 'in prison', 'during the storm', 'when pushed to our limits by circumstances totally beyond our control.'

We feel that God's faithful love will keep us out of prison, away from the storm, safe within our own comfort zones.

But we seldom get it! We sit in our cells or hang on for dear life in the midst of our storms or get pushed beyond what we believe to be safe or loving and wonder what in the world God is up to. But there is not only method behind the apparent madness ... there is a plan that will eventually exhibit genius behind every hill, hurt or horror.

For you see, God is positioning Joseph for a future he can't begin to comprehend and for a role in the salvation of His people that won't be fully understood for many, many generations.

Do you need to reaffirm your trust in the wisdom and faithful love of your Heavenly Father? Do you need to swallow your questions, quit looking around and let God's arms and heart carry you through this time in your life?

You may not end up as 'second in command' as Joseph did, but the storm, the prison, the circumstances will all end at God's timely command ... when the next part of His plan is ready for you.

May you find joy for your journey and peace in the midst of the storms!

Sleep On It

"The wise counsel God gives when I'm awake is confirmed by my sleeping heart." Psalm 16:7 The Message

All of the mighty promises of God are meaningless if we can't sleep on them. If God makes a promise to you, not only can you 'take it to the bank' but you can 'sleep on it' as well.

Sleep is not always a given anymore ... what with anxiety-riddled minds grappling with problems with no apparent solutions, world class dilemmas and scary scenarios that stay with us long after the televised news has been turned off.

There's a certain amount of guilt to be found in not doing our fair share of worrying, too. After all, it's the least we can do. But it's also a gross mismanagement of our time and energy plus a discredit to the God of Israel who 'neither slumbers nor sleeps.' *Psalm 121:4*

When looked at in the light of day, worry is about the dumbest thing any of us ever invest in. It's been documented that less than 6% of things people worry about ever materialize ... ever! A dense fog that covers a seven-city-block area one hundred feet deep is composed of very little water divided into multiplied millions of incredibly small drops. A minimal amount of moisture spread out can cripple an entire city area.

And so it is with worry and anxiety ... the matter in question might be rather insignificant, but when we invest heavily in it, we give it the power to rob the best portions of our lives. It would be good to heed the advice of the Apostle Paul who warned: *"Don't worry about anything: instead, pray about everything. Tell God what you need, and thank him for all he has done. If you do this, you will experience God's peace, which is far more wonderful than the human mind can understand. His peace will guard your hearts and minds as you live in Christ Jesus." Philippians 4:6,7 New Living Translation*

Today find some way of attaching that passage to your heart and mind. And then, sleep on it … every night.

> *"I am inwardly fashioned for faith, not for fear. Fear is not my native land; faith is. I am so made that worry and anxiety are sand in the machinery of life; faith is the oil. I live better by faith and confidence than by fear, doubt and anxiety. In anxiety and worry, my being is gasping for breath – these are not my native air. But in faith and confidence, I breathe freely – these are my native air." Dr. E. Stanley Jones*

And let that fill you with joy for the journey.

February 9

Let God Choose

It was easy enough. A nickel would let me hear the song of my choice. And a pocket full of nickels would assure me of hearing just what I wanted to hear for a long, long time.

It was called a jukebox.

I don't know the origin of the name but it was standard fare at some of my favorite eating establishment while growing up. Mind you, I didn't like a lot of the music contained in the machine, but as long as it was my money going in the slot, I got to choose.

There are people who would love for God's music and voice to come from a jukebox. You know, put your nickel in and hear God say, "I love you with an everlasting love." Another coin and choose, "Cast all you cares upon me for I care for you." And after another deposit hear, "I will never leave you or forsake you."

If God was a jukebox we could get only what we want to hear. But He's not.

There are times when other messages come from Him. Like, *"Make every effort to live in peace with all men and to be holy; without holiness no one will see the Lord." Hebrews 12:14 NIV*

And, *"Go sell all you have and give it to the poor, then come and follow me." Matthew 19:21* And what about, *"If you want to follow me, you must deny yourself, pick up your cross and follow me." Mark 8:34*

No, He's not a jukebox god, dispensing only self-serving and self-gratifying words. Instead, from the heart of a Father who truly loves us come words that we need to hear, not just what we want to hear. He loves us that much.

So put your nickels away ... stay close enough to hear well and let heaven's DJ choose the things you hear. They're all straight from his great heart.

February 10
Abnormally Normal

> *When the sub-normal becomes normal ...*
> *normalcy is thought to be abnormal.*

That's our world today. God sets the bar and establishes it as normal. The culture settles far below that standard until old benchmarks are forgotten and all the price tags have been switched. Chastity and integrity used to carry high price tags ... now they appear valueless. God placed the value of a pre-born or new-born baby so high that it was worth the death of his Only Son. Now, to some, they're throwaway inconveniences.

We live in a society very much like the community described in Mark 5:1-17. They were used to living sub-normally. In their neighborhood was a demon possessed man who lived among the tombs, rattled chains and refused to wear clothes. Talk about getting used to a sub-par existence. But they were used to it.

Jesus delivered the man of his many demons and when the good folks of the town came to see what happened to their newly demonized pigs, they found the man who probably kept them locked up tightly in their homes every night ... in his right mind, wearing clothes and listening carefully to Jesus.

And it scared them! Jesus reestablished normalcy to their lives and they called it abnormal and wanted Jesus to leave immediately!

You represent light and life amidst darkness and decaying death, so don't be surprised to be thought of as weird and out of touch. You are not part of that death, but of life and as the saying goes, "Nothing shakes up a cemetery like a good resurrection!" Walk in darkness as light ... walk among death as riotously alive!

> "Men and women who have lived wisely and well will shine brilliantly, like the cloudless, star-strewn night skies. And those who put others on the right path to life will glow like stars forever." Daniel 12:3 The Message

May there be joy and normalcy for your journey!

February 11
Delays

> "This vision is for a future time. It describes the end, and it will be fulfilled. If it seems slow in coming, wait patiently, for it will surely take place. It will not be delayed." Habakkuk 2:3 New Living Translation

Delay! How we detest that word and its impact on our lives.

To watch the "On Time" designation change to "Delayed" while waiting to board a plane is not good news. To be delayed by traffic, work overload or bad planning on the part of someone else is almost insufferable in this day of hurry and hurrier.

To admit to being 'delayed' is an embarrassment to most.

In 1958 and not too long before his death, Walt Disney was working on Pirates of the Caribbean for the newly opened Disneyland. His plan was for it to be a walk-through wax museum with static displays. Anyone who enjoys the current ride does so because of a delay.

Walt's' imagineers' were called upon to travel to New York for the World's Fair and while there were introduced to a new ride system using water. Then they discovered something called animatronics … giving life-like movement to the characters telling the story. Pirates of the Caribbean is hardly a walk through a wax museum … all because of a delay.

We easily forget that God's delays often precede an outcome far better than what we had expected. The prophet Elijah chafed to interact with the waywardness of his generation … but two long delays prepared him for God's real work. While waiting beside the brook Cherith and later in a humble home in Zarephath among strangers and aliens, he became the man who courageously faced down an entire godless nation and its counterfeit priesthood.

G. Campbell Morgan said it well: "Waiting for God is not laziness. Waiting for God is not going to sleep. Waiting for God is not the abandonment of effort. Waiting for God means, first, activity under command; second, readiness for any new command that may come; third, the ability to do nothing until the command is given."

Remember, if God has hit the 'pause' button in your life, trust Him to know when to hit 'resume.' And when He does, hang on … because you've never been on a ride like this one!

May you find joy for and in your journey!

February 12
Not My Will

> *"Instead, whoever wants to become great among you must be your servant, and whoever wants to be first must be slave of all. For even the Son of Man did not come to be served, but to serve, and to give his life as a ransom for many." Mark 10:43-45 NIV*

> *"...yet, not what I want, but what you want." Mark 14:36 New Revised Standard Version (Jesus in Gethsemane)*

Leadership in God's Kingdom doesn't look like today's corporate model. Nor should it.

Jesus taught an antithetical brand called 'servant leadership.' It's barely caught on in the church because we tend to use the method that the secular business community uses ... we just add Christian jargon to it and assume God will bless it.

I've been learning a lot about servant leadership from the book "Upside Down" written by Stacy Rinehart, vice president of the Navigators. But I learned even more from my two grandsons this week.

Papa and Mimi Walterman (that would be Joanie and myself) had our five and a half and seven year old grandsons for a couple of days to let their parents have a little 'alone time.' I had a chance to observe just how lacking my 'not-my-will-but-thine' Christian attitude was.

Most mornings I arise early, make a cup of coffee and sit on my back patio watching the sun come over the mountain while working through my prayer time and immersing myself in Scripture. Most mornings. But Weston (the five and a half year old) was up as early as his Papa and I probably don't have to tell you that his agenda did not include Bible reading, sun gazing and listening to the finches fighting over their food.

And that gave me an exquisite opportunity of putting someone else before my plans and goals. The prayer list got put away … the Bible closed and Weston and I ambushed flies, studied the path of ants, looked behind chairs for spiders and discussed the satellites we saw fly over our house the previous night.

Today I'm thankful to be challenged by Jesus' command to put others first. I do it seldom and poorly, but I am learning. It may not have been nearly as heroic as Jesus in the garden, but it's helping me break the "me first" mind set that Jesus came to challenge.

And my agenda? Would you believe it all got done in due time and Weston and I shared some memories that to him will last longer than I will!

February 13

Statues To Stupidity

"I will reduce Jerusalem to ruins, making it a monument to their stupidity. All who pass by will be astonished and will gasp … " Jeremiah 9:8 New Living Translation

We laugh at 'blond jokes' but the fact is, hair color has nothing to do with some of the dumb things we all do.

I have been ill-advised, reckless and rash on a number of occasions in my life. I have acted irresponsibly and then been caught off guard by the outcome because I actually hadn't con- nected my action or choice to the 'surprise ending' it brought about.

And on occasion I have driven my 'monument to stupidity' around town and parked it in my garage. Hindsight never pre- pares us for that embarrassment.

Being irresponsible is not the same as being 'heedless.' That kind of stupidity is in a class by itself. There are excuses to be made for overlooking the obvious … for not taking the time to make a careful assessment before acting … for failing to account for unknown factors. But to stick your fingers in your ears and refuse to listen to instruction, however, carries another stigma altogether.

And that was what the nation of Israel did quite regularly. God would give clear directions and attempt to pre-emptively steer them away from sin and its huge consequences. Yet even while he was instructing them they would be rehearsing the next verse of "I Did It My Way."

Nobody shines God on! Nobody. What you sow you will reap. The crop of a life lived in rebellion against God is often harvested by God and assembled as a monument … a statue in the park for all to see. View the 'before and after' pictures of the city of Jerusalem and compare its former glory and potential to the broken walls and devastation seen later. Does the word 'stupid' come to mind? It wasn't supposed to and didn't have to end that way.

Today, try to live smart … eliminating as many mistakes and reckless decisions as you can. But whatever you do, don't ignore God's instructions. Because if followed, they promise to become a garland around your neck, not a noose around your throat.

And there won't be that embarrassing statue in the park!

May there be both joy and wisdom on your journey!

February 14

The Tilt of the Heart

"Turn my heart toward your statutes and not toward selfish gain."

Psalm 119:36

How's your heart on this Valentine's Day? It's an important question.

The Bible says the heart is far more than a receptacle of mushy emotions and the purveyor of fine chocolates! It represents the groundwork of not only emotions, but of will and intention and determination. It focuses us on where we want to go with our lives. It provides not only the inertia for our trip, but the boundaries that encase our journey.

Here's the tricky part … our hearts can be rather fickle and unpredictable at times. Depending on the 'tilt' of our hearts, they can take us far a field from our original and noble intentions. Our hearts can turn us 180 degrees from our chosen destination. It's up to us to keep our hearts centered on God's Word … His purposes … the true moral high ground. Anything else turns us in both a destructive and selfish direction.

The same sun that hardens clay melts wax. It's the condition of the object upon which the sun shines that determines the outcome. A self-centered heart finds itself hardened by the very Word that used to warm and soften it. But even the most hardened heart if 'tilted' back in God's direction will again prove to be a heart safe to follow.

Allow God's Spirit to poke your heart for signs of hardening or soreness. If the poke hurts, ask the Healer to fix your heart, or under extreme conditions to give you a complete heart transplant.

"You have tested my thoughts and examined my heart in the night. You have scrutinized me and found nothing wrong." Psalm 17:3 New Living Translation

February 15
Sand or Sinew

Note the balance in the life of a believer between *"There is no new thing under the sun …"* (Ecclesiastes 1:9) and *"The Lord's mercies are new every morning … great is thy faithfulness."* (Lamentations 3:22,23)

The hourglass symbolism is not entirely accurate to use at the end of one year and the beginning of the next. Because there is more to our lives than sand and also because everything in our lives does not begin fresh on January 1st of each year.

In addition to the transitional sand ... the ebb and flow of life with the tide in and then out ... there are sinews of connectedness that tie one year into the next and indeed one decade into another.

Take friendships for instance. Aren't you glad that you don't lose every close friend at the end of each year, forcing you to begin building significant relationships in your life yearly? And wouldn't it be horrific to not be allowed to build this year from last year's resources? What if the accumulation of finances or knowledge or meaningful hobbies ran out on December 31st just as the sand runs through the hourglass?

So God builds continuity into life and that continuity ties our intentions to our futures. It connects our work and career to coming rewards and satisfactions. That ongoing 'sinew' of life even enables us to see the connection between time and eternity. There is a strong bond between 'then and there' and 'here and now.'

But with that flow of life and the repetitions that help us learn and improve, come the marvelous surprises of God ... like new mercies every sunrise ... like serendipitous moments of delight when God releases unexpected and undeserved blessings into our lives. For life is all about routines and newness. It's made up of faithful plodding combined with refreshing stops and breathtaking sprints. But it's all life and we've just been given a new year in which to live it.

February 16

A New Beginning

Revival: a new beginning of obedience to God

Few of us would argue the fact that America needs just such a new beginning. As a culture and unique social entity in our world, we have drifted far away from the simple things that God asks of people who desire his blessing.

What would it take to bring this kind of moral upheaval… dramatic spiritual reorientation to the land? What would it look like? Where would it begin?

Our temptation is to wish that Billy Graham was in his 40s and that Promise Keepers was still filling 20 national stadiums with 65,000 men at a time. We could envision churches holding 'revival meetings' as they did many years ago with neighbors flocking into those churches to respond to God's invitation to a new and totally different life.

But God seldom brings revival to the masses. It's been said that every great move of God throughout history can be traced to a single kneeling figure. True revival has a solitary and lonely point of origin.

Many decades ago, famous revivalist and preacher Gypsy Smith was asked how to start a revival. Here was his answer. "Go home," he said, "lock yourself in your room, kneel down in the middle of your floor. Draw a chalk mark all around yourself and ask God to start the revival inside that chalk mark. When He has answered your prayer, the revival will be on."

Today my goal is to quit watching for signs of spiritual renewal in those around me. Instead, in humble obedience to the One who has everything I need or really want in life, I will ask Him to rework me. All of me. Every attitude, habit, ambition and longing. Even the 'religious' part of me that sometimes actually gets in the way of getting closer to him is fair game for his probing. I really do want a new movement of obedience to God, and I desperately want its headwaters to be found in me first.

> *"Won't you revive us again, so your people can rejoice in you?"*
> *Psalm 85:6 New Living Translation*

February 17
My Contract

"Lord, I'd like to discuss my contract with you."

"Fine."

My life had more bumps than a black diamond mogul hill ... more stress, pain and questions than I felt I could handle. I needed to get some things straight.

"Father, I don't remember all the stuff I'm going through being discussed in the fine print in my contract with You. Isn't there some kind of a warranty program in the event something bad happens ... like a AAA roadside service available to get me out of them when they do?"

"Do you remember that contract," He asked. "Can you re-member what was on it?"

It had been quite some time since I had signed it and I had to struggle to bring it into focus in my memory.

"I remember there was a short message from you to me written across the top. Oh, it's coming back to me. It was a verse from Jeremiah, *"For I know the plans I have for you ... they are plans for good and not for disaster, to give you a future and a hope.' (29:11)* Aside from that I can't really remember anything else that was on that page."

"It was blank, He said. "You said that you trusted me explicitly with every part of your life. It was a huge step of faith for you to do that. Now let me ask you some ques-tions: Have I ever failed you? In the rough spots have you ever been totally abandoned? Is either my love or my ability in question here? This is not a contract ... it's a covenant between my heart and your life. Trust Me ... it's going to be all right."

February 18
Steps

"Guide my steps by your word, so I will not be overcome by evil."

Psalm 119:133 New Living Translation

Sometime during the first three months of 1944 I took my first unassisted steps. It didn't make the newspapers, but my parents were pretty excited.

Folks who come up with statistics say a typical man takes about 7100 steps a day. I probably didn't get up to that average until my second birthday, but I've been cranking them out ever since.

In the early years the steps were invariably fast and furious. Many were at reckless speeds. In my teens and twenties they were purposeful and usually swift. Later in life the steps were measured … there was more thought put into the destination than simply the speed at which it was reached.

Now, even though I still walk faster than most people I am around, it takes much more effort to get in my goal of 10,000 steps a day.

Asking God to guide my steps is no small matter. So far there have been over 200 million of them! Ponder these questions that I have been asking myself:

♦ How many of those steps were toward obedience to God's will or how many were spent moving along my own travel plans?
♦ How many steps were detours to help somebody or how many kept me selfishly moving toward only my preferred destiny?

- ♦ How many steps were taken with a peaceful soul or how many were accompanied by strife and the noise of a world gone wild?
- ♦ How many steps did I take fully aware of the Father's voice or how many were taken 'out of communication' with him?
- ♦ How many steps were taken with absolute confidence of God's leading and how many steps faltered and stopped as I insisted on an understanding of why we were going the way we were going?

Steps. Whether fast and frenzied or methodical and plodding, steps mark movement. But movement by itself isn't enough. Movement without direction is haphazard and lacks focus. May the God who not only wants to direct our steps, but takes delight in every detail of our lives (Psalm 37:23) make every one of your steps count!

February 19
Tracing His Steps

Though sometimes he leads through waters deep, trials fall across the way,

though sometimes the path seems rough and steep, see his footprints all the way.
Old Hymn Luther Bridges

I grew up singing this old hymn and when it came to mind the other day I laid it beside the story of the "Footprints in the Sand" that has been circulating for a while now.

We all love the part about God carrying us when only one set of footprints is discernible, but my focus this week is on detecting his presence when we're not strolling in the sand along the seashore. For often God's routing in our lives takes us into the water ... into deep water. No footprints there!

And at other times we climb at his direction high into the hills of conflict, discouragement and affliction and the rocky terrain gives no clue as to anyone's footprints. It's as if no one has ever taken this path before. Now where do I look for reassurance? The stony, uphill path gives no indication that there is Someone making the journey with me.

At times I feel very much like the storm-terrorized disciples. While fighting for their lives against a heavy threatening sea, they knew that Jesus was close ... just not close enough for what they were experiencing. And had I been there, it might have been me who posed the question to the recently-awakened Master, "Don't you care that we are dying?"

But as the sea subsided and became once again manageable, Jesus' followers discovered a truth about the care that comes to those who put their trust and hope in Him. He's never really sleeping. Note Isaiah's strong declaration of faith and confidence:

> *But now, this is what the Lord says– he who created you ... he who formed you ... "Fear not, for I have redeemed you; I have summoned you by name; you are mine. When you pass through the waters, I will be with you; and when you pass through the rivers, they will not sweep over you. When you walk through the fire, you will not be burned; the flames will not set you ablaze. For I am the Lord your God, the Holy One of Israel, your Savior." Isaiah 43:1-3 NIV*

So whether walking the seashore, clamoring up the rocky side of a mountain, fording a swift-moving river or even walking through the fire ... remember this: There will be times when footprints are missing ... comfort isn't felt ... loneliness is stalking ... and there's no obvious antidote to your misery. There's only faith.

And that's enough. Now be joyful along your journey!

Wants or Needs

"But my God shall supply all your needs according to his riches in glory by Christ Jesus." Philippians 4:19 KJV

Do you know the difference between needs and wants?

Every succeeding generation has a tougher time making the distinction. Consider my personal observation. When electric door locks came out for cars I snorted in disdain "If the day ever comes when I can't push four buttons down to lock my car ..." Or this faintly remembered statement: "It's just wimps that can't put up with a little heat. Who needs an air conditioned car?"

Not only have I eaten those words but my present list of 'needs that are critical to my basic survival' now includes not only air conditioning and power door locks, but a navigation system as well. So before my very eyes the frivolous moved into the 'want' column and now reside comfortably in the 'need' category.

Are we suckers or what? In these last six months of our pastorate we find ourselves living in a hundred year old farmhouse where the kitchen has just one electrical outlet and there isn't a garbage disposal, microwave or dishwasher in sight.

Have our lives ground to a halt by the absence of these 'essentials?' Interestingly, no. We have discovered that a couple of must-have items in our lives have fallen back into the 'it-would-be-nice-to-have' classification. And do you know what? I believe God smiles at such a revelation.

Let's make it a bit easier for God to come through with his promise to meet our needs by separating them from the ever growing list of entitlements that come from an ambitious and unsatisfied heart, not so much from a grateful one.

Remember, if we lost it all ... everything ... but kept Jesus, we'd have everything we need.

May you find joy (and contentment) for your journey!

Anticipointment

"Anticipointment" def: hopeful expectation turned upside down/sky-high hopes brought down to ground level

All right, so it's not a legitimate word. I made it up. But I bet you could have used it at several points in your life.

Who hasn't set their sights high...who hasn't entertained big, bold and daring dreams... who hasn't attempted to lasso the moon, only to have reality set in or someone with more clout knock the moon completely out of sight. It's so much a part of life that after several occurrences, especially within a short amount of time, we tend to give up. We sigh with resignation. Our shoulders slump. And our resolve grows to never allow that kind of disappointment to ambush us again.

So we lower our expectations. We make the bull's eye too big to miss. We live and dream in dreary black and white until we've downsized our dream list so small that we're absolutely certain to get whatever is on it. How understandable.

How pathetic.

Maybe the problem has been that your dreams and aspirations haven't been big enough! Maybe you need to trade in your old black and white set for one with radiant color. Just maybe your dream list needs to be 'up-sized' and your bull's eye needs to be made so small that you'll only hit it if God does the aiming.

Take a careful look at the dreams that you've given up on. Look carefully to see if they have "Engineered By God" engraved on them. If they do, shrug off the 'pointment' part of that new word and concentrate again on the 'antici' part of it.

Eugene Peterson in "The Message" captures this attitude when talking about Abraham's faith: *"When everything was hopeless, Abraham believed anyway, deciding to live not on the basis of what he saw he couldn't do but on what God said he would do."* Romans 4:18 The Message

Why not go looking for that moon again today?

A True Scale

A half century ago it was the wandering thumb of the butcher who could turn a fair transaction into one that heavily favored his profits. Nowadays, the scales are tipped in more insidious ways.

Somebody is moving the ancient landmarks…those guidelines that differentiated between right and wrong, between good and evil. Or as another writer asserts, "Someone has switched all the price tags."

And so now a bag of virginity and chastity sells for pennies on the dollar. Integrity in business dealings has been heavily discounted. It often costs to conduct business ethically …but have we got a sale for you! Waiting and patience used to carry significant price tags, but we can get it for you not only faster, but cheaper as well. The scales used to reflect equal parts of joy and responsibility for fathering a child. Now the balance is tipped, if not toward joy, at least away from responsibility.

There are some who consider plants and animals of higher value than humanity who God came to redeem. Although He watches over the rest of creation and finds value in it, He sent his Son to redeem us. Let's never be confused by this.

Will the chaos go on forever? Will the lines remain blurred for the rest of time and on into eternal destinies? No, for Scripture declares *"Honest scales and balances are from the Lord; all the weights in the bag are of his making." Proverbs 16:11 NIV* The Eternal Standard Bearer still holds the real weights in his bag. His is the final word. Consensus is not the ultimate determiner of right and wrong.

Someday everyone's life will be weighed on the only scale that counts. There will be no wandering thumb to sway the results...no judgment based on the opinion of our peers... no sliding scale that turns a "C" into an "A". This week I want to be judged by the weights that will ultimately determine the success of my entire life. It's what's in God's bag that carries the only weight that counts.

Patience Adjuster

What do you do when God says, "The check's in the mail?" Roll your eyes and mutter "Yeah, I'll bet" or keep checking your mail box to see if it's come yet? There are a lot of us hanging on to what we believe to be promised from God on our behalf. It's either something we have read from the Word (and God can't lie) or something that He has birthed deep within us that even months or years later still carries the ring of eternal authenticity as it quietly ricochets around our 'believing apparatus.'

Proverbs 13:12 tells us that *"Hope deferred makes the heart sick."* And nobody I know wants to run around with a sick heart. So what are my alternatives? How do I continue driving to the Post Office while harboring the lingering suspicion that my PO box might likely be empty again?

There are only two real alternatives. One...turn off your 'believer'...write the whole thing off as pure fantasy...quit driving and looking...don't expect anything and get God out of the picture. Or, do like Abraham who had had decades of empty mail boxes to dishearten him. *"When everything was hopeless, Abraham believed anyway, deciding to live not on the basis of what he saw he couldn't do but on what God said he would do." Romans 4:18 The Message*

The writer of the book of Hebrews is talking to some whose belief began with gusto. His words: *"Don't throw it all away now. You were sure of yourselves then. It's still a sure thing! But you need to stick it out, staying with God's plan so you'll be there for the promised completion. It won't be long now, he's on the way…" Hebrews 10:35-37 The Message*

Though it may be delayed, God can be trusted. When He tells us it's coming … it's coming! Don't allow the delay to discourage, but to build anticipation of its arrival. God can be trusted.

Keep checking your mail box!

February 24

Prayer

I dislike stuffy, pontificating prayers. You know…the kind prayed by 'prayer pros' who cast ecclesiastical eyes heavenward as they intone *"Oh thou beneficent Most High God, ruler of heaven and earth; incline thine ear to this thy servant, etc., etc., etc."* Be they ever so sincere and manage to cover all salient points, I'm still not comfortable with prayers like that.

Give me a 'straight-from-the-heart' and 'what-you-see-is-what-you-get' prayer. One not hindered or worried toward heaven by concerns of either political or theological correctness. The kind of prayer that believes that absolutely anything can be said and that even groaning will be somehow turned into eloquence by the Father's attentive listening.

Although the latter is my preferred kind of prayer, it is exercised with some measure of danger. And it is this: we must never lose the awe of getting to talk personally with God. He's more than "The Man Upstairs" or our "Good Buddy in the Sky." We must retain a bit of the mystery that David expressed when he pondered "What is man that You are even mindful of him?"

In Psalm 18 after expressing concern about the hostile world pressing in on him, David says the following: *"I call to God, I cry to God to help me. From his palace he hears my call; my cry brings me right into his presence – a private audience!" Psalm 18:6 The Message*

There is a balance called for in this breathtaking arena of 'God Communication.' I must stay amazed that He would even pause to listen…to take time to sort out what I really mean from what I have said…to actively involve Himself in my puny affairs. It's beyond amazing.

Yet He calls me to approach Him with the confidence and boldness that comes only through a loving relationship between Father and child.

February 25

Turn Down The Noise

The beat goes on. Does it ever!

Sitting at a red light with my window down, I suddenly felt agitated. Something was bothering me. And then I realized that I was a guest at three distinct concerts going on simultaneously in three separate vehicles around mine. All three were playing music loud enough to vie for my attention … and all three had driving amplified rhythms badly out of sync with each other.

It was the battle of the bands and I was the loser.

There are many beats going on in our world at the same time. We often have several that we march to in a given day. But more often than not their tempo is labeled "Faster." As a culture we seem paranoid about ever slowing down. It's like a steam roller is right behind us and constantly picking up speed. We have no choice but to crank up the tempo and run just a bit faster.

Oh but we do have a choice. In a far less hectic time when everyone walked … the day ended when the sun went down … and most of life was reduced to utter simplicity … Jesus saw the effects of pressure and stress on his disciples. Look at his instructions. *"Then Jesus said, 'Let's go off by ourselves to a quiet place and rest awhile.' He said this because there were so many people coming and going that Jesus and his apostles didn't even have time to eat. So they left by boat for a quiet place, where they could be alone." Mark 6:31,32 New Living Translation*

He's still saying that to us. It's time to come apart from it all before you come apart!

Here are my questions for you today: Where do you go to get away from the noise of life? Is there a way to turn off the music and trade entertainment for real rest? Can God's quiet voice even be heard above the man made roar that surrounds us?

There is a quiet place. It's in God's presence …but you have to go there on purpose.

February 26
Becoming Like Him

*"How great is the love the Father has lavished on us, that we should be called children of God! And that is what we are! The reason the world does not know us is that it did not know him. Dear friends, now we are children of God, and **what we will be has not yet been made known**. But we know that when he appears, we shall be like him, for*

we shall see him as he is. Everyone who has this hope in
him purifies himself, just as he is pure." 1 John 3:1-3 NIV

I'm a work in progress and so are you.

There's a statement about our relationship with our Heavenly Father that is key to so many things. It says, "God loves us just the way we are, but loves us too much to leave us that way." That's wonderful news and troubling news all at the same time. It means that God loves us so much that He intends to keep 'messing with us.'

We know (if our eschatology is correct) that 'when he appears, we shall be like him' and what a change that will be! But not all the changing will take place only at that instant. It's going on right now.

♦ Every challenge I face changes me
♦ Each temptation fought makes me a different man
♦ The sad, lonely experiences mold me into someone different from the old me

The transformation is gradual and incremental, yet continual. We have many agendas for ourselves. God has one - to make us into the image and characteristics of His Son Jesus. Eugene Peterson in The Message gives us II Corinthians 3:18 in this way: *"And so we are transfigured much like the Messiah, our lives gradually becoming brighter and more beautiful as God enters our lives and we become like him."* The ESV version says that we are being changed 'from one degree of glory to another.'

In walking, I can't recognize a one degree deviation in my journey, but God can and does. And every modification of my passage into his likeness is carefully attended to and noted with pride.

It's not my chronological journey that matters most to my Father, but the movement to 'Christ-likeness' that captivates his attention.

February 27
Walking With The Shepherd

Aren't you glad that the sheep never have to walk where the Shepherd isn't leading?

You may not know what this day holds for you, but if you follow the Shepherd 'not knowing' is not critical. Why? Because the Shepherd knows.

He sees forward with more clarity than we see backwards. And not only can He see forward, but He has planned forward as well. He said this about each of us in Psalm 139: 16 *"You saw me before I was born. Every day of my life was recorded in your book. Every moment was laid out before a single day had passed." New Living Translation* So you see, today is already an open book to God. Not just did He 'pre-see' it, but He actually 'pre-planned' it. Every day.

Your life has been scripted by God. He had a plan before you had a life! It's an awesome thought to realize that the Creator of the universe had you in mind before the universe was ever created! And what an honor and thrill to work alongside of God in the completion of that plan.

Now combine God knowing about your life's plan and then see his intentions for those plans in Psalm 31:19: *"What a stack of blessing you have piled up for those who worship you, Ready and waiting for all who run to you to escape an unkind world." The Message*

As the saying goes, if that doesn't light your fire, your wood's wet!

The God who has good things in store for you is going to be your companion throughout this day. Expect something special and hang on for the ride!

February 28
Buried or Planted?

Buried or planted? Every test in life puts us under. At least that's what it feels like when we get sick, lose a job, or lose a close relationship. A tragedy strikes and suddenly the bottom is above us!

But being buried or being planted are vastly different from each other. It has far more to do with our attitude and faith than with the circumstances arrayed against us. When you're buried you stay exactly the same, but when you're planted, you never come out the same as you go in.

When you're buried, you're gone. When you're planted, you're coming back.

When you're buried, hope dies. When you're planted hope stays alive.

When you're buried, there's no tomorrow. When you're planted it's still there.

You bury what's dead … you plant potential.

Technically you don't bury seed, you plant it. The difference is, you expect the life in that seed to not only reproduce itself, but to multiply itself. There would be no farming if not for this confidence.

God allows us to be 'planted' in the soil of difficulty because He knows that ultimately life will overcome even compacted soil and that a plentiful harvest will result. A quick look throughout Scripture confirms this truth.

♦ Joseph was falsely accused and planted in prison until he broke through the crusty trial to assume a position of authority.

♦ Job was planted in the soil of heartbreak, depression and misunderstanding until there was a harvest of vindication and blessing.
♦ Moses found himself planted in a wilderness, far from his privileged upbringing until he broke into the future God had planned for him.
♦ David was planted in the soil of treachery, running for his life for almost two decades until he was ready to ascend to the throne for which he had been anointed.
♦ Jesus was planted in the soil of obscurity for 30 years as He was readied for the work assigned him by the Father. And at the completion of that work they planted him in a break-out-proof tomb but at the appointed time he broke out far different than he went in and with enough life to share with the entire world.

Buried? Not me. I'm planted and have "Come Back" written all over me.

> "The one who plants in response to God, letting God's Spirit do the growth work in him, harvests a crop of real life, eternal life." Galatians 6:8 The Message

March 1
'But' – A Change In Direction

'But' … "a grammatical word used in the middle of a sentence to introduce something that is true in spite of either being or seeming contrary to what has just been said."

It's a direction turner … a grammatical U-turn that faces us in the direction of new possibilities and new realities. Especially when 'but' is followed by 'God.' Consider:

"Joseph replied, 'Don't be afraid of me. Am I God, that I can punish you? 20 You intended to harm me, **but God** intended it all for good." Genesis 50:19, 20

"David now stayed in the strongholds of the wilderness and … Saul hunted him day after day, **but God** didn't let Saul find him." I Samuel 23:14

"My health may fail, and my spirit may grow weak, **but God** remains the strength of my heart; he is mine forever." Psalm 73:26

"They put him to death by hanging him on a cross, **but God** raised him to life on the third day." Acts 10:39, 40

"It is beyond my power to do this," Joseph replied. "**But God** can tell you what it means and set you at ease." Genesis 41:16

Can you see the exciting possibilities this phrase makes in our lives? Here are five short examples out of many in Scripture. Each one reminds us that 'what is' doesn't have to be 'what will be.'

- ♦ Joseph: "Your intentions set my life in the direction of a curse and failure and anonymity. But God had other plans."
- ♦ David: "It was a foregone conclusion that I'd be found, but God had other plans for me."
- ♦ David: "There may be a natural process of deterioration going on here, but God has the long term taken care of."
- ♦ Jesus: "No one has ever had life after a cross experience, but God has the power even over death."
- ♦ Joseph: "I may have run up against an insolvable issue, but God isn't stumped."

Are you in need of a 'But God' change of direction? Ask Him to inject Himself into your dilemma, your question, your wrong direction, your impossibilities. He's not only willing, but able.

March 2
Chuck

I just returned from meeting a new friend. His name is Chuck and he presently resides at a local hospital's hospice center. In his own words, his prognosis is 'grim.' It usually is when a hospice is your current address.

He's at the end of three long years of critical illnesses which include prostrate cancer, a strange disease that caused three months of paralysis, open heart surgery and now pancreatic cancer. The 'whiny factor' should be huge.

You shouldn't be able to get near Chuck without getting an earful of medical-ese explaining how tough life has been and how the end should not come this way.

But there was only sweetness, thanksgiving and hope that came from him.

How does that happen? What gets into a man to cause him to downplay such horrendous recent history and look death in the face and do it all with serious yet unbounded faith?

First of all, there's the history he has with God. He's had decades of observing God's faithfulness, love and attention to the details of his life. The "Friend that sticks closer than a brother" has proven Himself to Chuck over and over again.

And then there's the matter of the future. You know … the 'eye hasn't seen what God has prepared' part. That seems to be pretty well settled with Chuck as well. And while it's true that eye hasn't seen and ear hasn't heard what's awaiting us when we leave here and get there (I Corinthians 2:9), we know enough about God's handiwork to know it will be spectacular. We know enough about his love to know we'll be ecstatically happy there. And we've known enough of those who have already gone there to know the fellowship that awaits us.

But the most significant thing Chuck knows about the trip is that Jesus, his lifelong Companion, Savior and Friend will be there to greet him. And that explains the smile on Chuck's face as I left his room.

> *"Even when the way goes through Death Valley, I'm not afraid when you walk at my side." Psalm 23:4 The Message*

March 3
Changes

> *"I think of the good ole days, long since ended, when my nights were filled with joyful songs. I search my soul and ponder the difference now." Psalm 77:5,6 New Living Translation*

I recently visited my alma mater...the place I received my formal Biblical training. Along with the cascade of flooding memories came the realization that a lot has changed in the forty years since I graduated.

- ♦ gas for your car is no longer $.25 a gallon (read it and weep!)
- ♦ a semester of school (room and board) is no longer $500
- ♦ you can't buy a brand new, fire-engine red Rambler American 440H sedan for under $3,000
- ♦ managing a small neighborhood grocery store now pays more than $.95 an hour
- ♦ you can no longer drive the 500 miles back to your home in Chicago for around $5 in fuel cost
- ♦ and just try to get a five-course, filet mignon dinner with all the trimmings for $1.95 and see how successful you are!

Yes indeed...times have changed. But the biggest change over those four decades? Something so dramatic and unsettling that no Bible school education could have prepared me for it.

It's the distance brought about by the tectonic shift between the sacred and the secular.

You could not have convinced me that the day would come when the bulk of my cherished beliefs would not be shared with the majority of people around me. I would not have been able to conceive of the notion that one day babies not wanted by either mother or father or both would be labeled "Throw-aways." It never dawned on me that in the years to come, each succeeding generation would show less interest in the church that I was about to give my life to see flourish. And I never envisioned a time when attempting to pull those people to the message they needed would consume so much of the time, energy and resources of the church.

I miss the old prices...but I grieve for the changes in the spiritual/ethical fabric of my world. But neither you nor I can afford to stand gazing fondly back to a life and time we liked better than this one. This is where God has us, and for good reason. There's an incredibly important and wildly exciting job that needs to get done.

So remember that while this generation may show little or limited interest in church... their spiritual hunger is still acute. They may exhibit a 'nonchalant' attitude toward our programs, but they really want a relationship with our God. Let's live today as it really is ...a strategic opportunity to touch this time...this place...this culture...with the presence of God.

March 4
Blessed To Bless

Genesis 12:2 (God speaking to Abraham) "I will cause you to become the father of a great nation. I will bless you and make you famous, and I will make you a blessing to others." New Living Translation

The word 'blessing' makes us feel good all over – the plural 'blessings' is even better. Our desire to be blessed is not only natural, but Scriptural as well. Remember Jabez… "Oh that Thou wouldest bless me indeed." It's 1611 King's English but it sets up a wonderful resonance in our hearts.

But while aspiring to live a life blessed by God, remember that it's not all about you. You are not to be the final destination of the good things that God sends your way. He told Abraham "I'm going to bless your socks off. Everyone who witnesses my care for you will be envious. But if my goodness to you produces only envy in others, you've missed my whole point. My blessings are to transit through your life and bless others as well. Blessed to be a blessing…that's my plan for both you and them."

This morning I took a large trash bag of empty pop cans and plastic water bottles to the recycling center nearby. It took ten minutes to feed all the cans and bottles into the contraption that separated the cans from the plastic and glass bottles. It then presented me with a voucher to a grocery store across the parking lot. I was thinking about what I would buy with the $7.66 when I almost collided with him. He was obviously a homeless man of indeterminate age. He had accumulated six bags of cans and bottles.

In spite of the dirt on his face, it reflected hours and hours in the desert sun collecting the throw-aways of others. For him to collect almost eight dollars worth of cans and bottles would have taken him many hours and possibly several days. God has blessed Joanie and me with the ability to purchase all the soft drinks and bottled water that we desire. They had blessed me once already when I consumed them…so instead of adding another layer of blessing on an already-blessing-rich life I asked the man if he would like my voucher.

Am I gloating over exemplary Christian conduct? No, I'm just glad that God gave me a spontaneous opportunity this week of sharing a little of what He's given me with someone else. I've been blessed so I can bless others!

Who You Gonna Believe?

For the last forty years or so we've had increasing difficulty believing our politicians. What they say isn't necessarily what they mean or know. Truth isn't quite as important as expediency or appearances.

And how believable are those ads promising instant relief from everything from acne to high blood pressure? Twenty years of high blood pressure and destructive eating habits erased overnight with a pill?

We must face the fact that the god of this world ... the one who sets much of the agenda we live with ... has been, is and will continue to be a liar. We can't take anything he says to the bank because the check will bounce every time!

Ah, but we do have a wonderful choice in this issue of believability. There is One whose word is true. We not only can take his word to the bank, we can sleep on it, too.

- ♦ When He promises peace, (John 14;27) He can deliver, no matter how much we're told by the commentators to "be afraid ... be very afraid."
- ♦ When He promises to supply all of our needs, (Philippians 4:19) that promise is backed by all the resources of heaven, not the liquidity of the Federal Reserve Bank.
- ♦ When He promises you rest, (Matthew 11:28,29) it doesn't come with side effects.
- ♦ And when He promises you salvation, (Romans 6:23) He doesn't leave you with a bill for the outstanding balance. It's been totally paid for in advance!

So it comes down to this: Who are you going to believe? Over-exposure to something tends to make it believable to us. If we hear over and over again that a certain life-style is perfectly acceptable, we eventually begin to believe it ourselves. When 'wrong' is labeled 'right' over and over and over again, it starts to blur our assessment.

That's why it's critical for those of us known as 'believers' to listen more to the One who is trustworthy than to listen to those to whom truth is relative. Woe unto any of us who give more time and attention to 'truth modifiers' than we give to the One who not only tells the truth, but is in reality "The Truth."

Shame on any of us who come to believe everyone and everything but the One who is constantly telling the truth, the whole truth and nothing but the truth!

> *"Jesus answered, 'I am the way and the truth and the life. No one comes to the Father except through me.'" John 14:6 NIV*

Enjoy the journey and don't believer everything you hear!

Foretaste

Hymn writer Fanny Crosby talked of a 'foretaste of glory divine' that belongs to us simply because we belong to Jesus!

Just imagine …

If in the midst of intense sorrow
    God can bring joy …

If during daunting trouble
    He can instigate deep peace …

If in the clamor of culture's noise
    He provides quiet …

If, while surrounded by antagonism and bullies
　　He can make you feel loved and safe …
If in the middle of foot tapping frustration
　　He can deliver patience …
If in debilitating desperation
　　He can fill with unquenchable hope …
Take a moment to look forward to the kind of care He will provide us once He deals forever with sorrow, trouble, sin, hatred and hopelessness. His care and love know no bounds now … catch a foretaste of what is to come!

> *"Now God has us where he wants us, with all the time in this world and the next to shower grace and kindness upon us in Christ Jesus. Saving is all his idea, and all his work. All we do is trust him enough to let him do it. It's God's gift from start to finish!" Ephesians 2:7,8 The Message*

May there be great joy and anticipation while on your journey!

March 7
Faith

I am constantly amazed and heartened by the resiliency of faith.

Not mine, but many around me. I listen to people praying for jobs for others when they've been unemployed for a year. Yet their faith is intact. There's the mother who like Abraham, "against all hope … in hope believed" for the healing of her infant son.

Faith is designed to go whatever distance is called for. It's meant to outlast the opposition, every time. Faith is not flimsy and fleeting. Faith is 'substance' we're told in Hebrews 11:1.

Abraham continued to believe long past what everyone around him thought was his faith's expiration date. Job's faith lasted until the testing was over and divine restitution had been made. And while the king may have been pacing in his worry about Daniel, Daniel's faith lasted until he had fallen fast asleep in the den of lions.

Shadrach, Meshach and Abednego had faith that lasted into, during and coming out of the fiery furnace. Caleb's strong faith only grew stronger as he was forced to trudge the weary desert with a million faithless until he finally won his inheritance.

How many more stories do we need to understand just how durable faith is? We're not some kind of debris floating helplessly on the sea of life … being driven wherever the wind takes us. Oh no, our faith is more than adequate to get us safely through any storm … any circumstance … any opposition.

The Apostle Peter says it well: *" … through your faith, God is protecting you by his power until you receive this salvation, which is ready to be revealed on the last day for all to see." I Peter 1:5 New Living Translation*

Find comfort and strength in the anchor of your soul … you have more than enough faith to complete the journey!

March 8
The Ledger

As of my last count I have lost the balance mechanism of my inner ear (thanks to a prescription for a bug caught overseas) … gotten arthritis in my left thumb … need glasses for everything … and don't bend easily at the waist anymore.

As I was ruminating over my considerable losses and doing a bit of internalized grumbling, I found myself counting stuff from the other side of the ledger. For instance, I've never broken a bone. Never had an operation. Never suffered through the passing of a kidney stone or had gall stones. There has never been an ulcer that I've had to contend with. I have not been nor am I presently fighting cancer.

I do not have diabetes, fallen arches, a spine injury or tonsillitis. I've never been treated for high blood pressure or gout. No doctor has ever prescribed anxiety-relief medication. When quizzed by a new doctor I answer "No" to sexually transmitted diseases, heart murmur, hearing loss, anorexia (are you kidding me?) or dementia.

There's lots more on the 'never had' side of the sheet, but suffice it to say that physically speaking, God's been really good to me. However, I'm fascinated by the side of the ledger that I started on. While grousing over four rather minor things that 'tribulate me' I ignore 217 positive affirmations of God's care in my life.

And so, I'm sitting here feeling very carnal … extremely embarrassed and with a growing sense of chagrin at short-changing God with my praise. And how about you? What have you been concentrating on? Is your *praise report* in the formative stage while your *book of whining* has already been published and in its third printing?

Let the Psalmist help each of us here. *"Let all that I am praise the Lord; may I never forget the good things he does for me."* Psalm 103:2 New Living Translation

May there be joy and gratitude for your journey!

March 9

The Witnesses

"Therefore, since we are surrounded by such a great cloud of witnesses, let us throw off everything that hinders and the sin that so easily entangles, and let us run with perseverance the race marked out for us." Hebrews 12:1 NIV

The eleventh chapter of Hebrews has introduced us to a remarkable assortment of true spiritual heroes. There we revisit Noah, earth's first flood insurance policy. We see Abraham whose "Yes" to God came at incredible personal pain and was born out of extraordinary faith and confidence in his God. Isaac, Jacob and Joseph come next … three men whose commitment to follow God's plan took their lives in some harrowing directions.

Next the parents of Moses see wonderful potential in their baby boy and engineer a plan to keep him alive. For his part, Moses makes a painful decision to side with God's people and turn his back on a life of ease and prominence in the great Egyptian dynasty. Later, Israel itself is praised for its willingness to walk through the sea, walk around Jericho and follow God into their inheritance.

These heroes " …toppled kingdoms, made justice work … were protected from lions, fires and sword thrusts, turned disadvantage into advantage, won battles, and routed alien armies." We're told of others who, " … under torture, refused to give in and go free … braved abuse and whips, chains and dungeons. Some were stoned, sawed in two, murdered in cold blood … wandered the earth in animal skins, homeless, friendless, powerless." And the writer says this world wasn't worthy of any of them.

After bearing witness of their lives, the writer turns the tables and informs us that this 'cloud of witnesses' now bear witness to our lives. Whether they are actually peering over the balcony of heaven observing us or not, the fact remains … their lives powerfully remind us that no sin, no distraction, no detour is worth it if it keeps us from finishing our race. This week, go all out. Don't let anything stop you from being all that God has in mind for you to be. Put some determined discipline into the effort. God Himself is the prize!

March 10
What's In Your Hand?

"What's in your hand?" God asked Moses. "It's just a plain old walking stick," he replied. (Exodus 4)

"And what's in your hand?" God asked David the shepherd. "A few worthless rocks," was his response. (I Samuel 17)

"And you, Shamgar" He asked. "What's that you are holding?" "Just an ox goad, God … good for little but moving stubborn livestock along." (Judges 3)

With each man, God asked permission to use those worthless 'hand helds'.

The God-anointed walking stick of Moses out-performed the best magic in Egypt, parted the Red Sea and provided drinking water for a multitude of thirsty travelers.

Just one of David's inappreciable little stones, with a bit of help from heaven's GPS, found the giant's forehead and reversed a nation's fortunes.

And Shamgar's ox goad? When God's intentions flowed through it, 600 Philistines fell dead and Israel's days of hiding in ditches and caves were over.

That is not an Old Testament question. It sizzles like a laser beam from God's inquiring heart to every believer on earth. "What's in your hand?"

Be very careful not to minimize your assumed answer. "Just a MBA in business … it's only a paltry ability to sing … it's a gift for telling stories to kids … it's a knack for fixing cars … it's only a love of giving to people in need … it's nothing but an interest in people in third world countries."

God already knows what it is you possess. He's simply looking for permission to add his power and purpose to it. Give that seeming inconsequential thing you hold to God and watch Him make the miraculous out of your ordinary.

"God has given each of you a gift from his great variety of spiritual gifts. Use them well to serve one another." I Peter 4:10 New Living Translation

March 11
Behind The Tapestry

Would God have a preacher study all week, come to the pulpit fully prepared and then aim all that work and energy at just one person and her need? Would God ever take a famous evangelist in the midst of a successful city-wide crusade and take him, his message and his commitment out into the countryside to speak to just one?

The evangelist Philip in Acts 8 was enjoying just such a successful ministry. 'Great crowds of people' not only listened to him but responded to his call for repentance and watched him perform miracles and wonders. And from this event pregnant with spiritual possibilities, God asks him to go minister to a single Ethiopian man struggling with his understanding of Scripture. Does that make any sense to you?

You see, that's precisely our problem. And it is a problem when our attempts at controlling events gets in God's way. We love it when things make sense to us...when we can trace from A to B and eventually arrive at E and know just how we got there. God does some of his most important work behind the scenes, with more insight and with an entirely different perspective than us. Not only does He have access to all potential information, but knows the end from the beginning. We see less and most often with no divine insight. We are, as the Apostle Paul stated 'seeing through a glass darkly.' Kind of like squinting in a dust storm.

But the day is coming when God's finished tapestry will be on display...his handiwork finally finished...his eternal masterpiece hung for all the world to see. He will gather all the threads that we have labeled "Makes-No-Sense-To-Me" and with them produce a finished product that will defy all human attempts at understanding and comprehension. When seen, it will cause every one of us to bow and exclaim, "What an awesome God!"

I look forward to that grand unveiling. And I'll let you in on a little secret. When I have gazed at God's tapestry for a time from the front, I plan on slipping around the back to see the mysterious and marvelous ways that God weaved it all together...especially those parts that didn't make any sense to me when they occurred.

> *"I've also concluded that whatever God does, that's the way it's going to be, always. No addition, no subtraction. God's done it and that's it. That's so we'll quit asking questions and simply worship in holy fear." Ecclesiastes 3:14 The Message*

March 12

Ten Commandments

Mention the phrase "Ten Commandments" around most people and immediately word pictures come to mind:

- ◆ Charlton Heston raising his walking stick over a fake Red Sea
- ◆ a set of stodgy standards that don't relate to our world anymore
- ◆ a list of do's and don'ts that severely threaten the potential for any joy in life

But none of the word pictures above give God the credit He deserves. He is not a capricious parent who loves the sound of his own voice…is impressed by the power of his control over others… whose edicts are often arbitrary and void of meaning or consequence. Every time God utters a command…every time…it is backed by both wisdom and overarching love. The Psalmist said it this way:

> *"God's laws are perfect. They protect us, make us wise, and give us joy and light. God's laws are pure, eternal, just. They are more desirable than gold. They are sweeter than honey dripping from a honeycomb. For they warn us away from harm and give success to those who obey them." Psalm 19:7-11 Living Bible*

So today and throughout this year, embrace the laws of God in your personal life, your business life, your social life… in every arena of living. Running from his words does not lead to freedom; instead it leads to total domination by the ugliness and depravity of a fallen world.

Never see God's counsel for your life as 'nit-picking' and confining. He's not a 'busybody' trying to mess up your life with confusing and trivial rules to follow. Instead, his great heart longs to see you complete your journey successfully and with joy.

The future is bright and filled with inconceivable possibilities when we operate within the parameters of God's thoughtful and careful care.

May joy mark your journey!

March 13
When Somebody Loves You

I know people who get powerful spiritual lessons from everything in life. They go to see a movie with a plot built around blowing up buildings and somehow come away with spiritual insight into dealing with their teenager. They pause at the supermarket to read the label on a jar of peanut butter and come away with a truth pertaining to the return of Christ.

I don't necessarily doubt their 'reads'   guess maybe I'm just jealous. And I'm not worried since ultimately every truth needs the authentication of God's Word. It will prevail when peanut butter labels have all disappeared.

But having said that, I did find a spiritual thought coming out of an old Frank Sinatra ballad. I had my iPod on shuffle, so along with soaring praise and worship there would come an occasional soft jazz sax solo or the Beach Boys extolling the virtue of California, its waters and its girls. (If this doesn't date me, nothing does, right?)

Then came Frank Sinatra, the "Chairman of the Board" reminding us that if someone is going to love you, they need to love you 'all the way.'

Although not written as theology, the Holy Spirit seemed to say to me, "Paul, that's precisely how God has loved you. When He determined to draw you in by his love, He went all the way … not stopping until the cross had proven forever that He was serious about his intentions toward you."

Partial love, intermittent commitment, half-hearted allegiance … that's not how God does anything. Let his example offer us the blueprint we follow with those we are committed to. May our children, our spouses and especially our Heavenly Father find us pulling out all the stops in the way we love.

> *"I paid a huge price for you … That's how much you mean to me! That's how much I love you! I'd sell off the whole world to get you back, trade the creation just for you." Isaiah 43:3,4 The Message*

May there be thankful joy for your journey!

March 14

Putting On Airs

> *So be content with who you are, and don't put on airs.*
> *God's strong hand is on you; he'll promote you at the*
> *right time. Live carefree before God; he is most careful*
> *with you. I Peter 5:6, 7 The Message*

I suppose we all do it ... put on airs. We attempt to look, act and actually be someone different from who we really are. And since it's now a cultural epidemic, we're getting awfully good at it.

We buy expensive sweat suits that we never sweat in ... but it gives the appearance of athleticism. We drive cars that we cannot afford ... but the image of affluence stays intact. We use big words that we don't fully understand ... but people assume we're well taught. We swagger through crowds with forced smiles ... but inside there is insecurity and heartbreak.

Even in our religion we put on airs.

In worship we sing as if we mean it ... while contemplating the buffet line. We nod at the pastor's challenge as if it has taken deep root in our heart ... while refusing to respond to the last half dozen spiritual admonitions we've been given. We treat struggling saints with disdain, pretending that we've got it all together ... while inside there hasn't been a notable victory in quite some time.

I know I am not speaking for everyone here. Hopefully not even the majority. But I am painfully aware of just how much grandstanding goes on in my own life. And all the time we spend 'acting as if' we move ourselves away from the One who has the power to really authenticate us. To make us real. To save us from the ongoing battle of trying to impress.

Self-promotion is illusory. There is no substance to it. Real promotion has always come from the One who knows us best … and still loves us.

> *"For promotion and power come from nowhere on earth,*
> *but only from God." Psalm 75:6 The Living Bible*

Get real. And experience God's joy on your journey.

March 15
Lighten Up

> *"In his unfailing love, my God will stand with me.*
> *He will let me look down in triumph on all my enemies."*
> Ps 59:10 New Living Translation

We need to 'lighten up' sometimes.

We who soldier on behalf of the cross … who daily carry on the battle of the Kingdom … who sometimes feel neck-deep in a spiritual war that appears unwinnable … need to take a 'time out' and revisit God's throne.

Coming in from the pressures of the conflict, having been dodging the fiery darts of the enemy, having had to deal with the constant intimidation and insults of the opposition telling us that we can't possibly win this war … we need to see what's going on at headquarters!

As we step into the throne room, with the smell of battle about us … with fatigue showing in the lines of our faces … and with no small amount of fear that the battle isn't going well at all … we find an amazing sight!

God is laughing.

He who knows beginning from end, who not only holds power but is Absolute Power holds the threats of the wicked in total disdain and derision. He sneers at their insolence. As Matthew Henry says, "Sinner's follies are the just sport of God's infinite wisdom and power, and those attempts of the kingdom of Satan which in our eyes are formidable in his are despicable."

Today, leave the battle front long enough to check out the atmosphere back at headquarters. No wringing of hands, no furrowed worried brow ... just a God who reminds us that 'the battle is his' and that the outcome is assured.

> *"The wicked plot against the godly; they snarl at them in defiance.*
> *But the Lord just laughs, for he sees their day of judgment coming."*
> *Psalm 37:12,13 New Living Translation*

> *"Why are the nations so angry? Why do they waste their time with futile plans?*
> *2 The kings of the earth prepare for battle; the rulers plot together*
> *against the Lord and against his anointed one.*
> *3 'Let us break their chains' they cry, 'and free ourselves from slavery to God.'*
> *4 But the one who rules in heaven laughs. The Lord scoffs at them."*
> *Ps 2:1 New Living Translation*

March 16
Meandering

> *"So I run straight to the goal with purpose in every step."*
> *I Corinthians 9:26 The Living Bible*

When I golf (which is seldom) I utilize the famous "Zig Zag" method. I believe I have refined it to an art form. Starting at the tee box I gaze at the distant pin then send the ball at acute angles into surrounding shrubbery and woodlands. I easily turn a typical 7200 yard scenic course into miles and miles of wilderness trekking where often a machete could have been quite useful.

I am aware that 'the shortest distance between two points is a straight line' but I've never applied that to my game.

However, I am far more concerned with how I am playing the game of life ... particularly as a follower of Jesus. When I forget the goal and let purpose get murky, I do a lot of meandering.

- ◆ I purpose to make Jesus Lord of my life ... until something else turns my head and heart and I veer off course.
- ◆ I purpose to keep joy as my constant companion ... until I allow a newscaster's words to steal it and I stutter toward the sidelines.
- ◆ I purpose to always take the high road ... until the alternative appears to get me further faster, and again, it's into the woods seeking that which can only be found by moving straight ahead.
- ◆ I purpose to keep heaven and its awaiting joys my focus and then believe the lie that I can make heaven here if I just work enough, spend enough and enlarge enough.

Today concentrate on moving forward spiritually in a straight line. Look ahead at where you want to be. See that flag way off in the distance? Aim for that!

The Apostle Paul had several phrases he used to help us here. *"Set your affections on things above ..." (Colossians 3:1) ... "press on toward the goal ..." (Philippians 3:14)*

If you have to meander, do it on the golf course, not with your life.

May you find joy and 'destination focus' on your journey!

March 17

Extravagant Worship

Don't be fooled by the title … this isn't about church or church music.

Worship is the worth you assign to anything or anybody in your life. Although there is only one God, there are many gods to whom we grant worth. Some worship the stuff in their garages, the children they are raising, their favorite sport team, the week-ends.

The level of our worship is determined by how much that thing or person dominates our lives. Cruising the night spots on Friday and Saturday nights takes all the energy and planning that some people put out all week long. Others 'live for' the start of the next sports season, or the immaculate condition of their yard.

'Extravagant' means *spending much more than is necessary or wise; wasteful; excessively high and exceeding the bounds of reason.* Not much in our lives is deserving of this kind of attention! It's not that we don't give it to some things… just that they may not be worth the extravagance of so much of our time and attention.

Jesus doesn't demand this kind of worship, but applauds it. When a woman poured a year's worth of insanely expensive oil on his feet as an act of adoration and surrender, Jesus told the money-pinchers to leave her alone. "She has done a good thing," he declared.

Extravagant worship involves loving Jesus so much that you are willing to put yourself completely at his disposal, allowing him to use you how, where and when he sees fit. You relinquish control, and control is something few of us give up without a fight. When I love Jesus with all my heart I long to do what he wants me to do … more than I want to do what I want to do.

Easy? Are you kidding? This is a "living sacrifice" agenda. A dead sacrifice stays put. A living sacrifice keeps trying to crawl off the altar. And therein lies the challenge.

I want to worship the only One truly worthy of my time, energies and attention. I want my worship to be sincere, focused and with enough energy to let the Lord and anyone else around know without a doubt that he is number one in my life.

Extravagance is only negative if the object or intent is not worthy.

> *"For since the world began, no ear has heard and no eye has seen a God like you, who works for those who wait for him!"*
> *Isaiah 64:4 New Living Translation*

March 18

Bow or Burn

> *"Shadrach, Meshach and Abednego replied to the king, "O Nebuchadnezzar, we do not need to defend ourselves before you in this matter. If we are thrown into the blazing furnace, the God we serve is able to save us from it, and he will rescue us from your hand, O king." Daniel 3:16, 17 NIV*

As a child it was a breathtaking story even on a flannelgraph board. It hasn't lost its high drama. Three young men facing the biggest and baddest threat of their lives … forced to make a decision between caving into culture or remaining on the high road of their moral and religious upbringing. The right choice would see them hurled into a furnace hot enough to kill the men who threw them in. The wrong choice would set them free to resume their privileged life styles.

Why couldn't the outcomes be reversed? Why indeed!

There appears to be no hesitation … no "Can we have some time to think this over?" Their collective 'you-can-burn-us-but-you-can't-turn-us' response ranks high in the closing statements of martyrs throughout history. There is something very special in the eyes of the Hebrews as they look unflinchingly at King Nebuchadnezzar's angry face.

One personal implication of this story to me is this haunting question: How big is my God as manifested by the faith I exhibit?

But there is a breaking development in this story that literally demands our attention. Notice the verse that follows their bold confidence. Verse eighteen says, *"But even if he does not, we want you to know, O king, that we will not serve your gods or worship the image of gold you have set up."* God can … but if He chooses not to, it doesn't diminish who He is and does not alter our belief system!

Great faith believes, but doesn't base that belief on getting what it wants, but on its confidence that God is God, regardless..

May there be joy and majestic, yet child-like faith for your journey!

March 19

If Only

God, I feel a bit worthless today … kind of ignored and maybe a little 'unloved.' What I wouldn't give for You to show up and help me feel loved again.

> *"I have loved you with an everlasting love; I have drawn you with loving-kindness." Jeremiah 31:3 NIV*

And here I am in the middle of a gigantic 'fear storm' in my life that seems to reach every boundary of my being. I know that if You were here, You'd have a word that would calm the crazy seas and restore my equilibrium.

> *"And the very hairs on your head are all numbered. So don't be afraid; you are more valuable to God than a whole flock of sparrows." Luke 12:7 New Living Translation*

Along with everything else going on I have about as much peace in my life as if I were spending today in a giant tumbling clothes dryer. Your child is getting banged around pretty good. If only You would speak to this issue!

> *My people will live in peaceful dwelling places, in secure homes, in undisturbed places of rest." Isaiah 32:18 NIV*

There's also the matter of my propensity to sin. Do You have any idea of how yucky and worthless and hopeless I feel when I 'blow it?' Do You have any idea of how desperately I need to know you still love me and will forgive me?

> *"Come now, let's settle this," says the Lord. "Though your sins are like scarlet, I will make them as white as snow. Though they are red like crimson, I will make them as white as wool." Isaiah 1:18 NIV*

If only this week I could find a way to hear your heart for me … to get a sense of your peace for my life … to have You calm the storm as You did for your disciples … to be able to feel your arm around me and sense your smile on my life.

If only there was a way to hear you. (A little 'tongue in cheek' here to remind us of the primary way God reveals his heart and his plan for our lives.)

God's words are as close as an open Bible and we really deserve the fear, lack of peace, sense of guilt and the feeling of being unloved if we fail to open it and let God out and into our needy lives.

Mountains and Valleys

Did you know that there can only be valleys if there are mountaintops nearby?

There are times when we're 'down.' Sometimes way, way down. The proverbial 'look up to see the bottom' kind of down. But it shouldn't surprise us. Life isn't lived on a perfect bubble level. There are ups and downs. We experience times when the tide is in and other times when it's out.

There are times when everything we touch, try or encounter leaves us feeling very good. But at other times the circumstances of our lives leave us feeling empty and very alone. If we were emotionless beings, we probably wouldn't notice these differences so acutely, but we're emotional to the core and so they matter.

But 'down' has a counterpart. It's called 'up.' There would be no valleys if there were not mountaintops somewhere nearby. And the mountaintop you are looking for and possibly desperately needing is not a place. It's a person. Psalm 34:19 says it well: *"The righteous face many troubles, but the Lord rescues them from each and every one." New Living Translation*

So whether you're descending… at the bottom… ascending… or standing tall at the very top, it's God that you need and will continue to need. He's the companion that your soul is always comfortable traveling with. It might be wise to contemplate a simple fact of life: "This too will pass."

That thought keeps us humble and usable during the great times, and aware that even the worst of times will have an ending. But overall, the trip is being superintended by God and so has a wonderful ending to contemplate.

March 21

Numbering Our Days

"Teach us to number our days aright, that we may gain a heart of wisdom."
Psalm 90:12 NIV

I started learning about numbers when I was about three. I'm still learning about them.

By averaging numbers we can figure out how long a light bulb will burn, how long a running shoe will last and how long a dollar bill will stay in circulation before wearing out. And according to Moses in Psalm 90, we can expect to live an average of 70 to 80 years.

Obviously that's the average and not a guarantee.

Some day there will be a stone marker bearing our name and two dates…date of birth and date of death. The dash between the two dates has far more meaning than either one because it will represent what we did with the life God gave us.

Longevity in itself is not the goal, although wanting to live a long, good life is a good goal to have. But consider Methuselah who lived 969 years, but very probably died in the flood along with the rest of the unbelievers and skeptics. Jesus lived 33 years and his life is still impacting this planet today.

"Numbering our days" is simply the recognition that we won't be around forever. And because of that realization, today becomes very important. We will make wiser decisions. We will choose relationship over 'stuff.' The future will take precedence over simply living for today.

Even though we all wish to live to a ripe old age, this week... think quality as well as quantity. And may you have joy for your unique journey.

Bringing God Up To Speed

I'm not sure which genre of prayer they come under, but you've heard some of them prayed in church.

"Lord, you are aware of what is going on in the Middle East … how the Arab nations are …"

"Father, we ask that you bless our upcoming potluck next Sunday the 18th between 1 and 3 p.m. …those with last names A-F bring a salad …"

"God, I have a really tough week coming. What with my travel to Cleveland, the report that is due on Thursday and …"

I call them "Prayers To Bring God Up To Speed On What Is Happening In My World." We all pray them. And while it's great that we know God on such an intimate Father/child relationship and can speak candidly to Him about anything in our world, we must guard against the temptation of thinking we must fill God in on details as if they're news to Him.

After all, He's got our hairs numbered. He accurately translates groans into 'on target' prayers. He knows how everything is going to turn out. He's the One who wrote out the script for our lives.

Instead, use some of your prayer time to let God bring you up to speed on what is going on in his world! If we had his perspective and better understood his heart, plan and purposes we would move into partnership with his intentions. Our hearts would become settled even as we moved obediently into the arena where He is working.

"For just as the heavens are higher than the earth, so my ways are higher than your ways and my thoughts higher than your thoughts." Isaiah 55:9 New Living Translation

March 23
The Question

"In late autumn, in the month of Kislev, in the twentieth year of King Artaxerxes' reign, I was at the fortress of Susa. 2 Hanani, one of my brothers, came to visit me with some other men who had just arrived from Judah. I asked them about the Jews who had returned there from captivity and about how things were going in Jerusalem. 3 They said to me, "Things are not going well ..." Nehemiah 1:1-3 New Living Translation

When Nehemiah asked the question "How's it going?" he didn't expect that the answer would define the rest of his life. He had no idea that the sorrowful, negative response to his question would begin to answer the age old inquiry that's in every person's heart: "Why am I here?"

Suddenly Nehemiah was caught in that powerful tension that often exists between what is and what could be. He could picture God's intentions for the beautiful city of Jerusalem ... the city that he and his fellow Jews had been removed from years before. Her former beauty could move him to tears instantly. And now he could hold this picture in his mind next to the reported picture of what had happened ... broken walls, no protection for the people of that city ... its ruins the laughing stock of those who did not share its history.

And from this tension came a call. The response to "How's it going?" became the answer to God's call on his life. He now had focus. The emotional response of how things could be suddenly had a moral imperative that said, "It not only could be, but it should be!" And within a short time Nehemiah had his life's work outlined for him. It came out of a question asked.

To a believer there is always a certain potential for danger, excitement and adventure when we ask someone this question and really listen to the response. How do we respond when the answer is:

"Not too well. My wife's fighting cancer."
"Not too well. My job has just been cut."
"Not too well. I'm so fearful that I can't sleep at night."
"Not too well. There is no satisfaction in my life."

God will open up tremendous and satisfying avenues of ministry to any of us who ask this simple question and then move toward the respondent with God's love and concern.

March 24
Underdogs

In 2013 a Nascar race was won by a 101 to 1 underdog. He wasn't supposed to win ... but he did.

In the 1980 Olympics a motley group of amateur and college hockey players were pitted against an elite group of Soviet professionals. There was no way they were to even be competitive, let alone win ... but they did.

The late 1930s found America coming out of hard times. She needed an underdog to surprise and give something to cheer about. She found it in an undersized, leggy steed named Seabiscuit ... ridden by an oversized jockey and trained by a 'past-his-prime' trainer. He wasn't supposed to be a contender ... but he was.

Three hundred Israeli soldiers equipped with clay pots, ancient horns and torches (improbable weapons of war to be sure) take on over one hundred thousand well-trained warriors in one of the Bible's most unusual battles. Of course they're not supposed to win ... but they did.

Teenager David carries his slingshot and five stones from the creek and walks toward Goliath. The giant is fitted with armor covering almost all of his body holding the best weapons available. Pound for pound, weapon for weapon, experience versus inexperience ... this shouldn't go well for David. But it did.

We thrill to the underdog overcoming all obstacles and opponents and view with amazement outcomes that shouldn't have come out as they did. But in the first three accounts above, we must factor in the toughness of human spirit, the lucky breaks that sometime give an advantage and much hard work behind the scenes.

And in the final two illustrations, we too easily ignore the most significant player in the drama ... God! Those we labeled 'underdog' were never thought so by God. They were 'shoo-ins' from the very start. Victory is always assured when God is on the team!

Today rejoice that you have a God with an unblemished winning record and that He wants you on his team!

"With God all things are possible" (Matthew 19:26).
"We are more than conquerors through Him that loved us" (Romans 8:37).
"(God) is able to do immeasurably more than all we ask or imagine" (Ephesians 3:20).
"I can do all things through Christ who strengthens me" (Philippians 4:13).

March 25

Speed or Distance?

There's a strange party game popular right now. It's called "Would You Rather" and it poses questions like:

♦ Would you rather be rich and ugly, or poor and good looking?
♦ Would you rather go without television or junk food for the rest of your life?
♦ Would you rather only be able to whisper or only be able to shout?

I always want to ask, "Are those my only alternatives?"

But a similar question/conundrum comes to mind. It goes something like this: Would I rather my life got exceptional MPG (Miles Per Gallon) or breathtaking MPH (Miles Per Hour)? Is distance more important to me than speed? In the world of the automobile, getting both at the same time is difficult.

A car capable of going 150 miles an hour probably won't pass up too many gas stations. While a car capable of achieving 50 miles per gallon probably won't pass up too many other cars!

Does God play this game with us in our lives? Are speed or longevity our only choices? I like to believe that when we were being formed in the secret place of our mother's womb that God gave us a gas tank that would give us the mileage to reach our intended finish line.

And through the powering of his Holy Spirit in our engine we have the appropriate speed for any part of our journey. We have 'putt-putt power' for those times when going slow and steady both fits his purpose and deals with our impatience. (Does it ever!) Yet when necessary we can break every speed record for our make and model. At those times we often feel like we're barely able to hold on as God seems to pull speeds out of us that amaze.

So endeavor to work with God to match your speed and mileage with his intended plan for you. If He's asking for slow and steady, quit revving your engine and rolling your eyes at him. And if his pace for you is faster than you're comfortable with, quit worrying about the mileage. There's enough for the task. Just hang on and steer.

And enjoy the variety that following our God provides. No child of his should ever get bored!

> *"The Lord will guide you continually, giving you water when you are dry and restoring your strength. You will be like a well-watered garden, like an ever-flowing spring." Isaiah 58:11 New Living Translation*

March 26

Be Quiet

> *Lord, my heart is not proud; my eyes are not haughty. I don't concern myself with matters too great or awesome for me. But I have stilled and quieted myself, just as a small child is quiet with its mother. Yes, like a small child is my soul within me. O Israel, put your hope in the LORD — now and always. Psalms 131:1-3 New Living Translation*

We speak often of being 'light in a dark world.' But it's almost harder to be 'quiet in a noisy world.'

We are told in the Word that in 'quietness and confidence' we would find our strength. But how do we find the quietness?

We are instructed to 'be still and know' but 'still' comes hard and 'noisy' comes easily. It's difficult to find any place that's quiet.

The planes roar ... the car next to us at the stoplight has a six million watt subwoofer that makes our car bounce as we wait the changing light ... the televised ads come on at twice the volume of the program we had been watching. And the beat goes on ... literally.

We are programmed to think that stillness is kind of like riding a bike ... if we get too quiet or slow down too much we'll fall over. However, the opposite has been proven to be true. It's the person who knows how to slow down, turn off the noise and be quiet before the Lord who has the best equilibrium and the most reserves for difficult times.

To push this rare commodity into your life, try these simple things. Remember that motion doesn't always denote progress.

On purpose push noise away. Turn off the TV. Give yourself permission to let the phone ring without picking it up. Listen to praise music and less talk radio.

Strain to hear God speak through the events of your day. He seldom tries to talk above the noise we've allowed into our lives and that makes hearing Him a challenge.

Begin to look at walks and trips to the park (and even vacations) as times of true recreation (re-creation rather than the sorry definitions that drive us into a frenzy trying to have fun and then spit us back into our routines in worse shape than when we began!)

God often does some of his most profound work in our lives in quiet times. Don't let our culture rob you of it. God's 'still small voice' still packs more power than all the noise around us.

March 27

God's Record

I love the honesty of the writers of the Psalms. Probably the most transparent and open to scrutiny is the King/Shepherd Boy David. He left us little to ponder as to how he was doing at any particular time.

If you're like me you find yourself in just about every Psalm you read. I'm either shouting "Amen" or "Oh me" with every chapter. When David is up, he flies very high. And when he's down it's a tragedy of un-plumbable depths. In Psalm 6 … *"O Lord, don't rebuke me in your anger.* In Psalm 13 … *"How long, O Lord? Will you forget me forever?"* And in Psalm 22 … *"My God, my God, why have you abandoned me? Why are you so far away when I groan for help?"*

When Samuel led Israel to a victory over the Philistines (I Samuel 7) it was but one in a continuing series of battles. Samuel placed a memorial at the point of the last victory and made a simple statement to the battle-weary Israelis: *"Up to this point the Lord has helped us!" New Living Translation*

It's a great confession that can be made by any of us who have walked with God for any length of time. Ask yourself: Has God ever forgotten us? Has there ever been a time when we have been out of his mind, let alone out from under his care? God's record is spotless … uncountable victories and no defeats.

And so we say with Samuel "I'm not sure what is ahead. I have no idea of the intensity of the next battle. My forward view is a bit cloudy but I'm 20/20 looking back and I can say with assurance that up to this point God has always come through.

Today recount the past with an eye on God's faithfulness and know that at any point in your future you'll be able to say "To this point the Lord has helped me!"

May you have joy and confidence for your journey!

March 28
The Ride

"Your road led through the sea, your pathway through the mighty waters — a pathway no one knew was there!"
Psalm 77:19 NLT

There are several rides at Disneyland that are not what they appear. To a very young child they could be terrifying. Consider the underground playground of the Pirates of the Caribbean. You find yourself immersed in a world of reckless pirates, pillaging, burning and threatening. You pass through a raging cannon battle that apparently puts you in harm's way.

Then there is the long-famous Jungle Cruise. Watch the face of worry on the youngest passengers as they come perilously close to man-eating crocodiles, boat-flooding waterfalls and hostile natives. The admonition to wave at those left behind at the dock because you may never see them again seems prophetic ... at least to the youngest voyagers.

We could relive the Indiana Jones jeep trip ... the intergalactic, out of control space ride Star Tours with an inexperienced droid at the controls! All with assured outcomes carefully programmed beforehand.

As a junior high student in the 50s, I watched the televised documentary on the building of the 'Magic Kingdom' and saw the tracks being laid before water covered them. There was never a question of the destination being safely reached.

And we watch with amusement as Israel, newly released from Egypt, finds itself on a ride never experienced before. The allusion at the Red Sea is similar to what the designers of Disney's attractions work so hard to convey ... there is no hope ahead, only danger. The attack is about to sweep over you and there is nowhere to turn. Maybe you were foolish to have embarked on the journey!

Ah, there is One who has designed the 'ride' and underneath are not only the everlasting wings, but the spiritual track that guarantees us getting to the destination safe and intact!

May there be joy (and excitement) on your journey!

The Heart's Contents

"The Lord does not look at things man looks at. Man looks at the outward appearance, but the Lord looks at the heart." I Samuel 16:7 NIV

Sometimes we are more aware of the bad in our hearts than the good. We know the propensity for evil that lurks there … but do we give much thought to the potential good that lies there as well?

Case in point: When I looked into the eyes of a cute twelve year old named Joan back in 1957 (I was a very mature fourteen year old at the time!) I saw no clue that an incredible grandma named "Mimi" was hidden in her heart. It took years for it to manifest itself, yet today she could easily pen a how-to book for aspiring grandmothers. Her capacity to love, pray for and envision extraordinary things for her eight grandkids is a spiritual and relational force to be reckoned with.

We hear stories of ordinary people who take a short missions trip after much cajoling from a spouse and find out that they are possessed with an insatiable hunger to see people meet Jesus. Others discover through hospital visits to a relative, that their hearts beat to the cries and disabilities of those who suffer physically. And still others discover later in life that they had much to offer a hurting world. They just never knew it was there.

Today's devotional is meant to sound an alarm in some of you. You may be living with an untried capacity to serve, to care, to give, to pray or to fill a vital and strategic place in God's expanding Kingdom. As one writer said, don't go to your grave with your song still in you. Ask God to show you the contents of your heart. Ask Him for his assessment of your potential. If and when He gives you a clue, pursue it … with all your heart!

March 30

My Amen

"Meanwhile … God's Spirit is right alongside helping us along. If we don't know how or what to pray, it doesn't matter. He does our praying in and for us, making prayer out of our wordless sighs, our aching groans. He knows us far better than we know ourselves …and keeps us present before God. That's why we can be so sure that every detail in our lives of love for God is worked into something good." Romans 8:26,27 The Message

"Would you like to pray for our meal?" I asked my recently turned three year old grandson Jackson. He pondered for a moment and then replied, "I don't think so."

I thought that was the end of it and besides, pushing a preschooler into public prayer before he's ready is most likely not a good idea. As I opened my mouth to do what he had declined to do, he spoke up and said, "But I'll say 'Amen.'"

I did my part and he added his and the Father knew that we were thankful for our lunch.

There have been times in my life (and there will be more, I'm sure) when I couldn't pray. It wasn't that I didn't believe in it … or because I didn't want to … I just didn't know what God really wanted in that situation.

And in those times, the Spirit of God who always knows what to say and how to say it, gets to compose the prayer. Sometimes He actually constructs it out of the very wordlessness of my confusion. At other times it's built on such deep emotional turmoil that all that comes out is a tired, dejected sigh … a groan, if you will.

I realize again just how important my 'Amen' is in the equation. My 'so be it' signifies my soul's partnership with the Father. It's my way of letting God know that whatever it is He is doing or wanting to do, it's all right with me. So if you catch me at a time when I'm hesitant to form a prayer because of my limited sight or knowledge, it is not a sign that my faith isn't strong. My 'Amen' speaks volumes about my confidence in my God.

March 31
Whittling or Carving?

I recently heard a speaker recount an experience as a young boy in the hills of Tennessee. He was at an old general store watching some locals sitting on the porch turning pieces of wood into piles of shavings on the floor.

"You've been doing that all day," he said to one man "and you haven't made nothin' yet."

"We're whittling," was the reply. "Whittling is when you turn something into nothin', but carving is when you turn nothin' into something."

Wow! What a depiction of the difference between the intentions of God's Kingdom and the kingdom of the evil one. Satan is into whittling. He starts with a person, a plan, a dream and when he's finished there is nothing but a pile of the shavings of despair, destruction and emptiness.

The Whittler is not content until he's stolen everything he can.

God, however, is big into carving. He begins with nothing, like the vacuous void before Genesis chapter one. And when He's done the seas shimmer, the mountains sparkle, the earth glistens with hope and possibility. In Mark 5 He begins with a shell of a man who was so much of a 'nothing' that there was room for a multitude of demons to live in him. When the carving is complete there is an evangelist who spreads the Gospel to ten cities!

God turns water into wine ... darkness into light ... poverty into 'more than enough.' He always leaves more than He starts with. In his presence is the power and resources to turn any nobody into a stellar somebody. And not just turn nothing into something, but into something very special.

Today ask the Creator Carver to reverse what the Whittler has started in your life. God is even able to turn shavings into lives of grace, beauty and eternal purpose.

> *"Abraham was first named "father" and then became a father because he dared to trust God to do what only God could do: raise the dead to life, with a word make something out of nothing. When everything was hopeless, Abraham believed anyway ..." Romans 4:17,18 The Message*

April 1

Be Not Afraid

It's been a long time since I had to assuage the fear of my young sons. There are no longer monsters under the bed or in the closet ... the forest is no longer foreboding, but delightful ... and girls turned out to be charming instead of terrifying.

But another generation of Waltermans has come along and a few of the grandkids still need a night light and steady reassurances about the spooky things of life.

Our Heavenly Father also must quiet the fears of his kids. And fears come in a variety of forms and to just about any age. The childhood fears are soon replaced by more obvious and threatening 'monsters.'

- ♦ Like making ends meet.
- ♦ Like taking a moral stand.
- ♦ Like watching a market swing take your retirement away.
- ♦ Like the fear of having your young love turn tasteless and even bitter.

There is a recurrent command throughout the Bible that is most familiar in the old King James Version ... "Be not afraid." And you'd be surprised at how often it is found; even more surprised at the circumstances where it is found.

Every time God tells us to stop being afraid, we're facing something that has made us afraid. The timing is explicit in Jeremiah 42:11 when God says, *"Don't be afraid of the king of Babylon, of whom you are afraid."* It's like God says to us: "Whenever you begin to be afraid, stop it!"

In Deuteronomy 20 God tells Israel that *"when you see the horses and chariots and the forces who strongly outnumber you ... be not afraid!"* Jehoshaphat in II Chronicles 20 gives God's people this prompt: *"Be not afraid nor dismayed by reason of this great multitude."*

Today if you have reason to be afraid of something ... be not afraid. When God says to stop worrying and biting our nails and looking over our shoulders it's because the enemy we fear is as harmless as that boogeyman under your bed!

April 2

Falling Is Not Failure

Falling is not failure to God.

We're not terribly surprised when a year old baby falls down. And even a stumble by a pre-teen is not all that unusual, especially when the size of their growing feet exceeds their peripheral vision.

Everybody takes a tumble periodically. Nobody's life is perfect. We don't always live up to even our own expectations. Some falls are accidental, others the result of walking on uneven moral or ethical ground or from wandering into places that are dangerous to our souls. But we all fall.

But falling isn't the same as failure in God's opinion. He fully understands our proclivity to fall and fall hard at times. Yet even after Jonah messed up badly in behavior that God expected, and although he paid a price for the mistake, the Bible says that "…the word of the Lord came again to Jonah." You see, He's a God of the second chance…and third chance and more as needed!

There is a 'sloppy grace' being advertised today, telling us that either God isn't looking or He isn't interested. Neither idea is Scriptural. God does call us to righteous living, but when we stumble there is great grace. God sees our hearts as well as the actions coming from our lives. His love reaches out.

To the woman taken in adultery (John 8:1-11) He acknowledges the broken law, then says, "I don't condemn you; go and stop sinning."

Do you find yourself needing another chance? Are you at this moment wondering if you should pick yourself back up and brush yourself off and try again? God's smiling and He's saying, "Yes!"

"At least there is hope for a tree: If it is cut down, it will sprout again,
and its new shoots will not fail." JOB 14:7 NIV

April 3
The God I Need

"...Abraham believed in the God who brings the dead back to life and who brings into existence what didn't exist before." Romans 4:17 New Living Translation

I need a God who takes death as a trade-in on life.

There is little need in my life for a god who simply re-arranges what's already there...a god who spray paints broken parts to cover the cracks and then declare them workable. I don't need a god who can cosmetically straighten my nose or give me more hair or make age spots disappear.

Oh no! My God has to be able to take dead things and breathe life back into them! He must have the ability to make quality stuff out of thin air...put something on the shelf that didn't exist before He went to work.

My God must be able to take dead emotions and bring life, expectancy and vitality to them. He must be capable of taking dead relationships...ones that haven't simply quit working well, but have been buried for years...and reconnect the synapse of neural responses so that they work again. He must be able to take dead dreams and desires and not only bring them back to mind and heart, but fulfill them in the process.

Life can be too tragic...too long...too disappointing...too con-fusing and too filled with my own blunders and inaptitude to settle for any other god than the One who can make all things new, and who speaks of tomorrow as if it were yesterday and who can create real and satisfying life out of brokenness, emptiness and death.

Aren't you glad that such a God is as close as the longings in our hearts?

April 4

When God Speaks

"Praise be to you, O Lord; teach me your decrees. With my lips I recount all the laws that come from your mouth. I rejoice in following your statutes as one rejoices in great riches I meditate on your precepts and consider your ways. I delight in your decrees; I will not neglect your word." Psalm 119:12-16 NIV

David seemed to have a love affair with rules and regulations.

Hardly the kind of person who adds much enjoyment to life ... so wrapped up in the fine print of all the legalities that they totally miss the joy of living.

But the rules David loved were the ones that came from his Father. They weren't given to restrict and take away freedom. Instead, by following them he found the greatest freedom he had ever known. God doesn't talk to hear Himself talk. He doesn't muscle his way verbally into peoples' lives because of a strong ego and need to be heard.

No, when God speaks two things are able to come together - his holiness and our wholeness and the two do go incredibly well together!

Here's how it works ... God speaks and his Word stands. It doesn't change according to the weather, the culture or consensus. It just is there. Now we face it and must come to grips with its implications. Many times it messes with our sense of independence, with our carefully planned future or with our pride. It's always a point of decision for us.

But as we mature in Him, we realize that God's will and our joy are inextricably tied together. He wants what will make me whole and happy (at a deep, spiritual level) and I want what He wants. It's a perfect arrangement.

So there are some rules you need to follow. Just make sure you know who wrote them!

April 5

Audacious Faith

Here's to audacious faith!

The kind exhibited by young Jonathan who in the company of his armor-bearer and one sword went out looking for a fight with the entire Philistine army.

It's the kind of faith that says, "If we need to feed a few people, we may as well provide lunch for these 5,000 men plus their family members."

Or David who decides that if he's going to fight a worthy opponent, it may as well be the guy who is eight feet tall with the booming voice that spreads panic among all who hear it.

How about Moses … who figures that if he's looking for a leadership position, why not answer the ad for the position that requires leading two million cantankerous, often rebellious people out of their captive nation into another one that doesn't even belong to them at the moment.

Caleb is another example. As an 85 year old military veteran with a distinguished career behind him, he bypasses the cushy job and asks to lead an attack on the heavily fortified hill country where the giants still reside.

And then there's Gideon who figures that if he's been tasked with leading three hundred 'soldiers' equipped with nothing more than party horns and flashlights, he may as well take on the entire 135,000 strong Midianite army.

And in every instance God was glorified and victory was won.

So … what are you believing for that is so daring, bodacious and illogical that it will take God's mighty hand to accomplish and put a smile on his face?

"When Jesus heard this, he was amazed. Turning to those who were following him, he said, "I tell you the truth, I haven't

seen faith like this in all Israel!" Matthew 8:10 New Living Translation

April 6
The Hurrier I Go

There's one of those 'it-must-be-true' quips that most of us have nodded our heads in agreement with. It goes "The hurrier I go the behinder I get!" But there's a spiritual corollary to that statement that says, "The hurrier I go the behinder He gets!"

Have you ever tackled something, gotten off to a quick start and while maintaining a dizzying pace suddenly realized that God wasn't keeping up? The One to whom even the speed of light holds no fascination often moves at a maddeningly sluggish speed.

But God isn't motivated by hurry. Timing and tight schedules and deadlines are all byproducts of clocks and calendars and To Do lists. In our frenzy we forget that it's us and not God who operate on a time line. God inhabits eternity and is not rushed, bothered or concerned with time or the lack thereof.

However, there is a Trusted Agent who can help us coordinate our concern with time and God's concern about eternity and its values. The Holy Spirit has been given to us to, among other things, help us with timing issues and to remind us that God is still actively involved in the matters of our lives.

The Apostle Paul gave good advice in his letter to the church at Galatia. Note what he says, *"Since we live by the Spirit, let us keep in step with the Spirit." Galatians 5:25 NIV*

So don't look over your shoulder with impatience for a God who can't keep up. Instead, keep in step with His Spirit … timing will take care of itself.

April 7

Beyond Our Obedience

"Because one person disobeyed God, many became sinners. But because one other person obeyed God, many will be made righteous." Romans 5:19 NLT

That first man, Adam, got us all into a lot of trouble. The Second Man, Jesus, rescued us in a dramatic and costly way. Two men. One disobedient … the other obedient to the point of death.

Disobedience still brings about death and obeying still opens the door to extraordinary things. Consider this statement that I heard not long ago. A good friend of mine, working through a very difficult period of his life when quitting made a lot of sense, said he didn't give up because "people were standing on the other side of my obedience."

I think I actually gulped at that statement with the realization that I possibly have left people standing on the other side of my disobedience. Left hurting people standing without comfort … left sinful people standing without knowledge of God's available forgiveness … left confused people standing without a sure word from God that would have made a huge difference in their lives.

When we realize that our refusal to obey hurts more than just us, we gain some spiritual maturity. The reality is that sin never only affects us. Our sin, our disobedience, our reluctance to bend our will to God's … always touches other lives.

Today ask God to show you who may be standing just the other side of your "Yes" to Him. Ask Him to give you a glimpse of the people to whom your "Not my will, but Yours" will mean the most. And then go out in joy and confidence knowing that your partnership with the Father is going to produce wonderful results.

"... one man said yes to God and put many in the right."
Romans 5:19 The Message

May there be joy for and obedience on your journey!

April 8

This God Lives Here!

The wily old monarch of the Old Testament – Nebechudnezzar – had a dream one night that scared him so badly that although he couldn't remember the dream, the horror of it wouldn't let go of him. He had to know what he had dreamt and what it meant to his kingdom.

Summoning his magicians, enchanters, sorcerers and astrologers he demanded an interpretation of his nightmare. "Fine," they replied. "Just tell us the dream and we'll tell you what it means."

"Can't remember the dream," he replied. "But you'll give me both the dream and its interpretation or I'll have your lives."

"Not fair" they wailed. *"No one on earth can tell the king his dream! And no king, however great and powerful, has ever asked such a thing of any magician, enchanter, or astrologer! 11 The king's demand is impossible. No one except the gods can tell you your dream, and they do not live here among people."* Daniel 2:10,11 New Living Translation

We commiserate with their dilemma, but have to laugh at their faulty analysis. Of course there is a God who can do what is being asked ... and of course he resides here among his people. In actuality, He lives within them!

Lesser gods are totally incapable of handling such 'impossibilities,' but our God takes the impossible in stride. And this good news is twofold. This God, our God, is able and He's readily available!

So while other gods are rewriting their resumes, our God is sometimes quietly, but always powerfully doing what they cannot do. While they are busy making up excuses for their impotency, our God is doing more than we can ask or even imagine. While they look for slight-of-hand, smoke and mirror responses to need, our God is meeting those needs.

Today you may be challenged with a 'can't do' assignment. You may be asked to do the unimaginable. The task may call for you to " ... *crush an army or scale a wall.*" *(Psalm 18:29)* But the story for us is never about what we can't do, but what God can do with us, in us and through us. Take courage!

April 9

Does This Look Like A Rescue?

" ... *rescue? Does this look like rescue to you?*" *Exodus 5:23 The Message*

God promised a rescue. A rescue is an event, right? Not an everlasting process of frustrating events. At least that's the definition in our dictionaries ... and Moses'.

He had hesitatingly signed up to lead this event and had somewhat reluctantly taken the first steps. He told Pharaoh what God told him to say and had waited for the rescue to take place. Instead, he ticked the Egyptian ruler off and in turn made bad conditions for his people many times worse.

And now he's the object of resentment and anger from the very people he is to lead. So his question to God is understandable: " ... rescue? Does this look like rescue to you?"

It was the same with Gideon who overcame severe reluctance to 'help God' rescue Israel from the Midianites. He, too, believed he would lead an event but instead witnessed a process in which God increased the odds against them from 4 to

1 to 400 to 1. And God's rationale? "I can't save Israel with this many soldiers"

Gideon's response? "… rescue. Does this look like a rescue to you?"

And on it goes. Daniel's rescue comes via a night with the lions. The three Hebrew children got rescued in and through a fiery furnace. Lot's rescue required leaving everything behind and running for his life.

Get it settled in your heart. If God promises a rescue, it will happen. But almost every time it will not be as you imagined it will be. God wants your rescue to be all inclusive … to accomplish all of his plans for you. Moses' rescue would have seen Israel leaving with the clothes on their back … God's rescue had them leaving with the plunder of Egypt in their possession.

Here's your promise: *"Then call on me when you are in trouble, and I will rescue you, and you will give me glory." Psalm 50:15 New Living Translation* Don't dictate the strategy of your rescue. Let God be God. He's extremely good at it!

April 10

Anger Management

Anger management. I admit it … I need some on occasion.

It's typically on the freeway when being passed on both sides by racers going 20-30 miles an hour over the limit. Or when someone is going 10 miles per hour slower than the posted limit in the fast lane (which I have reserved for my whole trip). My anger really spikes when someone driving foolishly threatens my personal safety.

That last scenario helps me understand that often my anger is precipitated by fear. Men aren't really good at emotions. Oh, it's not that we don't have them, it's just that we aren't sure how to display them. And so we stuff them until they erupt in anger.

Now another admission. I am angry at what is happening in my world … fist pounding, raised voice mad. I am miffed at being asked to pay the sin tax for people whose lifestyle I abhor. I rage internally at bullies taking advantage of those who are vulnerable. My resentment rises against different standards being applied to people because of their connections or friends in high places. I am particularly galled by those who openly display their wickedness and do it often enough that their lifestyles appears to be normal.

The moral slide of my world seems completely out of control and I feel helpless at times to fight it, let alone make a difference. And so I'm angry … because I'm afraid. Is this the way it's going to end? Will the enemy have the winning shot? Will Satan, standing on a mountain of sin and rebelliousness, be the last one standing?

Oh no! God has said, *"At the time I have planned, I will bring justice against the wicked." Psalm 75:2 New Living Translation.* God's counseling session to deal with our fear of sin's encroachment can be found in Psalm 98:8,9 from the New Living Translation: *"Let the rivers clap their hands in glee! Let the hills sing out their songs of joy before the Lord. For the Lord is coming to judge the earth. He will judge the world with justice, and the nations with fairness."*

The affairs of man are still under God's control. The ultimate outcome is assured. I need to remind myself that anger and fear over what is happening to my world are not my only choices. Instead I must feel compassion for those living the lies of the Liar and at the same time rejoice with the hills and rivers who are sure than redemption is coming!

"The Lord is my strength and shield. I trust him with all my heart."
Psalm 28:7 New Living Translation

April 11

Before and After

I love 'before and after' comparisons ... from the advertisements of weight loss programs to the makeovers of rooms or whole houses. My wife and I both love the 'before and after' pictures of diet programs, but for different reasons. I like them because I can dream about what I'd look like after I've lost weight. Joanie likes them because she can dream about what I'd look like after I've lost weight!

I've seen 'after' pictures that didn't show the 'before' and they don't carry much weight. (Pardon the pun ...) God likes to chronicle the entire journey!

But He doesn't hide the before pictures. Although He's incredibly into the 'after' picture in our lives, He never attempts to hide the start of our journey. I find that the 'before' picture is what gives me the faith to believe for my own success story.

And so God shows Abraham struggling with faith, just like so many of us. And when we see the 'after' picture of him in Hebrews standing as a strong faith warrior we personalize his journey and say, "And why not me, too?"

David is shown with the acne of sin and immorality scaring his life in his 'before' picture. But later on we see a clear, unblemished life and hear God saying "He's got a heart very much like mine!"

We gaze at Gideon's 'before' portrait and he's covered in wheat dust as he is secretly and fearfully thrashing the grain in a large vat, scared of being discovered by Israel's enemies. But when God completes his makeover we see a confident leader of 300 men taking on the fearsome hoards of the Midianites.

The list could go on and on, but the important lesson for us is that regardless of any of our 'before' pictures, there is a picture of us 'after' in God's mind and all of heaven's resources are available to complete this remarkable makeover in our lives.

"The Lord—who is the Spirit—makes us more and more like him as we are changed into his glorious image." II Corinthians 3:18 New Living Translation

May there be joy and anticipation of the final picture during your journey.

April 12

Consequences

The Biblical definition of who I am would be an 'exhorter.' One of the things that denotes is that I love to encourage and like everyone else, have a need for encouragement. But sometimes our behavior or choices don't deserve a word of encouragement … they require dire consequences.

God is not only a God who can and does smile with an "Atta boy!" and a pat on the back. He's also a God who instituted the law of sowing and reaping and applies it to our lives when necessary to remind us that He means what He says.

In Isaiah 17, at God's prompting, the prophet is foretelling the consequences of Israel's idolatry and alliance with the pagan Damascus. They've had warning and we expect that from a God whose first choice is to bless and grow us. But with fingers in their ears and hearts bent on disobedience God makes the following pronouncement:

"So you may plant the finest grapevines and import the most expensive seedlings. They may sprout on the day you set them out; yes, they may blossom on the very morning you plant them, but you will never pick any

grapes from them. Your only harvest will be a load of grief and unrelieved pain." Isaiah 17:10b, 11 New Living Translation

We can shine God on … smile warmly in his direction … and go ahead planting our own willful ways. We may even see initial evidence that God isn't paying attention and we're going to get what we want. But don't be fooled, because God isn't!

What we sow we always reap. And disobedient Israel thought they were planting grapes, but their real crop was a stubborn, wicked heart. They were about to harvest from that planting because they had " … turned from the God who can save … and forgotten the Rock who can protect." Isaiah 17:10a

Today, decide in advance what it is you desire to harvest and then plant accordingly.

April 13

Nevertheless

"Master," Simon replied, "we worked hard all last night and didn't catch a thing. But if you say so, I'll let the nets down again." Luke 5:5 New Living Translation

The obedience God calls for is not a 'blind obedience.' He doesn't require us to turn off thinking or ask us to suspend our ability to weigh outcomes. We aren't more spiritual by sticking our heads in the sand. When God speaks to us, He addresses us as rational, intelligent human beings. That's the way He made us.

But He does expect us to adjust our thinking to eternal principles. He wants us to throw his omniscience and his omnipotence into whatever it is we are weighing. Jesus wasn't angry that Peter's response began with a short critique of the way he viewed Jesus' instructions. But He would have been disappointed if that was as far as Peter went.

In the King James version, after Peter gives Jesus the reason for his reluctance to try again, we find the word 'nevertheless.'

It was a sign that he was going to follow through on the new directions, even though a part of him didn't think it would do any good. And that relinquishment of our will to His is what precedes amazing outcomes.

Sometimes the 'nevertheless' doesn't come on the heels of not understanding, but on the heels of being asked to do something very difficult ... even impossible. Consider Jesus in the agonizing hours prior to his arrest. What He is being asked to do is beyond comprehension, yet note his response to his Father: " *... if thou be willing, remove this cup from me: **nevertheless** not my will, but thine, be done.*" Luke 22:42 King James Version

There is no good alternative to bending and submitting to God's will for our lives. His word might be hard ... might be puzzling or even dangerous, but to say "No" to God is not a good thing.

C.S. Lewis said it this way: "There are two kinds of people: those who say to God, 'Thy will be done,' and those to whom God says, 'All right, then, have it your way.'

Weigh the options, but always choose the one that has 'God Approved' stamped on it.

April 14

Insiders and Outsiders

"So let's go outside, where Jesus is, where the action is – not trying to be privileged insiders, but taking our share in the abuse of Jesus. This 'insider world' is not our home. We have our eyes peeled for the City about to come. Let us take our place outside with Jesus, no longer pouring out

the sacrificial blood of animals but pouring out sacrificial praises from our lips to God in Jesus' name." Hebrews 13:13-15 The Message

In these verses, the writer of Hebrews is attempting to get insiders to go outside. As children of the Kingdom, the inside has gotten comfortable. Our friends are all in there. They sing our kind of music and hardly ever is heard a discouraging word. Who'd not want to stay inside?

Outside lurk 'them.' You know them ... all those who aren't us! It's dirty out there with sin on every corner. They curse outside and ridicule and belittle those of us from the inside. It's actually dangerous enough outside that someone could get killed.

Hebrew's author agrees wholeheartedly. Jesus went outside and was killed out there. The Scripture makes it clear that the same ones who killed the Son of God are still out there waiting for us. Make no mistake ... it's far safer inside. Yet our inside experiences are meant to prepare us for our mission. And our mission is outside.

Today some insider is going outside. What they will find is a world of 'outsiders' needing their world to be turned inside out by the Giver of Life. This brave insider, just by being willing to step outside, will find all the resources of heaven at his disposal, and armed with the special blessings of God which are reserved for those willing to crack the door ... will bring light to the darkness and hope to the hopeless.

"Make sure you don't take things for granted and go slack in working for the common good; share what you have with others. God takes particular pleasure in acts of worship – a different kind of 'sacrifice' – that take place in kitchen and workplace and on the streets." Hebrews 13:16 The Message

April 15

His Hand In Mine

Her name is Karissa. Chronologically she's fourth among our soon-to-be seven grandchildren. She and her "Papa" have been closest friends for all of her four years.

Several years ago we spent a couple of days in Palm Springs with Karissa, her three siblings and her parents. We had a wonderful time. Thursday, coming back from a late-evening walk we faced a terrifying crisis. As we entered the resort compound and began moving back toward our building, Karissa could not be found. Only moments before she had been a lively part of our procession. Now the surrounding darkness had somehow swallowed her up. Less than inadequate lighting on the paths left large areas completely dark. The inviting green of the golf course had now become a shadowy world of potentially dangerous ponds. With growing concern we shouted her name. And for the worst part of the next quarter hour our searching was fruitless.

No response.

Concern gave way to panic when the ensuing minutes gave rise to terrible mental pictures that the mind would not even entertain for more than a millisecond. The world does indeed come to a complete and horrifying halt in a situation like this. But fifteen minutes after it had begun, our crisis ended. Karissa had gotten a couple of bends in the sidewalk ahead of us…lost her bearings and thought she saw someone familiar up ahead. The reunion was one of enormous relief coupled with emotional trauma that probably hasn't fully subsided yet in her parents' hearts.

Scary story…happy ending. But it has caused me to ponder my walk with the Father. I can be quite independent myself (although it's tough to match the growing independence of a four year old.) But after this week I am resolved:

1. Never to get beyond a bend in the road to where my view of my Father is cut off
2. The darker it gets, the closer I intend to stay to Him
3. And finally, I will never take the security of the feel of his hand in mine for granted

"God is good, a hiding place in tough times. He recognizes and welcomes anyone looking for help, No matter how desperate the trouble." Nahum 1:7 The Message

There is joy available for you on your journey!

April 16

All These Things

"But seek first his kingdom and his righteousness, and all these things will be given to you as well." Matthew 6:33 NIV

It's always been a battle between the "Kingdom" and "all these things."

I've been consciously fighting that battle for more than four decades now. What's winning, you might ask? Wish my answer would place me on God's list of "People-I-Can-Trust-To-Always-Put-My-Kingdom's-Purposes-Ahead-Of-Anything-Else-In-Their-Lives." But alas, most of us have to honestly face up with the sad fact that "all these things" often take precedence over our involvement with God's Kingdom and his purposes.

It might hurt, but answer a few questions with me to see how well we do in putting God's business before ours:

♦ Is more time spent choosing our daily wardrobe than contemplating ways in which God might use us to extend his Kingdom?

♦ Are we more engrossed in meal-planning and menu-scanning than in making sure that God's instructions for our day are getting through?

♦ Does our physical thirst ever ignite in us a parallel thirst for God and his Word?

♦ Are personal 'kingdoms' draining our emotional, physical, financial and spiritual energies so there is little left to promote God's Kingdom?

At issue for the rest of our lives is this: Can we trust God enough to throw our energy into hearing his voice clearly… into following his directions carefully…into becoming faithful servants instead of bossy owners. He promises that if we will literally put Him first in our lives, He will make sure that "all these things" are handled personally by Him with care, love and generosity. And as you journey, be joyful in his leadership.

April 17

This Land Is Your Land

Song writer Woody Guthrie wrote a patriotic song about America, reminding us that 'this land was made for you and me.' That song, sung with waving flags helped instill pride in our nation.

But while this land was made for me, it's becoming much clearer that I was not made for this land only.

However, God has been preparing a land for me for some time now. It will literally and figuratively be 'out of this world.' The problem is that I know more about here than I know about there. And because of that, this world and its attendant culture takes on far more permanence than it should.

With my Dad now in the presence of the Lord, having heard the "Well done, good and faithful servant" that he had been listening for, and getting settled in the rhythms and splendors of that eternal city ...it's a 'no-brainer' that I've had heaven on my mind far more than I previously did. So I'm beginning to make some important distinctions between 'this land ' and 'that land.'

Since this world is not really my 'forever' home...I am simply a foreign traveler moving through it...I must never settle in for the long haul. The long haul for me must be the trip itself. But while I'm moving through, there is a God-given responsibility to bring as many with me to this 'city built by God.'

And I must view all of life...the good, the bad and the ugly... through an eternal lens. Every decision in my life has eternal consequences. My choices will ripple across years and take on eternal ramifications. An eye on heaven will affect just about every step I take. Spend a bit of time reflecting on Eugene Peterson's words in the Message, taken from Hebrews 11:13-16

> *"Each one of these people of faith died not yet having in hand what was promised, but still believing. How did they do it? They saw it way off in the distance, waved their greeting, and accepted the fact that they were transients in this world. People who live this way make it plain that they are looking for their true home. If they were homesick for the old country, they could have gone back any time they wanted. But they were after a far better country than that – heaven country. You can see why God is so proud of them, and has a City waiting for them"*

Enjoy the journey to that city!

April 18

God's Song

> *Zephaniah 3:17 "The Lord your God in your midst, The Mighty One, will save; He will rejoice over you with*

gladness, He will quiet you with His love, He will rejoice over you with singing." New King James Version

How does the thought of God singing over you make you feel? Uncomfortable? Are you suspect of this activity or do you have trouble believing that it actually does take place?

Or do you get caught up in side issues that have little to do with this Eternal Songster? Like wondering if God is a bass. (Every time we've heard his voice in movies, He's always a bass, right?) Continuing with this sidebar, would it bother you if God is a soprano? He may be, considering both male and female were created in His image.

But the real issue is God singing at all and what would cause Him to break into song. In this Old Testament passage a people who at one time feared the wrath of God, whose shoulders slumped in fear and anxiety suddenly find God on their side. He has come not with anger and vengeance, but with grace and power ready to put away all enemies.

And He's not coming begrudgingly, as a man with a job to do, but not too happy about having to do it. No, this Redeemer comes fully absorbed in the objects of His love. His care for them is not routine…not perfunctory…not with an "It's-a-tough-job-but-somebody-has-to-do-it" attitude. Here is a Savior who takes exquisite delight in those He is saving. So much so, that He breaks into song from the sheer joy of the relationship.

I don't know if you've ever heard God singing over you…but He does. Listen for His song. It will be a melody that flies in the face of life's circumstances…a sweet sound that seems out of touch with the activities of your life…an internal tune that assures you at the deepest recesses of your soul that you are loved and fondly cared for.

April 19
Who's Out There?

"What's out there?" I asked, peering into the cloudiness of my future. "I'm not exactly anxious about it, but am curious. And it is my future."

"Well," He said, "there's a lot out there and there are reasons why you can't see it all right now. Some of it might frighten you and some of it would make you so giddy with excitement that you'd quit living today in anticipation of later."

"But from where I sit I can see mountains you will have to climb that will test the very core of who you are. And with these climbs will be spectacular views that will bring joy and perspective to your journey. I see heartbreak, exquisite joy and delights from a thousand directions. There will be the heat of desert experiences and the cool refreshing of trusted friends."

"You will find great peace, times of confusion, bits of chaos and times of contentment so great that you'd almost think you're at Home with Me. But every part of it will have a purpose. Some will drive you to Me; others will convince you of my great love. And taken together they will mold you into my likeness. And that has been your prayer, hasn't it?"

"Yes it has," I responded thoughtfully. "So none of my future is wasted or unimportant to You?"

"Absolutely not," He assured me.

Hesitatingly I probed, "Is there anything else out there I should know about?"

"I am," He said smiling.

"I can never escape from your Spirit!
I can never get away from your presence!
If I go up to heaven, you are there;

if I go down to the grave, you are there.
If I ride the wings of the morning,
if I dwell by the farthest oceans,
even there your hand will guide me,
and your strength will support me."
Psalm 139:7-10 New Living Translation

April 20

The Moment

"She lived her entire life for this moment."

Prevailing intelligence and standard deductive ability would probably guess what this moment was. The winning of a Pulitzer? Perhaps receiving an Oscar before an adoring crowd? What about finally picking the correct numbers in Powerball and becoming a media icon for suddenly increasing your net worth by 140 million dollars?

Nope!

This statement was made about the moment she closed her eyes for the last time here and opened them to see Jesus face to face. That's right ... this was the moment she had lived her entire life for. That's a very wise woman because this is the most important moment in any life ... for in that moment you will hear either "Well done; welcome home" or "Depart from Me ... I never knew you and you never really knew Me."

To live for that moment makes sense, especially when that moment comes. But making eternal sense doesn't mean that living this way is particularly easy. It requires daily choices that often go against the grain of conventional wisdom. There are times when a conscious decision to please God sends your life at cross purposes with those around you, and can actually be dangerous as multitudes of martyrs can attest to.

Missionary Jim Elliot said, "No man is a fool who gives up what he cannot keep to gain what he cannot lose." Several years later he died at the hands of the Auca Indians in Ecuador. The corollary would contend that a man or woman is a fool who throughout life grabs what they can't possibly keep and in the process forfeits what they were meant to enjoy for eternity.

So today, reconfirm your ultimate objective. Live for that moment. It's not a matter of working harder and performing better, but of living in anticipation of God's smile. Because if He smiles at that moment, it means He's smiling now anticipating that moment as well!

> *"What good would it do to get everything you want and lose you, the real you? What could you ever trade your soul for?" Mark 8:36 The Message*

April 21

Dangerous

> *"When someone has been given much, much will be required in return; and when someone has been entrusted with much, even more will be required." Luke 12:48b New Living Translation*

The next time you are about to plunk yourself down for a service at your church of choice ... take warning! There should be a sign printed outside above the entrance and the same message included in the weekly bulletin: *BEWARE! SITTING IN ONE OF OUR SERVICES CARRIES POTENTIAL DANGER!*

But not everyone is exposed equally to that danger. If you are just there because someone is insisting you be there ... or if you're only there because of obligation to tradition and you won't be paying attention anyway ... then sitting there carries no more threat to you than possibly sitting through a piano recital.

However, if you in any way engage in the worship and pay any attention to the Word of God as it is proclaimed, then you need to be very careful and don't assume safety in numbers or later claim a faulty memory.

The truth is, whenever we're exposed to anything God says, we go away from that experience with much greater responsibility. We are no longer ignorant of that part of God's heart. Something must now be given in return for that increased knowledge and insight.

When we walk from that place of meeting … with new information now at our disposal … with more of God's heart and intentions and operating instructions now part of our lives … we are responsible for an obedient response! Jesus makes it clear in the verse from Luke that this response is required!

It's called 'discipleship' and God is serious about it happening in our lives. His goal? Turning us into followers who look and act and respond like His very Son. So as you contemplate attending your next church service, don't take what will happen there lightly. God doesn't.

"Great gifts mean great responsibilities; greater gifts, greater responsibilities." Luke 122:48 The Message

April 22
Deconstructing

Back in the Southern California desert my prayer walks are no longer taken along a flowing stream, surrounded by green trees. Our rural community is bisected by a two lane blacktop from which branch the myriad dirt roads (sand, actually) on which most houses sit. It's on these rough, corrugated roads that I do most of my walking.

With houses few and far between and with the incredible vistas offered in the clear desert air, I tend to keep my eyes on the sky, the surrounding mountains and the occasional cloud bounding past me. But at times I look down and what I've seen lately is thought-provoking. There in the roadway I am finding miscellaneous bolts … obviously fallen off the cars that bounce over these roads.

Cars deconstructing as they move through life! The washboard roads, the bumps and dips all contribute to these unwanted donations.

And isn't life sometimes like that? The potholes of living take their toll on us as well. Physically we know that we are in the process of 'deconstructing.' Strength diminishes … eyesight worsens … stamina runs out more quickly. And emotionally we feel the effects of living our lives in a fallen world. The process can be slowed, but not stopped. You may have a lifetime 'bumper to bumper' warranty on your car, but on you, there's another guarantee in place.

The Apostle Paul read the small print and announced: *"Even though on the outside it often looks like things are falling apart on us, on the inside, where God is making new life, not a day goes by without his unfolding grace." II Corinthians 4:16 The Message*

So today don't worry unnecessarily about losing a few nuts and bolts from your temporary chassis. Rejoice instead that the part of you that will never die is being exquisitely cared for and maintained by your Creator.

April 23

All Shook Up

"Why are you downcast, O my soul? Why so disturbed within me? Put your hope in God, for I will yet praise him, my Savior and my God." Psalm 42:5 NIV

How often do you talk to your soul?

The Psalmist did it when it was necessary. And he wasn't embarrassed to admit it. Our souls are that non-physical part of us that interplays between our spirits (where God lives) and our bodies … the only part we see in the mirror in the morning.

The soul is the residence of our personality. It encompasses our minds and emotions and our will. But put in a more practical sense, our souls are what get shook up over the current events in the world. Our souls react strongly to fears and innuendos and threats. Our souls tend to take on the agenda and aura of whatever or whoever feeds them.

And that can be a problem. The writer of this Psalm must have heard some disturbing news. Something that triggered wide-spread alarm. Some news item brought with it queasiness and disturbance to his inner man.

So he simply and in a straightforward manner addressed his soul as if talking to someone who should know better and needed to be corrected. "Hey, soul" he says, "who and what are we listening to here? As long as God is God, He provides the real story. You quit your worrying and settle down. Do you hear me?"

And the soul longs to be thus instructed. It was designed to be at peace. The Creator made it so. An agitated state is not its native environment. You just may need to turn down or turn off some of the offending media that brings anxiety and nervousness. It can be done and without moving to a monastery!

So how's your soul? All shook up? Bewitched, bothered and bewildered? Hunkered down in great fear? The word for us today is simply this: Put your hope in God!

April 24

My Pity Party

I wasn't mad or bitter … just disappointed. Someone had let me down and sorrow had scribbled all over the tablet of my life. I desperately needed to get to a "Pity Party."

The mistake I made at that point was to stop and ask Jesus for directions.

"What's a pity party?" He asked.

"You've never been to a pity party?" I queried in astonishment!

"No" He replied. "What do you do there?"

"Well, you mingle and look for people who appear to be sympathetic to your sad story. Then you recite it to them until they put their arm around your shoulder and tell you that they feel your pain."

Jesus asked, "Does it work? Do you feel better for the sympathy shown and does the pain go away?"

"No" I confessed with head bowed. It was dawning on me that the One I was speaking with knew well what unmet expectations felt like. He was the One who came to his own and they had no time for or interest in him. He was a Man of Sorrows and well acquainted with grief.

"What did you do with your pain?" I inquired, chagrined. "What did you do when people let you down?"

His eyes sparkled. "I overlooked the offense ... I forgave them. And when I did, the disappointment lost its ability to continue hurting me. And then," He continued with a broadening smile, "I invited them to my party!"

> *"You must make allowance for each other's faults and forgive the person who offends you. Remember, the Lord forgave you, so you must forgive others." Colossians 3:13 New Living Translation*

April 25
Do Gooders

> *"So let's not get tired of doing what is good." Galatians 6:9 New Living Translation*

We often feel that we are good for nothing. By that I mean we aren't recompensed fairly for being good, choosing right, making sacrifices for the good of others. Living a Godly life requires making decisions that cost us and appear to give us nothing in return.

And when compared to those who aren't trying, who aren't being good and make little effort to make their world a better place, it makes sticking to 'doing what is good' seem a bit futile.

But the reason for continuing to do good whether it seems to pay or not is found in the verses that follow the one above. *"So let's not allow ourselves to get fatigued doing good. At the right time we will harvest a good crop if we don't give up, or quit." Galatians 6:9 The Message*

It's like God recognizes that it's tiring being good in a bad world. It's tough taking the high road when the low road travels so easily. It can be a burden holding to a standard that others openly mock.

But ... there is a payday coming for the righteous. It will come at the 'right time'. If it hasn't happened yet, it's simply not the right time. The promise is secured by the tiny, two-letter word '**if**'. The prize won't come if we give up or quit.

It takes patience to exercise faith. Faith's motto is: "Hang on. It's going to be worth it."

Impatience counsels "Why wait? Just take what you can get now."

It's important to reaffirm our confidence in the law of 'sowing and reaping.' Behind it stand all the promises of God and the assurance that He is keeping accurate records and will reward faithful living.

April 26
The Voice

"The voice of the Lord is powerful; the voice of the Lord is full of majesty."
Psalm 29:4 KJV

If you think the voices of Jimmy Durante, Willie Nelson, Jimmy Stewart, James Earl Jones are unique, you should hear the voice of God! Really ... we all should hear the voice of God.

♦ God opened his mouth and hurled 50,000,000,000,000,000,000,000,000 stars across billions of light years. Counting them at one per second would consume the next fifteen hundred trillion years! (And these stars account for only about 1% of the total mass of the universe.)
♦ God's voice is able to break cedar trees (Psalm 29:5)
♦ God's voice called Lazarus, a man dead for three days, back to life with such authority that all the departed within earshot came out of their graves.

But there are other dimensions to God's voice. Consider:

♦ He beckons a young boy in the middle of the night and doesn't scare him! (I Samuel 3)
♦ Elijah (I Kings 19) doesn't connect with God in a mountain-rending, rock-breaking wind, nor in an earthquake or fire ... but finally hooks up with God's still small voice.
♦ And if you need guidance for life's journey and not a mountain-blasting voice, this verse in Isaiah 30:21 should encourage you: *"Your own ears will hear him. Right behind you a voice will say, "This is the way you should go," whether to the right or to the left."*

So whether you are facing a battle or enemy that requires the power of the 'star-hurler', the bunker-buster or resurrection-producer or simply quiet words in the night, God has a voice that matches your circumstances.

Give thanks that God has a voice and is willing to use it to rescue us, comfort us, inform us, discipline us and love us. Listen for it and then respond to it.

April 27

Our Amazing God

"The Word of the Lord came to me, saying, " Before I formed you in the womb I knew you, before you were born I set you apart; I appointed you as a prophet to the nations." Jeremiah 1:4 NIV

What do you say to a God who knew you before you were you? How do you respond to a God who set you apart for his purposes even before there was anything tangible to set apart? What is your reaction to a God so big that He single-handedly holds the cosmos together, yet relates to your aching tooth?

Can you comprehend the One who instructs the sea on how far up on the beach it is allowed to go and at the same time has the creativity to orchestrate a magnificent sunset over that same sea?

Can you explain how He can be and is the God of the 'big stuff' yet attend to the detail of an individual rhododendron blossom?

Are you able to fathom the way He can muscle the planet's weather systems … keep the lid on a volcano … satisfy the ravenous hunger of a lion and still pay undivided attention to a toddler's fall or a grieving heart?

The Psalmist exclaimed, *"I look up at your macro-skies, dark and enormous, your handmade sky-jewelry, Moon and stars mounted in their settings. Then I look at my micro-self and wonder, Why do you bother with us? Why take a second look our way?" Psalm 8:3,4 The Message*

Why indeed? And yet He does 'bother with us' and take even more than a second look. And that should be enough amazement for you for one day!

April 28
Your Faith's Shelf Life

What is the shelf life of your faith? Is there an 'expiration date' on it somewhere? Or is it so packed with preservatives that it can last a long, long time?

Bread can only stay on a grocer's shelf for so long. The same with milk, even though refrigerated. And any green grocer who doesn't move his produce fast enough will be throwing a lot of stuff out. But what about faith?

If you're like me, I begin to worry occasionally about running out of it before the crisis is over … prior to the answer arriving …just before God's dawn begins brightening the eastern sky. It's a scary thought.

Do you think the Apostle Paul ever wondered if he possessed enough faith to get him to the 39th bloodying stripe? Did he question whether he could endure his Mediterranean cruise without a ship, bobbing up and down while waiting rescue? Could his faith endure one more night in a cold, damp prison cell?

The encouraging Scripture to me on this subject is I Corinthians 10:13 where God promises through Paul's writing not to let more into our lives than what we can handle. He knows the expiration date on our faith better than we do and promises that nothing will get past that point.

Our confidence must be in Him and once we have even a small measure of it, we must not cast it away, regardless of circumstances, statements to the contrary or what our physical eyes and ears tell us.

Our faith is designed to go the distance, someday giving every one of us the same testimony of Paul who said, *"I have fought the good fight, I have finished the race, I have kept the faith."* II Timothy 4:7 NIV

April 29

He Loves Me ... He Loves Me Not

When 'puppy love' was in bloom and you were somewhere between twelve and fifteen ... it was often difficult to know how the object of your emotions really felt about you. So you picked a flower ... cast your entire future (at least it felt like it at the moment) to the fates and began plucking petals.

"She loves me ... she loves me not ... she loves me ... she loves me not." This went on until the petals were gone and the answer to your heart's burning question had been answered.

When reading the book of Psalms and holding it up alongside my life, I find that same sort of heart-wrenching, teeter-tottering, tug of war going on inside of me. Does God love me or not?

From *"Why, Lord, do you stand far off?" Psalm 10:1 NIV* to *"This poor man called and you saved him out of all his troubles." Psalm 34:6 NIV* It runs the gamut from *" ... do not ignore my plea ..." Psalm 55:1 NIV* to *"A righteous man may have many troubles, but the Lord delivers him from them all." Psalm 34:19 NIV*

Let me remind you that the apparent inconsistency is always with us ... always a part of a fallen world with all the 'stuff' that goes along with it. The up and down, in and out, does He or doesn't He ... is all on our side.

With Him there is only steadfast, unmovable consistency. *"Cast all your anxiety on him because he cares for you." I Peter 5:7 NIV* To Moses He promised, *"Certainly I will be with thee ..." Exodus 3:12 ASV* Through Jeremiah the prophet he said, *"I have loved you, my people, with an everlasting love. With unfailing love I have drawn you to myself." Jeremiah 31:3 New Living Translation*

And the promise given to us in Romans 8:39 says, *" ... nothing in all creation will ever be able to separate us from the love of God that is revealed in Christ Jesus our Lord." New Living Translation* That sounds encouragingly consistent to me.

So remember, no matter which flower you pick to pluck, the last petal will always say, "He loves me!"

April 30
Serendipity

> *"Every desirable and beneficial gift comes out of heaven."*
> *James 1:17*
> *The Message*

I had a 'serendipity' of sorts tonight. That's a fun word that's even more enjoyable when it happens to you.

The word can mean everything from karma to fate to fortunate luck to destiny. But it's usually used to mean 'an unexpected delightful experience.' Those delights can range from finding a twenty dollar bill on the sidewalk to showing up at the store looking for gym shoes that have just moments before gone on sale for 75% off.

For me it was a free dish of ice cream.

Joanie and I had taken the opportunity of visiting one of our favorite Northwest waterfront eateries… knowing that our times for doing so will soon be over. (There are few seaside restaurants in the Mojave Desert.) We had a wonderful meal with extra special attention from our waiter Robert. He was friendly, quick with the coffee refills and accommodating to our dining desires. Desert came with the meal. Joanie chose the ice cream with a bit of chocolate syrup while I chose the burnt cream. Neither would have made Robert Atkins proud of us. (You skinny people will probably not understand that last sentence.)

In the midst of 'ooohing' and 'aaahing' over our seldom enjoyed deserts, Robert showed up with another dish of ice cream. He had forgotten to tell us about a third choice and wanted us to taste it. It was worth leaving the other two deserts half eaten…it was that good. That extra little gift was unexpected.

It was a blessing from the freezer in the kitchen. But it was also one of heaven's little 'extras.' When we trace any of the good things in our lives back far enough, we will always find the loving and imaginative Father heart of God. God's Word says that He thinks about us constantly.

Always be aware of 'serendipities' that come into your life. Recognize them. Enjoy them. And then follow their origins back to a Father who loves entering our lives in small, yet wonderfully enriching ways. And then, in that secret place in your heart where much business is conducted, simply say "Thanks!"

May joy accompany your journey.

May 1
Night Drive

"Since God assured us, 'I'll never let you down, never walk off and leave you,' we can boldly quote, 'God is there, ready to help;'"
Hebrews 13:5 The Message

It is the end of an excruciatingly long and tiring day, which culminated a physically and emotionally draining week, which in turn capped off six months of transition, trauma and excitement.

The movers have left…the house has been cleaned for the new owners…the last of the trash has been hauled away and now we're driving through a rainstorm heading south toward a new chapter (possibly 'book') of our lives. The drive is already five hours old and it's in the middle of the night. Joanie is sleeping the fitful sleep of someone whose body desperately needs rest, but then won't let that rest come easily. Our Cocker Spaniel is sleeping in her bed on top of a three foot tall pile of clothes in the backseat.

So it's just me and the windshield wipers and an occasionally passed eighteen wheeler… and God. Though I'm exhausted and feel totally empty at the moment, I'm particularly glad that I have a Traveling Companion who doesn't need sleep. A Friend who through all the decisions, details and questions of the last months has promised me that He'd never for a moment leave me or move off in another direction.

God has a plan for each of our lives. Read Psalm 139 again if you need reassurance of that fact. From his vantage point He can easily see how all the twists and turns and delays and fast starts all blend into something wonderful that's been in the back of his mind for a long, long time. And so tonight, as the miles are pushed behind me and the sunlight of another day is quickly approaching…I'm pretty happy. This is the kind of night, and this will be the kind of week that the knowledge of his perpetual presence will warm my heart and sustain my spirit.

Tonight, indeed, there is joy in my journey.

May 2
Missed Opportunities

There is a powerful yet sad word picture portrayed in an old secular song by Tommy Edwards. The words give life to a fear that lurks within many of us…the fear of 'what if?'

In the song's text he tells of a boy and girl growing up on opposite sides of the mountain and ponders "What joyful bliss could have resulted had they ever known each other?"

Haunting, isn't it? What if my ideal soul-mate lived on the other side of the hill and we never met? We can add verses of our own, like: *What if I was supposed to have taken that other job instead of the one I have? What if I would have picked the bottle of soda behind the one I chose…might I have gotten the winning bottle cap? What if we hadn't purchased our house when we did…would the price have come down?*

To the child of God the 'what if' questions aren't wrong… if they're directed forward instead of back toward that which has already taken place. Going backwards with those questions is not only counter-productive but can lead to an emotional trauma. However, when you are walking with God and you launch a 'what if' question toward the future, the implications become wildly exciting.

What if this day contains the miracle I've been needing and looking for? What if God showed up in the life of my co-workers and met their deepest needs? What if God and I teamed up today to tackle a difficult social problem in my community? What if God used me today to tell the story of his incredible love to someone who doesn't feel very loved? What if this week ended the emotional or spiritual or financial draught in my life?

Indeed…what if? The wisest man who ever lived (Solomon) said "*Hope deferred makes the heart sick, but when dreams come true, there is life and joy." Proverbs 13:12 New Living Translation*

Today, remember to 'what if' toward the future. Don't allow your history to destroy your destiny. God has good things in store for you…count on it!

May 3
Bannister Grabbers

Author John Powell tells a rather poignant personal story about his mother's last days. Each evening at bedtime he would carry her up a flight of stairs to her bed. Invariably, as he began to climb with her in his arms, she would reach out and grab the banister. "Mother" he would gasp "don't do that. I am liable to drop you."

And she would reply "That's why I grab the banister…so you won't drop me."

Do you identify? Are you a 'banister grabber?' Grabbing at banisters is a product of distrust…distrust in both the ability and the intentions of the one doing the carrying. Being a Chrsitian involves being carried a lot. We are continually born-along on the strong arms and the mighty wind of God's Spirit. And at almost every point 'banister grabbing' becomes a temptation.

♦ We don't believe God can hold us...so we grab the banister.
♦ We aren't sure we like the direction He is taking us...so we grab the banister.
♦ His intentions seem a little murky...so we grab the banister.
♦ We forget the strength and history behind his arms...so grab the banister.
♦ We aren't sure He's completely thought through the next move...so we, well, you get the picture.

This would be an excellent time to sit down and reconsider both the Father's ability and his intentions. All of Scripture makes it abundantly clear to anyone (even former 'banister-grabbers') that He is both willing and able to get us to where we need to be. If God wanted to help us but couldn't...or if He were able to but didn't really care to, then grabbing at banisters would make more sense. But rest assured friend that *"He who has begun a good work in you will complete it..."* Philippians 1:6 KJV

Let go of the bannister and enjoy the journey.

May 4

I'd Rather

"One day spent in your house, this beautiful place of worship, beats thousands spent on Greek island beaches. I'd rather scrub floors in the house of my God than be honored as a guest in the palace of sin." Psalm 84:10 The Message

Life consists mainly of making choices … and then living with the results of those choices.

After a lifetime of studying the ways of God, the Psalmist made a choice: better to be a floor-scrubber in God's house, than hang out as a special guest in "Sin Palace." That would not be the choice of a normal person. Being a guest of honor always sounds better than menial work.

But I've now lived long enough (with an ear tuned to heaven's advice) to have come to some 'choice' conclusions of my own. Like:

♦ I'd rather have one friend who will tell me the truth, than several who will bend truth to keep from hurting me.

♦ I'd rather be in the presence of stumbling sincerity than exposed to professionally-polished hypocrisy.

♦ I'd rather leave where I am than to never get to where I long to be.

♦ I'd rather hang out where I'm celebrated than where I am tolerated.

♦ I'd rather become broken and then re-made soft and pliable than to be tough, unbending and uncaring.

♦ I'd rather spend time with people who support my hunger for God and his will in my life than give myself to self-made and selfish people who feel complete without Him.

♦ I'd rather be naively obedient to God's voice than be adamant about first knowing all the angles, stipulations and ramifications.

♦ And I'd rather hear God's "Well done, good and faithful servant" than receive the Pulitzer, Nobel Peace Prize and Publisher's Clearinghouse sweepstakes check all combined.

Find great joy and make good choices today.

May 5

Up To This Point

"Remember the things I have done in the past. For I alone am God! I am God, and there is none like me. "" Isaiah 46:9 *NLT*

I am fundamentally a futurist. I love to look out the front window. I would not pay money to sit backwards on a train trip. My destiny is not determined by my history.

Having said that, let me temporarily suspend those sentiments and say that sometimes looking back is not only good but vital to our future. Consider Israel as their long journey to God's promise and their new land came to an end. The last obstacle to face before the soles of their sandals touched their new homeland was to transverse the Jordan River.

A decade-old miracle is repeated and God parts the waters and they walk into their destiny on dry ground. One of the very first things they were instructed to do was to erect an altar of twelve stones ... piled up as a memorial to God's faithfulness.

"Why are we taking the time to build an altar?" they may have asked. "Because," came the reply, "the time will come when our children will ask us about its significance and we'll recount God's faithfulness to us and to his promises."

It is so easy to get caught up in living and growing and studying and predicting our futures that we forget how closely the future is tied to the past. When we look forward in faith, it is a focused view because of what we know about God from our past. Every past victory ... every answered prayer ... every spiritual test passed ... each a clear cut sign that our future is secured.

Go back if need be and do what Samuel did in I Samuel 7 after seeing God come through once again for Israel in their battle against the Philistines. Again, a stone was erected with these words: "THUS FAR THE LORD HAS HELPED US!"

Look back long enough to see God's hand in your life. It'll do wonders for your view of your future.

May there be joy for your journey

May 6
Some Need Help Believing

God says, "Because he has set his love upon Me, therefore will I deliver him; I will set him on high, because he knows and understands My name [has a personal knowledge of My mercy, love, and kindness - trusts and relies on Me, knowing I will never forsake him, no, never]." Psalm 91:14 Amplified Bible

After being a son of God for over five decades, I am beginning to feel like I know and understand Him...at least better than I did when a young man. As the Psalmist said, I have a personal knowledge of his mercy, love and kindness.

When I blow it, I believe that He views me and my actions through eyes of mercy. And I firmly believe that even when I'm a jerk and fail at impressing anyone, let alone Him, He still looks lovingly in my direction. And when life is tough and circumstances beat down on me, my belief system has taught me that my Heavenly Father will always be extraordinarily kind to me.

Yet after years of this incredible relationship, I still find it difficult to comprehend a God who is merciful, loving and kind to me. I trust His Word when it describes his character, but I believe it because I've experienced it.

My new friend who owns a small coffee shop doesn't know those things about God. Nor does the stroke victim that I treated to breakfast this last summer. And the neighbor whose three large dogs often run loose...he doesn't have a clue as to the

potential Friend he has in Jesus. And so, initially I must believe
for them. I begin to envision God working in their lives well before they imagine it happening. I see God smiling at them even
while they may be sure that God is mad at them. I pray for them
and allow them to see how well God takes care of me.

God's goodness to me is not intended to stop with me. It's in
the free-flowing stories and testimonies of God's care, that others are given the opportunity to 'see for themselves' the exquisite goodness of God.

Polish the reflective mirror of your life. Blind and dazzle the
eyes of the pre-Christians around you through your changed
life of thankfulness and witness. What you owe every seeker
is to first tell them about the One who has supplied you with
enough mercy, love and kindness to last you for eternity.

May 7

Landing Safely

If you take an airplane into the air and intend to fly it to another airport, there's an important thing you must do prior to
landing. You must recalibrate some of your instrumentation...
primarily the altimeter. Your altimeter tells you your altitude
and it figures the altitude out by knowing what the barometric
pressure is. So before letting down into your new surroundings,
you must know what the barometric pressure is at your destination. Otherwise, coming down through clouds you may expect
to break out into the clear at 800 feet when in reality you're
actually at 300 feet and you'll pop out of the clouds short of the
runway with maybe a large house in front of the windshield. If
not a crash, it'll be at the very least a lousy landing.

I've been in and out of changing weather patterns in my life
for the last few weeks. My instruments needed recalibrating.
Some of my landings were simply dreadful and some were down-
right scary. And so, I slipped in my ear buds, cranked up some

of my favorite worship music on my MP3 player and set out on a long walk through the desert. It wasn't long before I had the correct 'barometric pressure' for today and its various situations.

I'm quite sure that the Apostle Paul utilized God's Recalibration Shop on a regular basis, because he could claim *"I have learned the secret of living in every situation… " Philippians 4:12 New Living Translation* He could land safely at any airport because the instrumentation of his life was always correct.

So how do you know if your life isn't calibrated? You just know. And the people closest to you know it also. Let me offer you two sources of help. First, carve out enough time daily for God to be able to speak his directions and peace into your heart. And second, bring someone alongside you that knows you really well…a best friend, or perhaps your spouse or a work associate. And level with them about the 'foul altitude' that you've being flying at. They already are aware of your struggle and by inviting them to participate in the recalibration process, you'll get both accountability and some serious allies to keep you safely in the air until a safe landing can be assured. Enjoy the journey.

May 8

The Mirror

> *"So we're not giving up. How could we! Even though on the outside it often looks like things are falling apart on us, on the inside, where God is making new life, not a day goes by without his unfolding grace." II Corinthians 4:16 The Message*

Periodically, when I forget myself and glance in the mirror after my shower, I am stunned by what I see. "What are they doing to me?" I exclaim, greatly troubled in my spirit.

The 'they' I refer to is an amalgamation of forces arrayed against me whose sole purpose is to destroy me. Included in this dastardly group would be: age, gravity, poor eating habits, lack of exercise and I'm certain, the devil. Indeed, their pursuit of me is relentless and when I assist them in even the most minor of ways, they move even more quickly toward success.

But there is another 'mirror' that I glance into from time to time. It's far kinder to me than the bathroom mirror. It's the reflection I get when checking on my spiritual body. And for the most part, it's very encouraging. Again, 'they' have an ongoing role in my progress.

And who are 'they' in this case?

> Godly friends who long for my spiritual well being and speak truth and faith into my life.
> Assorted preachers, teachers and mentors who are used by God to build me up in my spirit.
> My own personal times when I allow God to speak directly to me through his Word or in prayerful conversation.
> Those trials and assorted irritants that keep my faith real and grounded and goad me onto a higher plateau of trust.

So I take courage in the steady progress of the spiritual man and agree with my wife that I don't have to surrender quite so easily to the forces that are working on me physically.

May 9
Uncle or Father?

When Jesus was looking for answers that weren't available, He didn't cry "Uncle."

♦ He cried "Father!" *"Jesus prayed this prayer: "O Father, Lord of heaven and earth, thank you for hiding these things from those who think themselves wise and clever, and for revealing them to the childlike." Matthew 11:25 New Living Translation*

When the cross loomed before him and he faced an obstacle requiring faith and commitment not normal in the circumstances, He didn't cry "Uncle."

♦ He cried "Father!" *"After saying all these things, Jesus looked up to heaven and said, "Father, the hour has come. Glorify your Son so he can give glory back to you." John 17:1 New Living Translation*

His friend Lazarus had been dead for three days and He faced a situation that everyone around him said was an impossibility, He didn't cry "Uncle."

♦ He cried "Father!" *"So they rolled the stone aside. Then **Jesus** looked up to heaven and said, "**Father**, thank you for hearing me." John 11:41 New Living Translation*

How often do we holler "Uncle" when calling on "Father" would change our entire situation ... restore sanity ... quell out-of-control emotions ... give an elusive perspective ... grant peace in turmoil ... heal a broken relationship.

Why is it we call for a relative who may not come through when we have a Father who always does?

Pride and deluded self-confidence keep some from calling for any help whatsoever. They stumble from one disaster to the next. A person wrapped up totally in themselves is generally a very small package indeed. It's tough to go it all alone.

But others call and wait in vain for the cavalry to arrive. In their growing panic they scan the horizon for signs of help approaching and are met with disappointment.

God's Word is quite deliberate in its instructions: *"But everyone who **calls on the name of the Lord** will be saved." Acts 2:21 New Living Translation* There it is – a simple directive of what to do when the world caves in, friends abandon, finances disappear, pressures build unmercifully, disappointment disheartens and hope dies.

The operative word isn't "Uncle" … it's "Father!"

Somewhere Between

Somewhere between 'we've never done it that way before' and 'we've done it one time in a row that way, why do it the same again?' … between presumptuous faith and scared timidity … between laying it all on the line and cautious hoarding … between giving it all away and keeping it all for yourself … between feeling like you deserve it all and feeling absolutely worthless … there is a position of balance.

We lose ourselves in the extremes, often getting into trouble in the edges of faith and life. It would be nice if there were published 'middle points' that were exact and correct in every circumstance … a place where we would never have to worry about going overboard or being too conservative. But with maturity comes the realization that there is no magic marker spot at which we should stand in every situation.

In one instance God's wisdom has us going slow. But days later the Spirit's prompting has us at warp speed and we can scarcely focus on the stuff going by us in a blur. We'd find a certain comfort in knowing where to stand, every time. But we'd also miss the thrill of learning to instantly follow the directions of God's incredible Holy Spirit.

Who but God knows where the next curve will be revealed in the headlights of life? And who else knows the safe speed to take that curve? And who knows the resources I will need in my life at my next spiritual assignment. And who best knows when it's safe to give it all away because there is a God-appointed oasis up ahead where financial, physical and emotional tanks will all be refueled?

The best balance in any of our lives is the keen awareness of God's awareness of all things, and our ability to both hear his directions and follow them explicitly. Remember the admonition in Proverbs *"Trust God from the bottom of your heart: don't try to figure out everything on your own. Listen for God's voice in everything you do, everywhere you go; he's the one who will keep you on track."* *Proverb 3:5,6 The Message*

May you experience wonderful joy on your journey!

May 11

Mom

Mom has Alzheimer's.

For the last few years she has been fighting a temporarily losing battle with this dehumanizing disease. I say temporary because she secured the permanent cure many years ago when she settled on heaven as her ultimate destination.

So while here in Atlanta visiting her, it's enough for me to see a smile cross her face when she sees me … or reach out in the car to pat my shoulder. Not huge things, but indications that I haven't been erased from that part of her mind and heart.

But not so with most of the rest of her life. Breakfast of fifteen minutes ago … a roommate to meet 'for the first time' time after time … the looks of confusion as she sits at a piano and the oldest hymns pose serious problems for her.

Sixty-plus years of ministry appear to be forgotten. Not even the memory of being a pastor's wife with five active children remains. Certainly not the cooking of some 54,000 meals for her family … or for playing the piano for thousands and thousands of services from the age of 12 … for sure she doesn't remember the names and faces of multiple hundreds of overnight house guests over six decades of ministry. Nor can she recall the many times the churches served couldn't provide adequately for the Walterman family and she left the home to work.

I have no idea when or how this incomplete story will end here on earth. I just know that there's an ending for her so spectacular … so immersed in God and His plan … that even the fact that she can't remember, won't be remembered.

As I honor her on Mother's Day this year she has a missing companion in my Dad who even now from the banister of heaven watches and waits and smiles, knowing that she *"… will never again be hungry or thirsty; she will never be scorched by the heat of the sun. For the Lamb on the throne will be her Shepherd. He will lead her to springs of life-giving water. And God will wipe every tear from her eyes." Revelation 7:16,17 New Living Translation*

May there be joy and anticipation on your journey!

May 12
He Doesn't Lie

It's been a minor disappointment, yet indicative of just how easy disappointment comes.

We now live in the arid Mojave Desert. Any moisture is a big deal to us. Obviously, we don't expect the weather patterns of Portland, Oregon or Seattle, Washington …but we do look forward to an occasional rainsquall blowing through.

So when the weatherman warned of a potential winter storm to sweep into Southern California from the Gulf of Alaska and slide over the San Gabriel Mountains and give us two to six inches of snow, we were more than ready for it. Granted, the southern end of the state tends to come to an abrupt stop with the advent of the first several flakes. But we need the moisture and eagerly looked forward to being 'snowed in' for the evening.

The winds blew … the temperature dropped … the world turned gray … and the weatherman never backed down from his prognostications. We waited and watched; then watched and waited …from early afternoon until bedtime and then into the next day. There were several moments of the appearance of snow, but short enough to make us wonder if we had actually seen any.

Foiled again!

And isn't life like that a lot of the time? Big promises, but little in the way of delivery. The portend of great events that turn out to be non-events. We hitch our wagon to a star only to have it (and our attached wagon) fall from the sky. Is there nothing or no one who can deliver? Is there anyone who makes a hamburger as gigantic as the one portrayed on the full color pictures? Does anyone make good on his promises …every time?

You know the answer. The writer of Hebrews admonishes us: *"Let us hold unswervingly to the hope we profess, for he who prom-ised is faithful." Hebrews 10:23 NIV* When Solomon was dedicat-ing the temple he reminded Israel that God *"has given rest to his people … just as he promised. Not one word has failed of all the won-derful promises he gave through his servant Moses." I Kings 8:56 New Living Translation*

So if you're going to stake anything at all on the words of somebody, make sure it's on the promises of the Somebody who always says what He means and absolutely means what He says. That … you can take to the bank!

And may that fill you with joy.

May 13

Ask Largely

Not long ago someone sent me some material from Charles Spurgeon's book on prayer. He speaks of praying while stand-ing in the palace, on the glittering floor of the great King's own reception room. Around us angels bow with veiled faces. In the presence of such a God, he challenges us with this question:

"Shall we come there with stunted requests and narrow, contracted faith?" He chides further with this admonition: "Do not bring before God stinted petitions and narrow desires. Ask, therefore, after a Godlike fashion, for great things, for you are before a great throne."

How many huge heart-hungers have I pared down to a tiny bite size? How many times have my large dreams been downsized into a humanized 'miracle' that even I could pull off? And how many times have I choked in prayer in asking God for what I really needed by backing off to petition for something so pathetic that even in me it produced nothing but a yawn?

If God is God (and He certainly is …) then He is big enough to be asked to do great things. I don't know about you, but the growing hunger in my heart is requiring a larger and larger petition. My world is too confusing, too hurtful and too demanding to let me ask for anything other than a bona fide miracle from a very large God.

I'm going to read the following passage several times until my confidence in God sees this kind of provision in my life and in the lives of the people who surround me. Don't ask small … believe as large as you can!

> *"In Jerusalem, the Lord Almighty will spread a wonderful feast for everyone around the world. It will be a delicious feast of good food, with clear, well-aged wine and choice beef. In that day he will remove the cloud of gloom, the shadow of death that hangs over the earth. He will swallow up death forever! The Sovereign Lord will wipe away all tears. He will remove forever all insults and mockery against his land and people. The Lord has spoken!" Isaiah 25:6-8 Living Bible*

May you have great joy for your journey.

May 14

Fighting or Hiding

"But the Lord is my fortress; my God is a mighty rock where I can hide". Psalm 94:22 New Living Translation

"In your strength I can crush an army; with my God I can scale any wall." Psalm 18:29 New Living Translation

Without a doubt David was among the greatest fighters to slip on sandals in the Old Testament. As a boy he learned how to fight …but as a man he learned how to hide. To any follower of Jesus there are times for both. Knowing when to do one or the other is a matter of spiritual maturity.

To the young, a good fight is always the best way to settle conflict. Whether using words, sticks or bare knuckles, an altercation shows what side you're on and reveals your passion for that position. But there have been fighters who have eloquently and powerfully made those points yet didn't make it out of the battle to fight another day. Being mighty does not guarantee victory. The Old Testament writer laments in II Samuel 1:25 *"How are the mighty fallen in the midst of the battle!" King James Version*

Sometimes there's wisdom in hiding out. While there are battles we are not meant to fight alone, (we need brothers and sisters at our sides) … other conflicts we are to stay out of completely! Listen to Moses' instructions to Israel when it looked as if they would have to fight to the death against the advancing Egyptian army: *"But Moses told the people, 'Don't be afraid. Just stand where you are and watch the Lord rescue you. The Egyptians that you see today will never be seen again. The Lord himself will fight for you. You won't have to lift a finger in your defense!'" Exodus 14:13,14 New Living Translation*

This day you may need divine wisdom to know if you are to draw the sword and take on the enemy (while depending entirely upon God) or if you should re-sheath the blade and slip into God's fortress during the battle (while depending entirely upon God). Can you see the common thread running through both scenarios? Whether sidelined and hidden, or thrust into the middle of the hottest battle zone, the outcome is always dependant upon God. Allow Him to put you where he chooses. And enjoy the fight!

May 15

Live Like You Are Dying

Tim McGraw wrote a thought-provoking song … recorded it well and most likely made a lot of money from it. More power to him.

It's a song that challenges the culture's sense of entitlement to immortality. The story tells of a man told he will soon die from a disease that ambushed him and forced him to consider his woefully shortened life before him. He makes the decision to 'live like he was dying' and hence the song's title.

It's a tale of cramming in now all the things you thought you'd get to later in life … because there will not be 'later.' "It's now or never" could be the subtitle to Tim's story.

But in spite of the positive contributions made to a society that generally refuses to think about the end of life, from a Christian's perspective the song misses a most essential point. God calls us to live life, not as if we've got to get it all in now … but that 'now' is simply preparation for what is coming when 'now' is over.

Solomon stated the following: *"Yet God has made everything beautiful for its own time. He has planted eternity in the human heart,*

*but even so, people cannot see the whole scope of God's work from begin-
ning to end." Ecclesiastes 3:11 New Living Translation*

We were made for eternity ... it's in our DNA. And though
the carnal part of each of us attempts to ignore it and the up-
ward pull it exerts on us (not just the pull 'up' to heaven, but
a spiritual prompting to be better, do better, please Someone
other than ourselves), eternity and its values reside within us.

So don't concentrate on the fragment that remains, whether
1 day or potentially 75 years. Don't just live like you are dying,
but let the enormity of eternity help you live like you are never
going to die!

May 16
Freedom From Stuff

Stuff ...

The seed of greed is found early in each of us.

- ♦ At one year of age we desperately want our cousin's toy -
  enough to hit him for it.
- ♦ At seven we're bringing some of our stuff to school for
  'show and tell.'
- ♦ By our teens our room cannot hold all our stuff.

And it only gets uglier as we get older. "Want to see all my
stuff? Most of it's in my garage but I've also got a 15' by 30' stor-
age unit for the stuff that doesn't fit in my home and garage.
I'm getting a raise next year and I'll be able to buy some of the
stuff I've really been wanting!"

There are several dangers in this gathering, hoarding, storing and caring for our stuff. First, we almost immediately quit
owning it and it all begins owning us. Second, we tend to tie
our identity around it. If I have a lot, it makes me feel better
about myself. Conversely, if someone else has something I don't

have, my life spirals down into depression and becomes fuel for covetousness, which is the big Bible word for greed.

We now have graphic reality shows on television where cameramen enter the homes (or attempt to enter them) of people who have never learned to let go. Their lives come to a standstill ... family relationships break down ... the joy of living succumbs to the habit of hoarding. Simple pleasures and possessions as they grow take on a malevolent personality. They demand care, maintenance, increased insurance, more and more space. And none of it really helps us feel secure or loved.

Might you consider parting with some of your stuff? Give some away. Throw some away. Sell some of it. Enjoy the freedom of having 'enough' and use the surplus to further God's work in your life.

> *Then he (Jesus) said, "Beware! Guard against every kind of greed. Life is not measured by how much you own." Luke 12:15 New Living Translation*

May you find joy and simplicity for your journey!

May 17
Why Me Lord?

As you read the above title, my guess is that you heard it in your mind being said in a whining, pouting voice. Maybe there's even a little lip quiver as we say it. Because that question is usually a form of spiritual complaining.

It's a self-centered lament and comes from the branch of theological inquiry that asks: How come bad things happen to good people?

But let's change directions. Instead of pondering why bad things happen to good people, let's consider why good things happen to bad people. The first question presupposes that we're good and deserve more than what we're getting.

The second supposition is that we are by nature bad and that it's only God's exquisite grace that keeps us from getting what we really deserve. The Bible says that " ... *everyone has sinned; we all fall short of God's glorious standard." Romans 3:23 New Living Translation*

Let's not use this question as a self-righteous inquisition of God. Let's use it as a doxology of high praise for God's goodness in our lives.

+ "Why me Lord? Why am I so blessed?
+ "Why me Lord? Why do I have health?
+ "Why me Lord? Why am I surrounded by good friends?
+ "Why me Lord? Why do I have a good job when others don't?
+ "Why me Lord? Why was I introduced to you when so many others have not been?
+ "Why me Lord? Why do I have a future and a hope that eludes others?

Why indeed.

Several decades ago, country singer/composer Kris Kristofferson got it right in his song "Why Me Lord". He contemplates his past and tries to figure out what caused God's grace and mercy in his life. It's a futile search that leaves out God's kindness to us just because He loves us.

We need to turn whining into worship by questioning the good things coming into our lives ... not the bad things that happen from living in a fallen world. Let's quit blaming God for things He didn't do and begin praising him for the things He has done!

> *"Every good gift bestowed, every perfect gift received comes to us from above, courtesy of the Father of lights. He is consistent". James 1:17 Voice Translation*

May there be joy and thankfulness in your journey!

The Finish Line

A race is defined as "a contest of speed or endurance." The Bible says it's both.

In a sprint (60 – 200 meters) where the difference between first or second place is often measured in hundredths of seconds, you don't have time to wave to your girlfriend in the stands! The eyes see only the finish line.

In a 10,000 meter race (almost 6 and a quarter miles) your eyes are still on the finish line, although it will take you much more time to get there. In a sprint you give it all up at once … you leave nothing in reserve for later because there is no later. But pacing and persistence as well as almost inconceivable conditioning required by all serious athletes are what matter for the long distance runner.

As Christians we're entered into both kinds of races. The many sprints seem to be imbedded in the much longer race that lasts our entire lifetime. The writer of Hebrews paints this picture: *"Therefore, since we are surrounded by such a huge crowd of witnesses to the life of faith, let us strip off every weight that slows us down, especially the sin that so easily trips us up. And let us run with endurance the race God has set before us." Hebrews 12:1 New Living Translation*

Those times when the gun goes off and we're battling impossible circumstances, hostility from a loved one, a looming financial disaster … our objective is clear: get to the finish line as quickly as possible; you can breath again later. Our creed is: "This too will pass."

But the longer race, the race of life itself, calls for a sure and steady pace … of letting go of things that would hold us back … of keeping the long range goal right in front of us where it dictates our life style, our priorities, our relationships and mostly our growing relationship with our Lord. Because He plays an extremely important part when our race is ended.

Hebrew's author reminds us to keep our eyes on Jesus. He was not only there when the gun sounded and we pounded down the track, but He'll be there at the other end to welcome and congratulate all the runners who kept the faith and finished their course.

May you find joy and strength and endurance for your journey!

May 19

Demas

> "*Demas hath forsaken me, having loved this present world.*"
> *II Timothy 4:10 King James Version*

The Apostle Paul thought he had a trusted comrade … a faithful companion … one who would share in the hardships of first century evangelism. Demas was committed enough to find himself in Rome during Paul's first imprisonment and whereas Paul and Epaphras (Paul's co-minister) were locked up, Demas wasn't.

Being a disciple and protégé of the greatest apostle ever was pretty heady stuff. The Bible doesn't record 'Peter-like' comments about dying for Christ or going all the way regardless of cost, but it's safe to assume that initially he considered himself a serious disciple of Jesus.

Until Rome, that is.

Now the comparison between the moldy, damp cell of Paul and his companion and the lure of the capital of the Roman Empire turned Demas' head … and eventually his heart. One of the most heartbreaking lines in all of Paul's epistles is the verse above: "*Demas hath forsaken me, having loved this present world.*"

Loving the world without loving the world is one of our biggest challenges. To love it as Christ did … willing to take on its pain, its problems and its sin is noble and our greatest calling. But loving its allure, its gaiety, bright lights and sub-par life style as Demas did is often our most daunting temptation.

This week, see the world for what it really is. It's a place of vast lost ness and short-lived satisfaction, promising much and delivering a pittance, populated by hurting people whose lives have been diminished and often destroyed by the very attractions that turned their heads in the first place.

They need you to love them, not the lifestyle that entraps them.

May you find joy and eternal purpose in your journey!

May 20
Just The Facts

In our "Me first" world, filled with every variation of "I want…I need…I deserve…I've been victimized…I'm the center of the universe", Max Lucado's words appear to bring the ego party to a screeching stop.

> *"God does not exist to make a big deal out of us. We exist to make a big deal out of him."*

Selah…reality check…a two by four to the forehead…whatever it takes to remind us that there is a God, and the solar system of our life must revolve around Him. Without that center there is no gravity to hold us; there is no light to dispel the aching darkness that often accompanies living; there is no hope of life taking on more meaning than simply a candle wick that flares for a moment and then is extinguished forever.

And so I am granted the awesome responsibility and privilege of making a big deal out of Him. Have you ever been called upon by the "Hype Committee" to make a big deal out of a little deal? You must add significance to an insignificant person or event. You must through hyperbole-filled ads increase the value of something that is valueless. I don't envy people who must do this for a living.

We, on the other hand, get to make a big deal out of the biggest deal of them all! All it requires to make a big deal out of God is to tell the truth about Him. Reflect his attentive care in your life. Tell about the way He has brought peace to your soul. Convey the message of what his love feels like to you. Explain simply to someone that He loved you so much that He offered his only Son to take the penalty for your sinfulness. Make a big deal out of his protection…the future He has planned for you… the incredible joy He has given you.

Today would be a wonderful time to make a big deal out of your Heavenly Father and the unique adopted role you have in his great family. No hype…just the facts. That's all.

> *"How great is the Lord, how deserving of praise, in the city of our God, which sits on his holy mountain!" Psalm 48:1 New Living Translation*

May 21

Reflect

> *The people walking in darkness have seen a great light; on those living in the land of the shadow of death a light has dawned. Isaiah 9:2 NIV*

Being somewhat of a 'past prime' techie, I was impressed with the new *Digital Light Processing system (DLP)* coming from Texas Instruments. It uses a chip containing up to 2.1 million tiny mirrors, each about one fifth the size of a human hair, and set one micrometer from each other. Now catch this: they are

individually moved by digital signals in synchronization with a
light source to project an image that can be easily seen.

If there is a better illustration of what God is endeavoring to
do through the multiplied millions who belong to His Body, I
don't know what it is.

Picture a multitude cornered by spiritual darkness. Their
antidote? A clearly recognizable picture of God's power, love
and mercy. But one mirror has a hard time reflecting the immensity of God. So heaven's R & D department comes up with
a brilliant idea. Use each believer … every one of us scattered
throughout the entire globe … and synchronize us to be moved
upon by the Holy Spirit to tilt in just the perfect direction, that
we, along with all those around us give an accurate reflection of
the Father.

Don't concern yourself over what the mirror thirty-four
micrometers down from you is doing. You just concentrate on
the signals you are receiving … make the adjustments called
for and stand amazed at the reflected masterpiece you helped
create.

In pitch black inky darkness, any old light will help. But the
full image of the Father's heart and plan will permanently dispel the darkness in anyone's life.

Reflect! And be joyful.

May 22

No Picture

*"We don't yet see things clearly. We're squinting in a fog,
peering through a mist. But it won't be long before the
weather clears and the sun shines bright! We'll see it all
then, see it all as clearly as God sees us, knowing him
directly just as he knows us!" I Corinthians 13:12 The
Message*

Forrest Gump said that his mama taught him that life was like a box of chocolates. You're never quite sure what you're going to get when you take a piece out of the box.

But recently the analogy that seems to be most appropriate in my life is "Life is like a puzzle." Here's the scene: it's a cold and windy night, perfect for staying inside … the table is cleared and you've got a mug of hot chocolate steaming next to you. You empty the pieces onto the table and begin turning them all over to see the various colors and patterns. You then prop the box's cover up only to discover that there is no picture!

You don't know if you're compiling a picture of boats at anchor in some exotic port, a covered bridge in New England somewhere, an impressionist's idea of a vase of flowers … there's no way to know. All you have are pieces to attempt to put together.

There are general steps that you can take like locating edge pieces and gathering certain colors together and trying to match straight lines. But the end result is not known.

It's a crude illustration of faith and the effort sometimes called for as we 'work out our salvation' with a certain amount of fear and apprehension; for we are not just assembling a two dimensional puzzle, but a multi-faceted life with eternal implications hanging all over it.

You can refuse to get to work while insisting on seeing the cover picture of the completed project, or you can trust the 'Puzzle-Maker' to guide you through the process. As the Apostle Paul said, sometime in the near future the weather will clear, the sun will shine and we will look down with satisfaction on what the Father's exquisite plan and our simple faith has brought about.

God is not building frustration, but faith. Work with Him!

May 23

Wheel and Throttle

In 2005 country singer Carrie Underwood released the song "Jesus Take The Wheel." It was the story of a young mother going through difficult times and her Christmas Eve drive to Cincinnati with her baby asleep in its car seat. As she hits black ice and loses control of the car, she releases the steering wheel and relinquishes control of her life and car to Jesus.

It has a good ending.

But I've discovered that Jesus needs control of the gas pedal, too. Both direction and speed are important elements to put under his control.

This Spring I had my nephew's young son Victor in front of me on an ATV (quad) for a ride in the woods. At age seven, he was becoming a man of the world. He wanted both the handlebars and the throttle under his control. But I found that having even one of them totally under his control could have been bad for our health and any plans we had for a long-term future.

So I manipulated the throttle as he steered … until a large rock loomed ahead on the trail. Or he handled the throttle as I attempted to steer over uneven terrain while the velocity kept approaching the lift-off speed of a rocket.

It's the same way for us spiritually. God deserves control over both speed and direction in our lives. Many don't seem to realize that without a destination, speed becomes meaningless. We must be going the right direction. And once pointed right, that does us little good if we sit motionless.

It's tricky business keeping us safely on life's uneven, potentially dangerous road of life.

I may feel confident about my ability, but have learned that only One can get me where I want to be.

This week, I must add to the label of Carrie Underwood's well-awarded song. For me, it now reads: Jesus take the wheel, and the gas pedal, and the brakes, and the turn signals and …. you get the picture.

> *"The Lord will guide you continually …" Isaiah 58:11*
> *New Living Translation*

May 24

Rest Area Ahead

> *"The steps of a good man are ordered by the Lord: and he*
> *delighteth in his way." Psalm 37:23 Kings James Version*

I was missing my Dad, so I picked up and opened his Bible to see if it would pull him back into focus in my heart and mind. And it did.

This wasn't one of his 'other' Bibles. This was the official one. The big one. The one he preached from. The Bible he wrote in while God spoke to him. The one he prayed over and dropped tears onto.

This extremely well-worn Scripture had my Dad and my God intertwined and mixed together on almost every page. They had gone extraordinary places between its covers.

When I came to the above underlined verse in one of his favorite Psalms, I had to smile. Because clearly printed in the margin were four words: *"and the stops, too"*

In an honest appraisal of my Dad's theology, he probably had more difficulty with God's stops than with God's steps. For a mover and shaker … for a 'never-let-the-grass-get-a-start-under-your-feet' kind of guy … for a highly motivated Type A personality, the stops don't come easily.

Yet they're always built into God's plan for us. He designed an automatic, built-in stop to come every seven days. He calls it Sabbath and tells us we will need it regardless of how much we have to do or how much energy we feel we have at our disposal.

In three years of demanding public ministry, Jesus practiced this holy rhythm of engagement and withdrawal. His steps would stop, but not his life's mission. He would find a rest area and come out of it energized and prepared. You can stop to rest without disrupting God's will for your life.

Learn to appreciate the 'stops of the Lord' even as you follow his steps. Be serious about a Sabbath break in your schedule. Be aware that you need physical rest on a regular basis, but also note that you need occasional spiritual rest from the constant blare of an alien culture that takes far more from us than it gives.

Don't sneer as you drive past the rest areas of your life, assuming that they're only for wimps that don't have your constitution. They're for you, too.

May you walk refreshed on your journey!

May 25

Jesus Disguised

It's amazing how many places Jesus is able to sneak into. Even places where He is not welcome nor expected. But they are always places where He is needed.

Why just yesterday He showed up in the presence of a politician who really didn't want his company, but desperately needed his advice. Then there was the Chinese village where the rules stated that He didn't exist and if He did, He wasn't welcomed. But the people there were hungry for his love and healing touch.

Later that same day Jesus showed up in a third floor hospital room. He spent a considerable amount of time comforting one of his children making the transition from earth to glory. And then He was off to the local college where He gave a masterful dissertation on authentic faith to a somewhat skeptical group of students.

On and on it went ... Jesus showing up in unexpected places but always with a message of life, hope and a call to live better. He is suddenly in the middle of a conversation that needed turning ... in the midst of a problem that had no discernible solution ... exactly in the place where peoples' needs and their awareness of those needs were coming together.

He's in the right place at the right time.

How is He able to accomplish these things? It's ingenious, actually.

You see, He comes disguised as you!

> *"Now all of you together are Christ's body, and each one of you is a separate and necessary part of it." I Corinthians 12:27 New Living Translation*

May 26
Till Somebody Loves You

The pop hit "You're Nobody Till Somebody Loves You" was written in 1944 and although recorded by over twenty vocalists, was made popular by Dean Martin in 1964. The opening lines makes it clear that we're nobody until somebody loves us.

There is a marvelous parallel and validation of this theme in Paul's letter to the church in Ephesus. These spiritual orphans ... these 'gate-crashers' to faith ... these interlopers of a divine inheritance became somebodies when they fell under God's gaze and grace. Listen to Paul explain the phenomenon: *"Long before He (God) laid down earth's foundations, he had us in mind, had settled on us as the focus of his love, to be made whole and holy by his love ...Long before we first heard of Christ and got our*

hopes up, he had his eye on us, had designs on us for glorious living."
Ephesians 1:4, 11 The Message

What deliciously desirous news for those of us who can still remember feeling 'out of sight and out of mind.' What a riotously thrilling ending to a story of bleakness, isolation and desolation. Somebody had his eye on us! Somebody saw potential in us! Somebody organized a mind-boggling future for us! Somebody looked at us ... not through us or around us.

So what is the reaction of a 'nobody' who is now a 'somebody' because 'Somebody' embraced him and invited him to become part of his growing family and spend eternity with Him? Not pride, because 'nobody' can pull this off by himself. He knows that until Somebody loved him, there wasn't much to him.

Today live in unbridled praise and thankfulness in the presence of the One who turns 'nobodies' into grateful somebodies.

May 27

Memorial Day

Memorial Day! It's a day to preserve the memory of fallen and still standing heroes who pay the price for our freedom.

And that's what a memorial is all about ... something to help us remember a person or event. We're surrounded by memorials. Washington D.C. has more than you can visit in a week. Every headstone in every cemetery is a memorial. There are tiny handprints set in sidewalks that take us back many years. A faded tassel from a graduation ceremony keeps that event fresh.

Memorials got their start early in the Old Testament when God put a rainbow in the sky to both remind of the flood and of his promise to never again destroy the earth in that way. The Ark of the Covenant served as a memorial for Israel to remind them of their deliverance from Egypt and their new-found land.

And then there were the rocks. (Joshua 4). Israel is to cross the Jordan River and enter their promised land. God again piles up water as he did at the Red Sea many years before and gives Joshua instructions to have one man from each of the twelve tribes carry out of the river bottom a large rock. They were to stack the twelve stones at Gilgal where they spent their first night. And the reason for the rocks?

Joshua's explanation: *"We will use these stones to build a memorial. In the future your children will ask you, 'What do these stones mean?' Then you will tell them ..." Joshua 4:5,6 New Living Translation*

The stones were a 'nudge' to help them remember the faithfulness of God in their midst. And when the next generation asked about them, it was the responsibility and the honor of the fathers and mothers to explain how God has dealt with them.

Here are some questions to answer: Are there memorials around your house and within your customs that would cause your children to ask about them? Have you placed a flag in the ground at historic points of God's intervention? Has every God-rescue been given a place of recognition in your family? Is God's deliverance and guidance something celebrated or simply assumed and forgotten?

> *"I remember the days of old. I ponder all your great works and think about what you have done." Psalm 143:5 New Living Translation*

May you find joy for your journey!

May 28

Sucker Bait

I met Anthony at Starbucks this morning. That's the half-way point of my morning prayer walks and provides me with a restful place to spend time studying and meditating.

Anthony asked me for $.85 and I gave him the $.30 change that I had gotten back after purchasing my coffee. He then lit up a half-inch stub of somebody's discarded cigarette and plopped down in the chair next to mine. His story was typical of many in our day, yet to him it was intensely personal… after all, it was his story. In the last years he had lost his mother, a sister and then a girlfriend. He was an unemployed construction worker who said he was also battling AIDS. The bottle was not on his side, either.

Before leaving him I asked if he had talked to God about his life. "Every morning when I wake up I ask the Lord to help me get through the day" he replied. As I stood up I asked him his name and promised that our small group would pray for him. I then gave him a five-dollar bill and requested him not to use it for smokes.

Do I believe his story? Why shouldn't I? It's the condensed story of the lives of millions of people who are living without Jesus in their lives. Believing his story was easy for me (but then, I'm the one who buys the 'miracle chamois' at the state fair year after year knowing that they don't work, but always impressed by the sales demonstration!)

I've determined to attempt to stay vulnerable to the stories of people. Can I be taken advantage of and 'suckered' out of money? I can be and I have been! And yet, I'd rather err on the side of compassion and give cynicism a wide berth. My model is Jesus, who at his greatest moment of self-imposed vulnerability and openness…with arms stretched wide making himself an easy target…gave all of humanity the right to take advantage of his compassion.

Both Jesus and I may be 'sucker bait' for someone trying to beat the system. But somewhere down the line…love and compassion will win the day. Enjoy the journey.

"And the King will say, 'I tell you the truth, when you did it to one of the least of these my brothers and sisters,

you were doing it to me!'" Matthew 25:40 New Living Translation

May 29
Our High Priest

For we do not have a high priest who is unable to sympathize with our weaknesses, but we have one who has been tempted in every way, just as we are—yet was without sin. Hebrews 4:15 NIV

It's almost impossible for me to imagine God identifying with what I go through in my life. It seems almost sacrilegious to picture God, through his Son Jesus, experiencing devastating depression …the strong emotions of exclusion …the cutting pain of being totally misunderstood. But He experienced it all.

He knew the absolute weariness that precedes giving up. He felt used and abused; debased and lonely. He, like us, looked for encouragement from those around Him. Sometimes He found it, but often did not.

In the most emotional and spiritual battle ever fought by a human being, just hours from the searing pain and utter humiliation of the cross, He asked his closest followers to help him bear the great struggle in the garden.

And they fell asleep.

No … there is nothing I have faced or will face that He hasn't been tempted with already. And that's precisely what makes Him such an incredible high priest. He is touched with the feelings of my infirmities. He fully understands broken hearts, ruptured dreams and smashed relationships.

When He places his arms around me, it's not the cold, clinical touch of a 'paid professional' whose "I feel your pain" is void of sincerity. He really does feel it … every bit of it. And the best news is that He knows the value of hanging on and believing 'in spite of' the circumstances, because He went the distance and knows the glory of ultimate victory.

Don't give this Shepherd a hard time. Yield to his loving care. Listen to his words of encouragement. Let Him pull you close to his side and allow his smile to eradicate any vestige of doom and gloom that may have gained access to your heart. And allow Him to flood your heart with joy!

> *"What is the price of two sparrows—one copper coin? But not a single sparrow can fall to the ground without your Father knowing it. And the very hairs on your head are all numbered. So don't be afraid; you are more valuable to God than a whole flock of sparrows." Matthew 10:29-31 New Living Translation*

May 30
Tumbleweeds

I love "The-Glass-Is-Half-Full" people.

I tolerate "The-Glass-Is-Half-Empty" people. They bore and drain me and do not speak to the quest in my own heart.

Bob Nolan comes to mind here. He observed a common, ugly and prickly weed that when dried breaks off from the root and is sent by the wind scurrying along until it meets a fence or other obstruction where it awaits removal while dropping its seeds into the ground to help continue to torment and aggravate people.

Bob witnessed this obnoxious weed and chose to memorialize it in song recorded by Roy Rogers and the Sons of the Pioneers … "Tumbling Tumbleweeds." It's quite a leap to go from clearing a fence line of these troublesome weeds to the words of Bob's last verse where he romantically paints a picture of rolling along with these noxious weeds.

I honor those who can pull victory out of defeat … who can pluck something good from something decidedly bad … who can see through tough times to good times beyond. The Apostle Paul had this attitude. When told that his enemies were preaching with good success he replied, "Good … at least the Gospel is being spread."

James talks about coming through turmoil and temptations not only intact, but with faith stronger and maturity maturing. The Psalmist made this statement in Psalm 112: "Light shines in the darkness for the godly."

Keep this truth in mind this week: If there can be beauty in a tumbleweed, then there can be purpose and joy in the seeming ugliness of life. We know the ending to the story and it tips riotously in our favor. For when all is said and done, the glass and our joy are not just half full, but overflowing with the goodness of our Heavenly Father toward us.

> *"I have told you all this so that you may have peace in me. Here on earth you will have many trials and sorrows. But take heart, because I have overcome the world." John 16:33 New Living Translation*

May you experience joy on your journey!

May 31
Whatever, Wherever, Anything

> *"I can do all things through Him who strengthens me." Philippians 4:13 NASB*

That verse spells victory though surrounded by calamity. It spells hope in the middle of doom. It's a sweet smell in the most putrid of circumstances. And it puts vibrant muscle on atrophied flesh.

The man writing those words was not an armchair theologian residing in a dark paneled library. No charmed life ... no one smoothing the bumps of life for him ... no shielding from the cruel blasts of real living.

Oh no! The Apostle Paul is a man who at one time or another was pummeled, hounded, hurt, tormented, beaten, trounced, broken, thwarted, exhausted, footsore, weakened, over-worked and under-appreciated. If this verse were written by anyone else, it would not excite me like it does.

In Eugene Peterson's The Message it reads like this: *"Whatever I have, wherever I am, I can make it through anything in the One who makes me who I am."* I find myself gravitating to the words 'whatever', 'wherever' and 'anything.' They touch virtually every experience in my life ... the good, the bad and the 'ugh'. Nothing lies outside the parameters and power of God's provisions.

This is fantastic news from a God who assures us that nothing can take us out of his hand or from under his care. This is more than heart-warming – it's life-altering!

So I'm not looking for trouble, but if it comes, it will come to a trusting child, confident that my trust in "Him who strengthens me" is enough to see triumph, not defeat.

June 1
I Want ... He Wants

Don't you just love it when what you want and what God wants coincide? When the match is perfect? When both you and He are zigging and zagging absolutely in parallel. When you begin with the question "Father, would it be possible for me to ...?" and He interrupts with a smile and says, "That's exactly what I was thinking!"

Such scenarios indicate an incredible convergence of God's will and ours.

The reality, however, is often quite different. A good friend of mine in the Seattle area wrote these words to me recently: *I want to scream and He wants me silent. I want to run and He wants me to sit. I want to talk and He wants me to listen. I want to be angry and He wants me to be thankful. I want to feel sorry for myself and He wants me to think of others. I want to fight and he wants me to surrender. I want to doubt and He wants me to believe.*

What do you do when this spiritual conundrum takes place in your life (and don't tell me it never does)? The obvious options are: 1. Stall 2. Feign a loss of hearing 3. Negotiate and explain to God your position 4. Pout pitifully 5. Respond like softened clay in the hands of an expert Potter.

Going back to my friend's choices above, what would you rather be? A screaming angry babbler, running off in all directions trying to find and attend your own pity party while filled with doubt? Or … a silent, contemplative, thankful secure and surrendered child who believes steadfastly in his Father's plans and care?

Those appear to be our only choices. Dragging our feet, arguing with the One we call 'Lord', insisting on understanding every detail … or yielding patiently and gracefully to the One who has our backs (and our futures!)

I can't see … He can. I don't know … He does. I care, but He cares more. I do believe I'm safe in His plans for me!

"God saved us and called us to live a holy life. He did this, not because we deserved it, but because that was his plan from before the beginning of time—to show us his grace through Christ Jesus." II Timothy 1:9 New Living Translation

June 2
Grace On The Road

They owe us an apology!

Let's face it...we've all been hurt by sin and sinners. Our godless culture puts significant hits on us every day. They flaunt their immorality...offend us with their language...speak disparagingly and irreverently about the very One who gave His life on the cross for us...they make stupid decisions (that often adversely affect us) based on unfounded theories, conventional wisdom and outright lies...much of what they say and do is designed to hurt us, or at the very least, annoy us.

They owe us an apology! We should open up USA Today this week and find a multi-page ad taken out on behalf of all the ego-driven, mean-spirited, irreligious people who make our life so difficult at times. Late night television hosts should open up their monologues tomorrow night asking the family of God to forgive the entertainers who have made reputations and a lot of money taking crack shots at Godliness and morality. And although she told the truth about us in parody at times, the Church Lady should come back on Saturday Night Live and apologize for making fun of Godly people.

But don't hold your breath waiting for those apologies!

Want to know your toughest assignment today? It's extending grace before it's even asked for or recognized as a need. We must forgive before being asked to. If you're at all like me, your first response is "OK...as soon as they apologize I'll forgive." But that's reciprocation, not grace. "If you'll...then I'll"... is how business is conducted in our society. Our modern marriages are made of it. Any old warm body can return kindness for kindness or meanness for meanness. That comes naturally.

Unlike the couple caught up in the "If you'll...then I'll" routine, each stuck in the cold, lonely winter of waiting the other out, let's take the initiative. Let's proactively take grace on the road. Extend patience and kindness longer than their normal shelf life. Give somebody another chance. Remember that what Jesus said about the fickle crowd is still generally true…they don't know what they're doing.

> *"Most important of all, continue to show deep love for each other, for love covers a multitude of sins." I Peter 4:8 New Living Translation*

June 3
Between Yesterday and Tomorrow

> *"There is a time for everything, a season for every activity under heaven. A time to be born and a time to die. A time to plant and a time to harvest. A time to kill and a time to heal. A time to tear down and a time to rebuild. A time to cry and a time to laugh. A time to grieve and a time to dance. A time to scatter stones and a time to gather stones. A time to embrace and a time to turn away. A time to search and a time to lose. A time to keep and a time to throw away." Ecclesiastes 3:1-6 New Living Translation*

I just went outside to close our front gate for the night. After temperatures in the nineties today, the westerly breeze brought a welcome relief from the heat. With elbows on the rolling gate I enjoyed the last little bit of light as it silhouetted the mountains in the distance.

At times a feeling of melancholy and nostalgia hits me at sunset. It's probably a strange mixture of the day's unmet expectations and disappointments combined with good memories from many of the day's activities … knowing that, whether good, bad or rather neutral the day is over and can never be lived again.

But guess what. If I stand at that fence for the next nine hours and then peek over either shoulder, the sun shows up behind me, and with it another day.

Here's the tension … letting go of today knowing that it will soon become yesterday, while anticipating tomorrow. None of the three is unimportant. Yesterday can help me live both today and beyond. The Bible speaks much of 'remembering.' There are things in yesterday that I never want to do or experience again. At the same time, there are occurrences in my past that I want added to my life again and again if possible.

But I can't afford to spend all my time, elbows on the gate, staring backwards in time.

There is a new day coming. I must be ready to receive it. So I let yesterday's mistakes and today's insufficiencies go and reach forward to God's gracious gift of tomorrow. There are opportunities coming that never dawned on me yesterday. And there are unique challenges awaiting me tomorrow that today helped prepare me for.

On this day feel the tension that comes from successfully living today with yesterday's lessons … fully anticipating the kind of tomorrow that only God could create.

June 4
When Afraid

> " … *many are boldly attacking me. But when I am afraid, I put my trust in you.*" *Psalm 56:2, 3 New Living Translation*

This devotional isn't about being afraid. There is a lot to fear in our world today and fear comes without much coaxing. The issue here is moving from fear to faith. That is often a more challenging journey. Many fear. Few trust.

I believe the Psalmist's next words hold a key for us. "O God, I praise your word," he declares. Faith requires knowledge of what God has said. There are promises not fulfilled because we aren't aware of them … hence we cannot put our trust in them. But when we know what God has said, we can then hold that sure word up against the thing that brought fear and make a conscious decision to respond to one or the other. Depending on our choice we move either toward fear or faith.

Just as we cannot serve both God and materialism simultaneously, we cannot trust God and the circumstances at the same time. They rarely run parallel to each other. Almost always we choose one to the exclusion of the other. And every time we side with God and come down on the side of his Word to us, trust is occurring … faith is growing … confidence deepens.

"So then faith comes by hearing, and hearing by the word of God." *Romans 10:17 KJV* So take stock today. You are surrounded by fear-producing circumstances (such as the price of a gallon of gas!) … but you also have easy access to God's Word. In which direction are you naturally moving? Circumstances change randomly. But the Word of God stands firm for every generation.

You can put your trust in it!

May there be joy for your journey!

June 5
The Seen and Unseen

So here's the deal. We Christians are the true 'dual citizens' of this planet.

We have citizenship in our country of origin and in heaven. One places us squarely in the 'seen' world, the other in the 'unseen.' Which should carry more weight? The Apostle Paul said it this way, *"So we fix our eyes not on what is seen, but on what is unseen. For what is seen is temporary, but what is unseen is eternal." II Corinthians 4:18 NIV*

That's always been easier said than done … at least for me.

The 'seen' world is obvious … in your face … up front and center. The 'unseen' we reach for in faith, sometimes even having to ignore the obvious. It's not that we practice a 'mind over matter' philosophy, but we're simply aware that what is here and now and apparent isn't even half the story.

We're in danger when the 'seen' gets all of our attention. The real is what we don't easily see but has eternal weight and significance. So the 'seen' says, "The economy is in shambles. Be afraid … be very afraid." But the 'unseen' says, *"And my God will meet all your needs according to the riches of his glory in Christ Jesus." Philippians 4:19 NIV*

The 'seen' says, "Did you hear what the doctor just said? It's critical and it's lethal. Be afraid … be very afraid." But the 'unseen' says, *"He sent out his word and healed them, snatching them from the door of death." Psalm 107:20 New Living Translation*

The 'seen' says, "There is little to no good news. You have every right to panic at this point in history. Your sleepless nights? They're what you get with what's going on in the world." The 'unseen' says, *"You will keep in perfect peace those whose minds are steadfast, because they trust in you." Isaiah 26:3 NIV*

Two worlds … always two conflicting viewpoints. The obvious and that which requires a reaching out in faith, trusting the words of the Creator. Two choices. Now tell me, where's the obvious in this choice?

June 6

Not There Yet

Not that I have already obtained all this, or have already been made perfect, but I press on to take hold of that for which Christ Jesus took hold of me. Brothers, I do not

consider myself yet to have taken hold of it. But one thing
I do: Forgetting what is behind and straining toward
what is ahead, I press on toward the goal to win the prize
for which God has called me heavenward in Christ Jesus.
Romans 3:12-14 NIV

To have to admit that you haven't 'arrived' is hard on the ego.
Especially for someone as driven as the Apostle Paul. Or for
someone like me.

My quest is not centered on the 'already been made perfect'
part, as much as it is concerned with taking hold of that for
which Jesus has gotten hold of me. Do you spend much time
pondering the plan that God has for your life? Is it important
to you to know what that plan is? Even the great Proclaimer
Paul at this late stage of his life still doesn't feel like he's fully
grasped it.

But then comes the kicker…even though his complete mission statement is still indistinct and the point of completion
can't be seen, he shifts into the highest gear possible and says,
"But it's out there and I'm going to give myself fully to both the
discovery and fulfillment of that mission. Out of my way…I'm
going for the prize!"

I've been stressing over a 'fuzzy future' with blurred lines,
uncertain dimensions and foggy directions making the forward
look less than satisfying. Conventional wisdom says it's a good
time to sit for a while until the air clears or until God decides
to make it plainer to my questioning heart. But faith must kick
in. My hope must be anchored in the quest God has placed in
my heart. And my faith must find its foundation in that hope,
whether visibility is 'unlimited' or just a few feet in front of my
face. And so, guess what?

So I'm moving forward…not hesitatingly and although not
without doubts or a bit of apprehension, still with firmness
in step and demeanor. And if God gives me the grace for it,

there'll actually be a bit of 'straining' to grasp the mission for which I have been created.

And I'm looking for joy to accompany me!

June 7
Alpha, Omega and Middle

> *"The Lord will guide you continually, watering your life when you are dry and keeping you healthy, too. You will be like a well-watered garden, like an every-flowing spring." Isaiah 58:11 New Living Translation*

The consistency of God's presence in my life is something very special to me. That word 'continually' in the opening Scripture passage has a way of calming my anxieties when his proximity isn't being picked up by any of my natural senses. We acknowledge that God is both Alpha and Omega...the beginning and the end. But if we're not careful the enemy of our souls implies that although God might indeed be present during the initial sound of the starter's gun, and He'll likely be in the stadium when we come staggering across the finish line, those lonely times between start and finish are lonely because we indeed are all alone.

Not true.

Listen to God preparing Jacob for the destiny that was his. Jacob had found a suitable place to spend the night in the open...had located a comfortable rock (an oxymoron to be sure) on which to lay his head and had fallen into a dream-filled sleep. He saw a ladder stretching into heaven with angels going up and down on it. Then God spoke words to him that are part of the spiritual constitution of the Jewish people. He said,

> *"I am God, the God of Abraham your father and the God of Isaac. I'm giving the ground on which you are sleeping*

to you and to your descendants. Your descendants will be as the dust of the Earth; they'll stretch from west to east and from north to south. All the families of the Earth will bless themselves in you and your descendants. Yes, I'll stay with you, I'll protect you wherever you go, I'll bring you back to this very ground. I'll stick with you until I've done everything I promised you." Genesis 28:13-15 The Message

You just may need to be reminded that although God certainly is not only *at* the beginning, but actually *is* the beginning...and is the Completer and the end, He is also very much in the middle. And since that's where most of life seems to happen, that's awfully good news. When God lays a dream in our hearts, He stays right with us until its full and exciting completion.

June 8

Contented

"Better to have little, with fear for the Lord, than to have great treasure and inner turmoil." Proverbs 15:16 New Living Translation

It wasn't much to look at, but it was our first car. Our 1957 Volkswagen Beetle was one of 380,561 produced that year. We got it in 1963, the year we were married. It was salmon colored (salmon steak grilled to 'medium rare'), and featured 'four on the floor' with a gear shift handle whose travel covered most of the area between our knees as it searched for the next proper gear. The rear window was the size of a porthole and the car was narrow enough to put your elbows on the windowsill on both sides simultaneously. And with its powerful, quiet 36 horsepower engine it was able to reach speeds in excess of 50 miles per hour, if wind and incline were allies.

It was a jewel.

Never in my wildest imaginations could I have conceived of someday having a car where the passenger door was almost beyond my reach. Or that I could lock that door with a button on my side. Or that I could unlock all doors from down the street! For audio pleasure we hot wired an old six inch oval speak into our AM radio ... mounted it in a wooden box and positioned it between us near the wandering gear shift pole. The thought of mega watts of stereo coming through 17 speakers throughout the car escaped my imagination.

Add navigation, 'On Star' emergency communications, 24 hour commercial free radio of any genre imaginable and engines powerful enough to drive an ocean liner and, well ... you get the picture. The basics of transportation with additions and improvements added at a dizzying rate.

I'm pondering how my 'need list' and 'want list' are morphing. In terms of the car I drive I had very few needs at one time. Oh, there were several improvements I kind of wanted. But now, at least 84 of my 'wish-I-could-have-that-feature' items have somehow moved onto my 'need' list. And it keeps happening in every section of my life. And I wonder if God's promise to supply every need has been keeping up with all those changes. Are all my necessities considered necessary from His viewpoint and plan for my life?

Somewhere I suppose that contentment has to show up. After all, the real wealth in life is said to be 'Godliness with contentment' according to I Timothy 6:6. May I learn the quiet heart attitude of thankful contentment and may it put to permanent rest the restless desires of a discontented, thanklessness.

Enjoy the journey as you enjoy what you have!

June 9

Qualified To Be Useful

When God called Gideon to lead Israel out from under the rule of the Midianites, He didn't exactly find a Type A self-assured leader oozing with charisma or confidence. Though the angel called him a mighty hero, Gideon does a double-take with a "Who, me?" glance around him. (Judges 6)

"I'm from the weakest clan in the weakest tribe of Manasseh. Furthermore, I am the least qualified of my pitiful family" he stutters.

At a time of national disgrace for Israel Samuel approaches young Saul and tells him that he is the focus of all Israel's hope! Saul's reply? *"But I'm only from the tribe of Benjamin, the smallest tribe in Israel, and my family is the least important of all the families of that tribe!" I Samuel 9:21 New Living Translation*

It sounds like both Gideon and Saul had the same script writer.

In a culture that looks for the most suave, the most articulate, the strongest, the most handsome or beautiful ... and denigrates those who don't fit those qualifications, it's no wonder that we don't feel we measure up.

But God doesn't page through GQ to find his man. He doesn't consult the latest volume of Who's Who In America to come up with his candidate. Prestige and political connections are meaningless to him. He could care less about physical attractiveness, physical prowess or the ability to be philosophically sophisticated.

What kind of credentials is he interested in? His answer could put the public relations industry out of work. *"... but this is the man to whom I will look and have regard: he who is humble and of a broken or wounded spirit, and who trembles at My word and reveres My commands." Isaiah 66:2 Amplified Bible*

If we're not careful we shun the very attributes God is searching for!

Pay careful attention to the words of the Apostle Paul: *"Take a good look, friends, at who you were when you got called into this life. I don't see many of 'the brightest and the best' among you, not many influential, not many from high-society families. Isn't it obvious that God deliberately chose men and women that the culture overlooks and exploits and abuses, chose these 'nobodies' to expose the hollow pretensions of the 'somebodies'? That makes it quite clear that none of you can get by with blowing your own horn before God."* I Corinthians 1:26-31 *The Message*

As you present yourself to God, give Him something He can really work with and blow your horn for God, not yourself!

June 10
Seeds For The Future

You might say there's a perpetual rip in the bottom of our seed bags.

We're sowing seeds all through our lives … at times on purpose and at other times accidently. We sow seeds that will make us proud when they're harvested. And at times seeds that will produce things that will disappoint us, cause us to hang our heads in shame.

The spiritual law of sowing and reaping is intractable – *"You will always harvest what you plant."* Galatians 6:7 *New Living Translation*

This would make us less concerned if we lived only to ourselves. But our lives do affect others; our sins impact those around us. Consequently the seeds that we sow will ripen. Whether we sowed them on purpose, without thinking, in a drunken stupor, while in an uncontrollable rage or while giving in to passions that were uncontrolled.

Once planted, those seeds will grow.

Yesterday I witnessed some good seed that I had sown begin to produce a good harvest in the lives of my two youngest grandsons as they stepped into the waters of baptism to pro-claim the Lordship of Jesus in their lives.

Seeds carefully planted in their dad's life through his forma-tive years are now invested in their lives. I must look behind me and be reminded that those behind me are living in the harvest of the things I have planted.

So we run the race not just for ourselves, but on behalf of those coming along behind us. The legacy of a life lived well is beyond price. May all who follow us through life thank God for our faithfulness.

As I look behind me, I want to see people who are finding it easier to embrace God and walk with Him because of the words and actions of my life. It is not only my responsibility, but an awesome privilege to pass the faith along!

June 11

Misunderstanding God

Misunderstanding God ... it's done from time to time, ei-ther accidentally or recklessly on purpose. But never to our advantage.

God says "Wait." We selectively hear "Proceed with caution."

God says "Proceed with caution." We read "Better stop."

God says "Better stop." We think "The road looks clear to me."

In Psalm 50 we find a classic case of misunderstanding God. He is chiding the religious pretenders of that day for their hy-pocrisy and wickedness and says to them, *"I remained silent, and you thought I didn't care." (verse 21 New Living Translation)* We don't escape God's scrutiny or his discipline that easily.

Some of our most complex and confounding life situa-tions can be traced to our misunderstanding God's instruc-tions. He points left ... we continue straight. He pulls on our reins … we take it as a release. He closes a door … we think 'barging ahead in faith' is what is being called for. He whispers vital directions … we miss the information by immersing ourselves in frantic, blaring urgencies and manufactured emergencies.

It's enough to make you feel sorry for God.

Life is far too short to keep going around the same mountain, misreading the directions that would put us on the right road. There isn't enough time or energy in any of us to meander purposelessly over the same route-less ruts … forever lost in the miasma of look-alike scenery and meaningless trudging.

I've walked in unison with God's heart enough to know that's where I really want to be … in unison with his heart. So I'll turn life's raucous noise down enough to hear his voice. I'll silence the instructions of those who don't know where they are going, let alone have God's directions for me.

Today I will seek to understand God clearly.

June 12
Going The Distance

In a great recent sermon on the importance of community, an old Native American adage was given: *If you run alone you run fast; if you run with others you run far.*

Now the people who weave in and out of freeway traffic at ten to twenty-five miles per hour over the speed of the pack… they'd probably pick the 'run fast' track. Getting someplace first, well ahead of everyone else does have its perks, for the moment at least. But life can never be lived entirely 'for the moment.' I have always been concerned that we trade our futures for some short-lived pleasure. We need to be concerned with 'going the distance.'

If lasting long and finishing strong is important to you, then community must win and loneliness must lose. It's only in movies that the 'strong, solitary, silent types' do well. In real life we always take a hit when we go it alone. John Eldredge in his book *Epic* makes a case for community when he asks, "Why else would we have come up with solitary confinement as a punishment? We are relational to the core."

The part of me that has bought into the macho image of today's loner would love to be seen as a rugged man, alone on a windy hilltop, staring resolutely into the future with the knowledge that whatever is out there…I'm fully able to handle.

But the other part of me…the part wired into reality and aware of eternal wisdom tells me something far different, like:

♦ *Hold my wife's hand tighter and depend on our partnership more*
♦ *Make the circle of those with influence in my life wider*
♦ *Always be on the lookout for a new 'good friend'*
♦ *Listen to others…conserve the flow of my words and listen carefully to the wisdom of others*
♦ *Be aware that God can give me information and direction through just about anybody and in almost any situation*
♦ *Stop acting like now is more important than later by recognizing that my words and actions take on a life of their own and will survive after I'm gone*

Let us seriously consider the words of the wisest man who ever lived. In Ecclesiastes 4:9,10 Solomon says, "*Two people can accomplish more than twice as much as one; they get a better return for their labor. 10 If one person falls, the other can reach out and help. But people who are alone when they fall are in real trouble.*" *New Living Translation*

Go for community and relationships!

June 13

Selective Obedience

Ever heard of 'selective obedience?' This is different than the misunderstanding God spoken of earlier.

This kind of partial obedience been an infection running through humanity right from the beginning. When God told King Saul (I Samuel 15) to destroy the Amelekites, He wanted every vestige of these ungodly people gone. He preceded the verb destroy with the adverb 'utterly.' So Saul obeyed … partially.

Some of what was to have been eliminated appealed to Saul and he took it home with him … presumably to give back to God as an offering. As if God lacked donkeys, sheep and fat calves! No, what God was waiting for was not the smell of stolen livestock cooked on the altar of disobedience. He longed for a heart of submission that took his commands seriously.

I'm afraid there's a bit of Saul in all of us. There are occasions in each of our histories where 'selective obedience' can be found. Part of us has gone along with God's instructions … and the other part, the part that is saying 'yes' while doing 'no' has shown that we struggle with heart problems …sometimes harboring stubborn and hard hearts.

When we play this 'half way game' we often compound the issue by offering back to God a portion of the illegal booty. Like: "I'll give God a tithe of the money I cheated the IRS of!" But we serve a God who has little interest in our money or possessions. He runs a Kingdom that needs none of that to thrive. Instead, He and his purposes need only the obedient hearts of those who call him King. With those kind of hearts and surrendered wills, He can accomplish anything his great heart desires.

When King David had played and lost the 'half-hearted' game, he declared with new insight: *"You would not be pleased with sacrifices, or I would bring them. If I brought you a burnt offering, you would not accept it. The sacrifice you want is a broken spirit, a broken and repentant heart, O God, you will not despise." Psalm 51:16,17 New Living Translation*

May your offering make God smile …not hold his nose.

June 14
Our Fathers

I was raised in a loving, supportive environment … in a climate of acceptance and possibilities. My parents believed in me and backed up that belief by planting in my life attitudes and confidences that I still draw upon six decades later.

Not everybody had as positive a launch as I had.

A young man confided in me that in the years spanning his T-ball to American Legion league baseball play … spanning some twelve or thirteen years … his father had never attended one of his hundreds of games. Not one. There was not one time when he looked into the stands and saw an interested father. Not once did he hear words of commendation for his considerable skill on the diamond. A father disinterested and removed.

Another man told me that standing by the hospital bed, the last words he ever heard from his father's lips were: "I never have liked you." Hours later the father died leaving an emotional crater for this man to deal with for the rest of his life. A father angry, puzzling and now gone.

My Heavenly Father has my picture on his refrigerator!

For me, my physical Dad set me up to respond to the Lord who is *"like a father to his children, tender and compassionate …" Psalm 103:13.* He modeled to the best of his ability this God who knows what I need before I even know it myself and loves to meet those needs.

Regardless of your paternal heritage, celebrate the Father who has eyes for you … who sees you as successful and satisfied

... who loves the presence of your company and who watches with great interest every detail of your life.

"The Lord is like a father to his children, tender and compassionate to those who fear him." Psalm 103:13 New Living Translation

June 15

Been There, Done That

"For we do not have a high priest who is unable to sympathize with our weaknesses, but one who in every respect has been tempted as we are, yet without sin. Let us then with confidence draw near to the throne of grace, that we may receive mercy and find grace to help in time of need." Hebrews 4:15,16 English Standard Version

'Been there ... done that.' It's a phrase of identification. It means that we both have a common experience that we share. I can understand your elation, your awe, because I've been to that same spot with camera in hand. I empathize with your grief and frustration, because I've been right where you now are emotionally. There is a common bond that connects us at this point.

So when we stand alone in a hospital corridor with the enormity of our loss beginning to sink in ... when we face the greatest test to our morality we've ever experienced ... when there appears to be no responses to our prayers or answers to our most troubling questions, Jesus says to us, *"I've been there. I am not out of touch with your realities." Hebrews 4:15 (The Message)*

But there's more to this issue. The 'done that' part is seldom part of the equation as far as Jesus is concerned. For when his world disintegrated, when his friends proved fickle, when the

darkness became overwhelming and even when it seemed like
his own Father had turned His back on Him, Jesus didn't quit.
He didn't fold. He didn't give in to the easy urges. He didn't
throw in the towel.

He kept following the Father's plan and believing the
Father's promises.

Remember today that the key to successful identification
with Jesus will be found in confidently drawing near … approaching his throne to find the very grace and mercy we need
to go through what we go through in life without quitting or
going under. Let the One who preceded us in the testing come
back alongside us to get us through victoriously. We're meant to
go through, not go under.

June 16

Masters At Mending

"The broken become masters at mending."
Rev. Mike Murdock
"All praise to the God and Father of our Master, Jesus the
Messiah! Father of all mercy! God of all healing counsel!
He comes alongside us when we go through hard times,
and before you know it, he brings us alongside someone
else who is going through hard times so that we can be
there for that person just as God was there for us." II
Corinthians 1:3,4 The Message

So here's how the system works. You go through troublesome
times, either difficulties of your own making or brought on
by others. You call on God to remove the suffering …undo
the damages … restore normalcy … forgive your actions …
heal your body … change lousy attitudes. And God comes

alongside you with his healing, soothing, forgiving and power-ful presence.

The tide turns. The adversary leaves. The accusations stop. The body heals. The relationship is restored. And life climbs out of the deep pit it had been in. All because we've been 'come alongside' by the One to whom nothing is impossible.

Then God says, "Now you try it!"

And into your life comes someone who is suffering … they have been physically laid low … an important relationship in their life has fractured … they have sinned grievously …life's circumstances have knocked them lower than they can imagine rising from …they have lost every one of their tomorrows. And you come alongside them, carrying both the Person and the life change He brought about for you.

You walk with them and cry with them and pray with them and tie a knot between them and the God of your comfort. You become a savior representing the Savior. You act as the comfort-er on behalf of the Comforter. And God's redeeming work and his great love transfer into ever widening circles.

Let God use you as a 'come alongside' and allow your heart to become the conduit through which his heart flows. And find great joy in this.

June 17
Get The Bait Out

> *"In the same way, let your light shine before men, that they may see your good deeds and praise your Father in heaven." Matthew 5:16 NIV*

Last Friday morning found my two sons, my two oldest grand-sons and myself fishing for trout in a lake almost 10,000 feet up in the eastern Sierra Nevada mountains. Any normal grandpa can live on the memory of such an experience for a long time.

But while we fished...I also watched. We were fishing with weights about two feet up-line from our bait. You cast, let the weights settle, pull in the slack and wait. But when you're eight and ten years of age, the word 'wait' has very negative connotations and in your mind, it has very little to do with catching fish. So it was almost impossible for my grandsons to leave the bait where it belonged for any length of time. After a short wait of perhaps 10 to 15 seconds, they would feel the need to "check on the bait...feels like it fell off" or "I'm going to bring it back in so I can get it out further."

Hence, while both Dads were catching trout, both grandsons managed to keep their bait out of the water for much of the time. The moral of the story? You'll never catch fish with your bait out of the water!

The implications are enormous for those of us who follow Jesus Christ and wish that many others knew Him well enough to want to follow Him also. Jesus says that we are to let our lights shine and our good deeds be shown before men, where the bait will do some good. I'm afraid that most of our 'testimonies' and good works are confined to church and religious activities. We do our preaching to the choir. (The fish we're after aren't in the choir loft...or most of our other church functions!)

Maybe this would be a good time for you to analyze the 'bait' of your life...you know, the part that shows off the goodness of God through the things you say and do. And if that bait is spending most of its time on shore, resting alongside fish that have already been caught, ask God to show you how to get it out where the fish are.

I'm convinced that the reason so many of us have had so little luck with sharing our faith with those who need to discover it for their own lives is because we 'can't catch fish if our bait is out of the water.'

June 18

Enough Strength

> *"Then the angel of the Lord came and sat beneath the*
> *great tree at Ophrah, which belonged to Joash of the clan*
> *of Abiezer. Gideon son of Joash was threshing wheat*
> *at the bottom of a winepress to hide the grain from the*
> *Midianites. The angel of the Lord appeared to him and*
> *said, 'Mighty hero, the Lord is with you!' …Then the*
> *Lord turned to him and said, 'Go with the strength you*
> *have, and rescue Israel from the Midianites. I am sending*
> *you!'" Judges 6:11,12,14 New Living Translation*

Let's learn an important lesson from a man named Gideon …
a man truly unimpressed with himself. In this day of 'self-
made-and-proud-of-it' testimonies all around us, it's initially
refreshing to meet someone with genuine 'Ah, shucks' humility.
Gideon exhibited such a spirit when he met the angel of the
Lord looking for Israel's next hero.

"Who me?" he utters in amazement. "And cut the 'mighty
hero' stuff, too. It's making me uncomfortable. And besides, I
don't have the stuff that heroes are made of."

What Gideon had seemed woefully inadequate for what
was required. To free Israel from foreign domination and an
army that numbered 132,000 professionals would require more
guts, more nerve, more ability, more experience and far more
strength than what he could bring to the table.

But with Israel's future on the line, he discovers an amazing
and transforming truth from the angel messenger. He was to
go with just the strength he had. He didn't need more because
God was sending him and in that call to service would be found
all the strength necessary to complete the assignment.

David didn't need more weaponry to take on Goliath. Jesus
didn't need more bread and fish to feed the multitude. Moses

didn't need a bigger stick to challenge the waters of the Red
Sea. And this week, you don't need anything you don't presently have to move out in obedience to any task God gives you.
His simple "Go" is accompanied by the arsenal and abundant
supplies of heaven.

May you find joy for your journey!

And Then Some

While praying this morning for a family going through turbulent financial waters, I asked God to "meet their needs, and
then some."

Some of you only know God in the realm of met needs.

There's nothing wrong with that.

It's a great place to meet the Father and gain an understanding of his faithfulness and timeliness. There is something
hugely comforting in Philippians 4:19 *"And my God will meet all
your needs according to his glorious riches in Christ Jesus."* NIV

But there's more! There is something hugely compelling and
almost preposterous awaiting us. Ephesians 3:20 says, *"Now all
glory to God, who is able, through his mighty power at work within us,
to accomplish infinitely more than we might ask or think."* New Living
Translation Now we've moved from 'needs' to "and then some."

"And then some" is both an environment and an outcome.
God operates in that stunning intersection of "Beyond Enough"
and "Infinitely More!" And from that place of abundant provision comes more than enough. Psalm 68:19 states that the Lord
loads us down daily with benefits.

The Apostle Paul tells Timothy to tell people seeking to be
rich *"to go after God, who piles on all the riches we could ever manage—to do good, to be rich in helping others, to be extravagantly generous."* I Timothy 6:17 The Message

God wants each of us to move beyond needs met and into 'and then some.' His abundance in our lives is meant to enable us to move with abundance into the lives of people around us.

Sometimes 'just enough' isn't enough for what God has in mind.

A Robin's Song

Even for a robin his voice is somewhat pathetic. There is no fluid songbird melody. It seems a bit forced with bird equivalent 'coughs' every once in awhile.

But it does not deter this little feathered guy from putting out and at high volume!

He appears to believe with all his tiny being that he is personally responsible for the praise of his Creator every morning from 4:00 a.m. until 5:00 a.m. Somebody in our neighborhood needs to acknowledge the care and provision of God and evidently nobody else will take those early, pre-dawn minutes. It's his duty and above that, his privilege to honor the God of the universe.

In Luke 19, Jesus is approaching Jerusalem on a colt. The crowd and his close followers are swept up in a crescendo of praise to heaven's King in their midst. The detractors challenge Jesus to get his disciples under control. Such exuberance is too boisterous and certainly out of place.

But Jesus says, *"If they kept quiet, the stones would do it for them, shouting praise." (Luke 19:40 The Message)* And I'm positive that if man's praise stopped and the stones took over for them, that my backyard friend would have added a loud obbligato part with them!

Here's the issue today. Nobody can praise the Creator like the redeemed can ... for creation can only appreciate creation.

What makes our song supreme is that it is the song of the redeemed. We've been both made by the Creator, then adopted into his very own family.

When I hear my robin sing at 4:00 a.m. something within me wants to make it a duet!

The Blame Game

> *"Lord, why have you allowed us to turn from your path?*
> *Why have you given us stubborn hearts so we no longer*
> *fear you?" Isaiah 63:17 New Living Translation*

It's hardly ever my fault … really! I've been taking the fifth since I was small. My major defense has been "I didn't do it!" Fortunately, there's always somebody else to blame for whatever is wrong in our lives.

Our pointing finger gets used more than the rest of them combined. (Except when I use all ten for two clenched fists of frustrated sidestepping.)

Israel appears involved in a genuine and sincere penitence. But even while admitting to sin and stubbornness and a host of other affronts to God, they reach out that pointing finger to try to implicate and share blame with another. And they pick God!

How preposterous!

"Why have you allowed us to turn from your path?" they wail. But allowing a turn and ordering it are two different things. It's like blaming a burglary on the owners of the house. "Hey, it's not my fault they had that stuff so readily available. It almost forced me into their home in the dead of night and take what was there!"

And how about the accusation of 'giving us stubborn hearts?' If I read Scripture correctly, we are responsible for the contents of our own hearts. We let it harden or keep it soft. We fill it with what we choose (and sometimes are deeply embarrassed by the evidence of our lives that displays the heart's contents.)

Remember ... take God's side against sin, not sin's side against God. I John 1:9 promises us that if we confess our sin (quit blaming anyone else for it) that God will deal with it. It may feel good to be able share blame, but to get rid of it altogether is priceless. And God can do that only if He's not a co-defendant but your defense attorney.

June 22

Your Last Three Paragraphs

> *"And we know that God causes everything to work together for the good of those who love God and are called according to his purpose for them. For God knew his people in advance, and he chose them to become like his Son ... Romans 8:28, 29 New Living Translation*

Margaret Mitchell took almost a decade to write *Gone With The Wind*. It's been said that she wrote the last three paragraphs first and wrote the rest of the book aimed at that point! If that rumor is true, then everything in that narrative would conclude just how and where she intended.

Likewise God wrote the final three paragraphs of Joseph's life long before the full account played out. And heady paragraphs they were! Joseph was destined to be a ruler that even his father and brothers would someday bow before.

But no story or life starts at the end. It proceeds to the end. And along the way the scenery seldom looks like it will at the end. As a matter of fact, the journey may appear totally detached from the conclusion. Do you think there could have been a disconnect in Joseph's mind between the dream ending he'd been promised and his actual life experiences? You think!

What do betrayal, slavery, accusation of rape, imprisonment and broken promises have to do with the last three paragraphs? More than we realize at first.

♦ in his brothers' betrayal he learns to put his faith in God
♦ in slavery he learns how to follow and then give orders
♦ in false accusations he learns that the high road isn't always smooth but is the right road
♦ in imprisonment he hones his people and management skills
♦ and in broken promises he refines his skill at hanging on to God's promises

So when the final three paragraphs take place and he is indeed elevated to the second highest position in the land, he is ready for it. For every obstacle, every set back, each bitter disappointment has been divinely used to properly prepare him for his future.

This week, ask God to help you understand the current contents of your life within the context of his bigger plan. Before you holler "Uncle" or think that God is goofing off at your expense, remember that He is actively getting you ready for those final three paragraphs. He's been excited about your future for a long time.

We can't always be looking around analyzing. We must also look ahead anticipating!

June 23
Sorry I'm Gone

I've been reading through the Old Testament this year. I would like to say it's blessing me beyond belief but in reality all those people with unpronounceable names producing more people with unpronounceable names is kind of boring. And Israel's spiritual ups and downs makes me dizzy. Not that I haven't had my ups and downs as well, but compressing their history into short narrations really makes their backslidings and revivals come at breathtaking speeds.

Bad people were sorrowful when bad kings died. They lost their excuse "but the king said it was all right." And the godly people sorrowed when Godly leaders died. Because with the exodus of the good king usually went the blessings of God on their lives. But there was seldom consensus among all the people over any one king.

Until Jehoram that is. Here is his sad epitaph: *"Jehoram was thirty-two years old when he became king, and he reigned in Jerusalem eight years. No one was sorry when he died." II Chronicles 21:20 New Living Translation*

That must be one of the most pathetic tombstone engravings in all of recorded history. It sends a shiver down my spine!

My goal is not to sound ego-centric here, but I'd like everyone who knew me to be sorrowful at my passing. And don't you want the same thing? I want my wife to miss the great love I had and exhibited for her. I desire my sons to miss the influence I provided and their wives to miss my support and appreciation I have for their powerful impact in our family. I want my grandkids to miss 'crazy grandpa' and his antics, but especially his prayers for them.

I want my friends to miss my loyalty and the confidence they enjoyed in the intertwining of our lives. I want my pastor to miss my words of encouragement. I want the baristas at Starbucks to miss my ready smile, even early in the mornings.

So I propose to live and act and pray and respond and love so that when I'm gone there will be people standing along the trail of my life who are sorry that I'm gone. That's not morbid … it's a godly legacy to want to leave behind.

June 24
Pasture Time

"Trust in the Lord and do good; dwell in the land and enjoy safe pasture." Psalm 37:3 NIV

With convoys in Iraq being ambushed ... the dangers of just passing through some areas of our cities ... the quest to 'just get through' this life and get on to heaven, it would seem like a better reading of this verse would read: "... and enjoy safe passage." I do believe most of us would add an enthusiastic "Amen!" to that rendering.

But the verse says to enjoy safe *pasture.*

Passage speaks of activity ... pasture speaks of rest.

Passage speaks of tension ... pasture speaks of quiet confidence.

Passage speaks of perpetual motion ... pasture speaks of the cessation of striving.

Passage speaks of margin-less living ... pasture speaks of room to unwind.

Although our journey through this life is a constant, it doesn't need to lack 'pasture time.' Our motto today is often: 'Put the pedal to the metal and don't stop for anything.' Lost on us is the quiet command to 'be still and know that I am God' and the accompanying revitalization of our spirits as well as our souls and bodies.

Listen to God's desire for his people: *"I will bring them out from the nations and gather them from the countries, and I will bring them into their own land. I will pasture them on the mountains ...I will tend them in a good pasture, and the mountain heights of Israel will be their grazing land. There they will lie down in good grazing land, and there they will feed in a rich pasture ... I myself will tend my sheep and have them lie down, declares the Sovereign Lord." Ezekiel 34:13-15 NIV*

Today would be a good time to see if you've gone around enough laps to merit a pit stop ... a spiritual stop to refresh and renew. Remember, it's those who 'wait on the Lord' (read: stop for a bit of 'pasture time') who will renew their strength and finish their journey strongly.

June 25

Chosen To Clap and Cheer

Seven year old Jamie was trying out for a part in the school play. And although his heart was set on being in it, his mother was afraid that he would not be chosen. On the day the parts were awarded she drove to school to pick him up. Jamie rushed up to her, his eyes shining with pride and excitement. "Guess what, Mom," he shouted as he jumped into the car, "I've been chosen to clap and cheer."

What an inspiration for those of us not chosen for life's 'school plays'. It's a poignant reminder that the ranks of the 'chosen' ... the 'movers and shakers' ... the luminaries that make the team, speak the parts, sing the solos and fill the most visible positions are actually a very small part of the whole.

Most of us have been chosen to clap and cheer.

Truth be known, there's more than fame in the spotlight. There's also isolation and loneliness ... there is the perpetual threat of being misunderstood ... being a leader isn't always what it appears to be.

Behind a weary Joshua were a couple of guys chosen to clap and cheer. They held Moses' hands up until victory came. (Exodus 17) Behind a persecuted and often jailed Apostle Paul was another given the role of clapping and cheering. His name was Onesiphorus (II Timothy 1) and he kept Paul's spirit buoyant as did Fortunatus and Achaicus in I Corinthians 16. The Apostle, who benefited from their unique ministry said that such deserve recognition.

So always thank God for those in your life who clap and cheer. They deserve your recognition. And if, instead, you go through life with sore hands and a hoarse throat from filling your role well and cheering on those on stage, on the field or in any leadership position, be assured also that your labor is not in vain in the Lord.

> *"The brothers and sisters in Rome had heard we were coming, and they came to meet us ... When Paul saw them, he was encouraged and thanked God." Acts 28:15 New Living Translation*

June 26

He Gives and Takes Away

> *"I came naked from my mother's womb, and I will be stripped of everything when I die. The Lord gave me everything I had, and the Lord has taken it away. Praise the name of the Lord!" Job 1:21 New Living Translation*

I know people whose testimony is "The Lord gives ... blessed be his name!"

Satan thought that's the kind of man Job was. "Oh course he thinks the world of you; You've given him everything he's ever wanted. But just see what happens when life isn't so good to him anymore!"

And so the story began ... and continues to this day. If our relationship with God is a one- way street built on a spiritual 'sugar-daddy-to-me' expectation, the bond between us will seem tenuous and transitory. Anytime the flow of blessings slows or stops, we immediately wonder why we're not loved anymore.

While some need the constant attention of a doting Father (not to say I don't love it as well), I want to be able to be sustained on his promises alone, if necessary. My confidence must be secured around all the edges. If He said He would never leave me (Hebrews 13:5) and that underneath me are the everlasting arms (Deuteronomy 33:27) and that all things will always work out for good to those who love God (Romans 8:28) … then I have a choice to make.

And I've made it. Today and from now on, I want my faith to stay strong if gifts are coming into my life or going out from my life. I want my contentment to be in God alone, whether the tide is in or the tide is out. In all honesty I prefer the blessings over the absence of them. But they are not the prime indicators of my Father's heart toward me. Otherwise the Scripture would read "For we know that good things, not all things, work together for good …" and it would leave out some of the most difficult but meaningful occurrences in our lives.

May you have joy for your journey.

June 27

Accidental Encounters

I've 'bumped into' Jesus on many occasions.

> Standing alone…wrapped up in my own little world… I sense something or Someone nearby. I glance over my shoulder and there He is, quietly waiting.
> In church, but with my mind many miles away…suddenly the words of a song or point of a message will penetrate my reverie and there comes an awareness of His presence.
> Lost in a problem without a solution and feeling hopeless to the core…someone who cares drops a Scripture into my life and it brings Jesus near.

I love those 'chance encounters' with the Lord, but I've got a better model to emulate.

In Luke 8 we are introduced to a woman who had been hemorrhaging for many years. She is part of a large crowd of people who were doing what crowds mostly do...crowd. Jesus stops in mid-stride and asks, "Who touched me?" Peter is incredulous. "What do you mean 'who touched you?' You're being mobbed!"

Jesus responds with a statement that makes my 'accidental encounters' seem pretty immature. He says "No, somebody touched me deliberately."

There in the mingling masses of 'we'll-see-what-happens' was a woman going after Jesus on purpose. She couldn't afford to wait and see if anything developed in her relationship with Jesus, so she took the initiative. I want to be like her. I'll take any encounter with Jesus and be happy for it, but I want to pursue Him deliberately...every day.

> *"The Lord is close to all who call on him, yes, to all who call on him sincerely."*
> *Psalm 145:18 New Living Translation*

June 28
Waiting Patiently

There's an enormous difference between "God is no where" and "God is now here." It's as vast as the gulf between despair and hope ... between victory and complete annihilation ... between getting up in the morning prepared for whatever comes or pulling the covers over your head for protection.

And yet the difference is simply one little space and where you put it.

I think I found that 'space' in Scripture. It can be seen in Psalm 40:1 where David writes: *"I waited patiently for the Lord; he turned to me and heard my cry." New Living Translation* At first God is no where to be seen, felt or experienced. But by the second half, God has arrived. My cry has been heard and responded to.

How difficult that 'space' can be for us ... the time between our cry and his response. It can seem interminable, like it will never end. At times we are sure that our prayer hit a leaded ceiling and is still bouncing around the room where it was uttered.

Waiting is one of our least favorite things to do. After all, we have things to do, places to go and people to see. We have a schedule.

So does God!

He's the very one who made something extraordinary out of blackness and chaos. His is an ordered schedule never hurried and absolutely never late. It's in trusting that that we can wait patiently ... idling our engine when we feel like stripping our gears.

There is a bright future for those who wait patiently. Look at David's personal testimony from his "God is now here" experience: *"He (God) reached down from heaven and rescued me; he drew me out of deep waters. He rescued me from my powerful enemies, from those who hated me and were too strong for me. They attacked me at a moment when I was in distress, but the Lord supported me. He led me to a place of safety; he rescued me because he delights in me." Psalm 18:16-19 New Living Translation*

Make sure you go the distance ... all the way from "I waited patiently" to "he turned to me and heard my cry."

June 29

And The Winner – Light!

"It was a dark and stormy night ..." And so began another of Snoopy's attempts at writing a novel. The fact that Charles Schultz used this line from an 1830 Victorian novel doesn't minimize the word picture it creates.

Dark ... stormy ... these two words seem made for each other. The reference to darkness describes the difficult times of our lives quite well. Darkness in the early part of Genesis connotes that God hasn't shown up yet. It was the arrival of darkness that prompted the closing of city gates, keeping those inside safe from danger. Romans 13 depicts despicable deeds whose choice environment is darkness.

Truly, many of the roughest chapters in our lives could easily have started with the words: "It was a dark and stormy night."

But where did darkness originate? We are first made aware of it in Genesis where we read: " *The earth was formless and empty, and darkness covered the deep waters.*" *Genesis 1:2 New Living Translation* The only reason there was darkness is because there was not yet light. "Duh," you say. What a brainless observation, Paul! But stay with me here.

Light is not the absence of dark, but dark is the absence of light. Light was created, dark wasn't. When you open the back door on a pitch black night, darkness does not come cascading into the room ... light breaks out into the darkness.

Never assume that dark is the opposite equal to light. Their respective powers are vastly different. Light will always annihilate darkness. If someone were to light a small candle, your eye would be able to pick out its flickering wick from 30 miles away. Surrounded by dense darkness a tiny bit of light stakes its claim and asserts its power over its surroundings. Impenetrable darkness? Hardly. Light will always win.

Rejoice in the fact that "*... He (Jesus) has rescued us out of the darkness and gloom of Satan's kingdom and brought us into the kingdom of his dear Son.*" *Colossians 1:13 The Living Bible.* In the toughest of times that Light at the end of the tunnel is never a train coming to finish you off, but a Savior coming to your rescue.

June 30
Righteous

"But when the kindness and love of God our Savior
appeared, he saved us, not because of righteous things we
had done, but because of his mercy. He saved us through
the washing of rebirth and renewal by the Holy Spirit ... "
Titus 3:4,5 NIV

I attempted to make a complete list of all the 'righteous' things
I had done in the last month or so. The list was painfully short
(actually non-existent) so I moved the start date back a bit to
see if I could plump up the data. No luck at all.

Many young people use the term 'righteous' to mean a lot
of things, few of them spiritual. It has become an adjective
meaning 'special, way cool, drastic or awesome'. It is not God's
definition.

We pile up activities that we feel have deep spiritual value ...
you know, the kinds of things that make us irresistible to God. We
go out of our way to help someone, we read extra chapters in our
Bibles, we suppress our angry streak, we hold back from hitting
someone who has made us mad and yell at them instead ... all in a
feeble attempt to win God's approval.

But alas, our sacred pile of deeds is seen by God as nothing
but dirty linen ... old paint rags. It adds up to nothing in comparison with his expectations for us. And we're left with a blank
sheet of paper, a dismal assemblage of worthless endeavor.

Then Jesus appears. He who never displeased the Father,
who actually was righteous, comes to us with a preposterous
plan. He will assume our failings, sins and futile attempts at
goodness ... He will take it all on Himself. And in return, He
will give us his righteousness. Free for the asking.

Today we stand, not condemned, not embarrassed beside our pile of worthless fake goodness ... but beside the cross where the Father smiles at the relationship we share with His Son ... and pronounces us 'righteous'.

July 1

There's More

They don't know there's more.

They just know that the bird feeder is empty, not a speck to be found no matter how many times they leave and come back to investigate. There are perhaps sixty finches, close to fifty blackbirds and even two pair of doves that consider my backyard their primary source of food.

But I know there's more! As a sub-supplier for their ultimate Supplier who personally watches over every aspect of their little lives, I know that as long as I have the finances and Costco keeps selling 20 pound bags of bird seed, there will be more. No question about it.

And so it is with the resources of our lives. The pantry gets low on food. The bank account moves from black toward red. The physical strength that we need and expect begins running out. And we wonder ... is there more?

So we consider the words of Jesus in Luke 12:24, *"Look at the ravens, free and unfettered, not tied down to a job description, carefree in the care of God. And you count far more."* The Message He who has unlimited resources without a Costco in sight .... who sees us as His treasured children ... who knows how to give good gifts to those who ask ... and who has promised to supply all of our needs according to His riches, not ours ... knows when our bird feeder gets low.

This week, don't waste unnecessary concern over whether or not there's more. There is not only more, but more than enough. You've got God's promise on that one.

May there be joy and sufficiency for your journey!

July 2

Servanthood

"The evening meal was being served, and the devil had already prompted Judas Iscariot, son of Simon, to betray Jesus. Jesus knew that the Father had put all things under his power, and that he had come from God and was returning to God; so he..." Luke 22:2-4a The Message

Put yourself in the position of Jesus for just a minute.

♦ you are hours away from an angry mob, trumped up charges and a trial
♦ the end of your life is right around the corner
♦ a close personal friend has just sold you down the river
♦ and you've just had all things placed under your power and authority!

A lot of possibilities come to the mind of this often carnal-minded writer of devotional thoughts, like: call down several legions of angels to deal with the injustice and one-sidedness of this situation. Like: use the power to at least defend my reputation or even possibly settle some long-standing scores with some of the godless religious leaders. And I can certainly imagine pulling Judas up short and holding him accountable for his two-faced act of ultimate betrayal.

In the interest of setting forth a better Kingdom model, I am certainly glad that the 'so he' in verse four wasn't describing my response to having all power granted to me! Instead, in one of the most exquisite depictions of 'servanthood' ever written, we find Jesus, with the knowledge of who He was, and what He was capable of, taking off his outer robe, grabbing a towel and water basin and washing the feet of his disciples.

Ouch! What a comparative jolt to our systems! What a 'non-politically correct' response to the possession of authority! What an indictment to the way we often use power and responsibility irresponsibly!

I want to be a servant. Oh, I know that as a child of God I have been afforded 'sonship' and a degree of power and authority. I know that the devils are subject to the power I possess as a Kingdom kid. I am aware, too, of the relational position I have with the Father through the Son and energized by the Holy Spirit. But none of that will make any difference to this dying, decadent and disturbing culture if it isn't showcased in true humility and with a servant's spirit.

Presumption and Planning

> "Now listen, you who say, 'Today or tomorrow we will go to this or that city, spend a year there, carry on business and make money.' Why, you do not even know what will happen tomorrow. What is your life? You are a mist that appears for a little while and then vanishes." James 4:13,14 NIV

God isn't against planning ... He's only warning us against presumption.

The difference as I see it is that planning is a partnership while presumption is a sole-proprietorship. Biblical planning takes God's will and purposes into account, while the sin of presumption is all about us.

Our happiness. Our satisfaction. Our future. Our plans and purposes.

We don't see very far into the distance, unsure if we will need an umbrella tomorrow! There is no way to know what the price of a gallon of gas will be next year. So when we make decisions and plans based on what we don't see but only presume, it quickly slides into the sin of presumption.

When we presume to know the future we are often blown away with what turns up in our lives ... things that we never expected to happen. Take Lot for instance. When Lot and his uncle Abraham (Genesis 13-19) needed to part company because of the size of their flocks, Lot chose selfishly by picking the well watered plains and moving his family into Sodom. He presumed the outcome.

For the place he chose put him right in the middle of waring kings and his family became political hostages. After being rescued he returned to the same home only to have his chosen city end up in the cross-hairs of God's impending judgment. Forced to flee he lost his wife, all of his possessions and both prospective sons-in-law. Genesis chapter nineteen says that he ended up with his two daughters living in a cave in the mountains.

God could have helped him choose more wisely.

God knows about the future and since there's ample proof that He cares deeply about the way my life will turn out, why risk missing out on his loving care by making presumptions that exclude his directions. Today I will relish the relationship that exists between a loving Father and this son ... the kind of partnership that will ensure that life stays together and fulfills all of God's great plans for my future.

July 4

Down To Go Up

"Peter said to him, 'Even if everyone else deserts you, I never will.' ... A little later some of the other bystanders confronted Peter and said, 'You must be one of them, because you are a Galilean.' Peter swore, "A curse on me if I'm lying—I don't know this man you're talking

*about!" And immediately the rooster crowed the second
time. Suddenly, Jesus' words flashed through Peter's
mind: "Before the rooster crows twice, you will deny three
times that you even know me." And he broke down and
wept." Mark 14:29, 70-72 New Living Translation*

We don't like break downs, whether on the highway in our
cars, with our appliances (whose warranties have typically
just expired), or more painfully the emotional or spiritual
types.

And Peter has just experienced such a break down. Soon
after capturing the bragging rights from his peers by proclaim-
ing his loyalty and allegiance 'unto the death' he wilts before a
servant girl in the cold night of Jesus' betrayal.

There are several steps to his reconstruction spiritually from crushed and guilt-ridden to powerful and fearless preacher just seven weeks later. For one thing he was
singled out by Jesus after his resurrection for a little extra
dose of much needed grace. *"Now go and tell his disciples,
including Peter, that Jesus is going ahead of you to Galilee. You
will see him there,"* (Mark 16:7) said the angel to the women
at the tomb. Peter needed the assurance of Jesus that his
failure was not final .... that his history did not determine
his future.

Another step from failure to fulfillment in Peter's life
was the outpouring of the powerful Holy Spirit on the Day
of Pentecost. The promised power came through as he could
never have imagined it. This is not the same man in Acts 2 as
we last saw at the end of Mark.

However, notice where this whole transformation begins.
It starts with a breakdown. Peter broke down, wept and re-
pented. We may not exactly like the process, but we go up in the
Kingdom by first going down. The last will be first (Matthew 19)
... the greatest among you must be a servant ... those who humble themselves will be exalted (Matthew 23)

Consider today the possible cost of getting where God wants you to go. It may require a break down.

"So humble yourselves under the mighty power of God, and at the right time he will lift you up in honor. Give all your worries and cares to God, for he cares about you." I Peter 5:6,7 New Living Translation

July 5
Training Wheels Faith

Mark 9:24 "Immediately the boy's father exclaimed, 'I do believe; help me overcome my unbelief!'"

You don't teach a young child to ride a bicycle by starting them on a unicycle. You start off with training wheels.

Those bolt-on 'balance enhancers' aren't the end ... just the means to an end. A unicycle may be in their future, but the present requires a bit of help to get there.

Now a believer for over six decades, I'd love to report that my faith is at the unicycle level. I would love to testify that I now regularly model the centurion of Matthew chapter eight fame. Jesus told him He would come to his home to pray for his sick servant and the soldier replied, "You don't need to do that ... just speak the word and it will happen!"

Pretty impressive faith.

But often I'm more like the father in Mark chapter nine. He had enough faith to bring his demonized son to Jesus, but not quite enough to believe Jesus actually could make a difference. So with training wheels firmly attached he says to Jesus, "If you can do anything, please help us!"

"If I can?" Jesus responds. "All things are possible to those who believe." (Even to believers running on four wheels instead of two or even one – *my addition*).

The idea is for faith to continue to grow … to find it easier to trust God now than it was earlier … for your expectations of his intervention and his power to be greater as time goes by.

At some point it's appropriate for the training wheels to get taken off. It's normal for the bike to grow with the rider. And some do actually graduate to the unicycle. That's what I'm aiming for … unicycle faith.

Today recount what you know about God's ability, from Scripture and personal experience and the testimonies of those around you. You may occasionally lose your balance, feel the bike tip and think you're going down. But then the Fathers' hands reach out to steady you and you regain balance and momentum.

Your faith no longer requires training wheels!

May you experience joy (and balance) for your journey.

July 6
Fenced In

It was a nicely worded request, actually. Just "Private Property. No Trespassing." The land owner had every right to ask for compliance. The knocked over and destroyed sign displayed another message entirely: Nobody can tell me what I can or cannot do! In a culture that touts a bumper sticker reading "Question Authority" it's becoming common behavior.

That's an attitude that Satan recognizes and promotes. It was behind his expulsion from the presence of God. Living 'lawlessly' is what many in today's world are doing. Even as government's role in our lives increases and we're being told what we can eat, what we ought to think, and how we aren't smart enough to make decisions about our health, the rebellious part of us is chafing under any instruction or standards.

And that's dangerous.

At the end of the day, no one wants to live completely lawless. Consider a trip downtown in your economy car with no speed limits, no stop signs or traffic signals ... and glance at that behemoth monster truck next to you ... the one with the bumper just above your eye level. Or how about a trip to the supermarket where no one checks expiration dates on the meat, no one must show contents of ingredients ... where there is no standard for safety in the foods we consume.

Oh now, a bit of oversight is needed. And when it comes to spiritual things, a great deal of oversight is required. And because God loves, He puts up fences. John the Beloved wrote: *"All who indulge in a sinful life are dangerously lawless, for sin is a major disruption of God's order." I John 3:4 The Message* Let the emphasis first be on the adjective 'dangerously.' Lawlessness is eternally dangerous and doesn't make the present particularly safe and secure either.

Then contemplate the last two words of that verse: "God's order." God's order ... his standards ... his regulations always have our best interests at heart. Always.

And so on one side of his fence (the outside) stand the lawless, mindlessly chanting their mantra, "Nobody is going to tell me what I can or cannot do!" On the other side (the inside where protection is guaranteed) are those of us who say, "What incredible security I have, knowing that God's loving plan is safeguarding me from the chaos on the other side of this fence!"

Don't let anyone tell you you're 'fenced in.' Instead remind them that you live in a freedom only available to those surrounded by God's steadfast love.

July 7

Learning To Plod

"Nevertheless I must walk today, and tomorrow, and the day following." Luke 13:33 KJV

Plod: To walk or proceed in or as if in a slow, heavy-footed way; to work doggedly or laboriously.

I had a "Three Stooges" experience while sitting down to put these words to computer keyboard. It went something like this: "I'm trying to think but nothin's happening!" Some weeks my thoughts bubble excitedly to the surface. There's an idea that just can't be ignored. But not this week. My mind was abysmally normal...adequate, but just.

Look at the definitions of 'plod' above. They fly in the face of how we picture ourselves living life. A lot of inspirational writing reminds us that we are eagles, meant to soar. Life is to be one grand adventure after another, with our feet rarely hitting the ground. The primary danger in life, we're told, is the lack of oxygen at the heights to which we stay 'soar-ed.'

Alas, that isn't life as most of us know it. And to be Biblically honest, it wasn't the normal experience for most of our Scriptural heroes. Oh sure, Peter and John brought a lame man to his feet in front of a large crowd. But what were they doing on the previous 42 days? Probably plodding. How many days do you suppose there were between those times when God and Abraham stood looking into the night sky talking about descendants more numerous than the stars? And what was Abraham doing in the 'between times?' Most likely plodding.

There's a lot of plodding called for in life. Simply putting one foot in front of the other. It's called "keeping going" and it fills a large part of our lives. Thank God for the epiphanies... rejoice greatly in the times of special spiritual insight and break-throughs...relish those times when God is closer to you than your spouse or your ministry. But remember, the monotonous plodding is what ultimately keeps us heading toward our dreams and our goals.

If this is plodding time for you thank God for the direction your dogged and laborious steps are taking you. Ask God to give you great joy for the journey...even the plodding.

July 8
Biblical Worldview

"In those days Israel had no king, so the people did whatever seemed right in their own eyes". Judges 17:6 The Message

I think it's safe to say that we've arrived at this point in this land we call America. George Barna, the researcher/pollster confirmed recently that only 4% of Americans make their decisions based on a Biblical worldview. That means that the basic tenets of my life...the superstructure upon which my entire life is built...the basis on which I make all of my decisions...is not shared by 96% of the people around me.

People don't act like Jesus because they're not thinking like Jesus.

Greed, lust, selfishness, gluttony, character assassination, robbery, cheating on tests and income tax forms...none of these things are particularly wrong if your worldview tells you they aren't. The problem with living our lives apart from God's perspective is that it inevitably brings pain and suffering to the human condition. Live selfishly and you will hurt those around you. Cheat your way through life and your getting ahead is always at the expense of others. Everybody pays for the shoplifting at Wal-Mart! We never sin just to ourselves...never.

Living according to Godly standards does two things: it guarantees ultimate success for the person living it and it makes living easier on everyone around us. God is only King when He is obeyed. Otherwise He's simply a name on our coins or the false BMW hood ornament on our Ford Fiesta lifestyle.

So what about today? Maybe it's time for those of us who are hanging on to the old-fashioned notion that there is a loving God who has proposed a standard for living life that is good both for the one living it and people around him...maybe it's

time for us to show by our obedience to Him that His ways
are best. Nothing sells like success. There are many around us
who aren't necessarily sold on what their worldview is doing for
them...they're just hanging on waiting for something better to
come along.

May your journey today be a time when you take God's show
on the road!

July 9

Authority and Freedom

*"After Jesus said this, he looked toward heaven and
prayed: "Father, the time has come. Glorify your Son,
so that your Son may glorify you. For you granted him
authority over all people that he might give eternal life to
all those you have given him." John 17:1,2 NIV*

*"You, my brothers. were called to be free. But do not use
your freedom to indulge the sinful nature; rather, serve one
another in love. The entire law is summed up in a single
command: 'Love your neighbor as yourself.'" Galatians
5:13,14 NIV*

They are two of the most sought after commodities in our culture today – authority and freedom.

Oh, what we couldn't do if we just had those two things! If I
possess the authority it means that someone else does not. That
would make me (I love this part ...) the Boss. And having freedom means getting what I want and need at any time and in any
way. Pretty heady stuff!

But beware! Man possessing authority and freedom without the constraints of Godliness can turn into a despot ... a
tyrant ... a dictator of family, business associates and even
entire nations. Both of them must be under divine control or

they quickly roar out of control and become weapons of mass destruction.

Jesus was given ultimate authority over all people. God knew his Son would not waste it and indeed, Jesus used that authority to provide eternal life for anyone who asked for it. His authority could easily kept him from the cross, but he used it for eternity's highest good.

In the same way freedom is not to be squandered on our own whims and fancies. We can use it to gratify our sinful natures, but within a short amount of time that investment turns on us and we become slaves to our own 'freedom.' Instead, we are to use our freedom to serve one another. And in so doing we liberate those we serve. Everyone gains freedom when it's used for the good of all.

Mother Teresa was bandaging the rotting nose of a leper in Calcutta and being followed around by a Life Magazine photographer/writer. As the interviewer watched her use her freedom by helping one of life's most pitiful, he said as he turned away from the squeamish sight "I wouldn't do that for a million dollars." To which Mother Teresa replied, "Neither would I."

There will always be those who do not understand the thrill and deep satisfaction of giving yourself away through both your authority and freedom. And I do not want to be one of them.

July 10
The Coming Kingdom

"The seventh angel sounded his trumpet, and there were loud voices in heaven, which said:
"The kingdom of the world has become the kingdom of our Lord and of his Christ,
and he will reign for ever and ever." Revelation 11:14 NIV

We live in the transitional zone between 'the kingdom of the world' and the one that 'has become the kingdom of our Lord and of his Christ.' The reigning over this incredulous kingdom will be Christ's great honor and our great delight. We will live in eternal astonishment and grateful wonder at what God's plan has brought forth.

But make no mistake. We're not there yet.

This is 'no man's land.' This is the tectonic-shifting, temporary, yet terrifying world of great change. What 'is' is 'becoming' and everyone of us who claim Jesus as our King are a serious part of it.

The King we serve has served notice on the current administration that He's taking over. It isn't to be by popular vote … no caucuses need be held … political expedience will never fuel this campaign.

The only 'primary' that matters is the one held the day He died, descended into hell and took the keys away from the corrupt usurper. That was the day the outcome was assured. There would be a change of power. The old is coming down and the new King will reign for ever and ever. There will never again be a regime change. All challengers and challenges will be gone for good.

And our part in all this? According to Matthew 11:12 " … *from the days of John the Baptist until now, the kingdom of heaven has been forcefully advancing, and forceful men lay hold of it.*" *NIV* So the violence of the cross continues in those of us who came into this Kingdom through the cross's power. By our obedience and steady commitment … when obeying comes hard and staying the course is tremendously difficult … we continue to move more and more of the kingdom of this world into and under the jurisdiction of our King.

"May your Kingdom come soon. May your will be done on earth, as it is in heaven." Matthew 6:10 New Living Translation

July 11

The Ultimate Oxymoron

Do you get a kick out of an oxymoron as I do? You know…words used together that have no business being in the same room, let alone the same sentence. Here are a few that make me smile: 'jumbo shrimp'… 'all natural artificial flavor'… 'Dodge Ram'… 'tight slacks'… 'authentic reproduction'… 'detailed summary'. It's a strange language that lets you use opposites to get a meaning across, but our vocabulary is full of them.

There is one oxymoron however, that doesn't bring a smile to my face. I actually think of it as the ultimate oxymoron. It's this: "No, Lord." What a terrible juxtaposition of words, let alone concepts. You can say "No" to God, but you cannot address Him as Lord if you do.

How do we say "No" to Almighty God? Hardly ever with the actual word 'no' and seldom in a head to head confrontation. As we get spiritual, we move to more sophisticated ways of giving God a 'thumbs down.' Sometimes we act as if we haven't heard. Ignoring God is just another way of telling Him 'No.'

Another way to shake your head negatively in God's direction is to attempt to change the subject, most likely hoping He'll get sidetracked and forget what He's asking. Won't work! We can also say 'yes' but do 'no.' Ever done that? The verbal response moves in his direction even while the intentions are going the opposite way. *"Not everyone who says to me, 'Lord, Lord,' will enter the kingdom of heaven, but only the one who does the will of my Father who is in heaven." Matthew 7:21 NIV*

Would this be a good day to make sure that our spiritual vocabulary and the way we're living our lives match up? The future is bright for all those, like the young and unmarried Mary, who responded to God with *"I am the Lord's servant, and I am willing to accept whatever he wants. May everything you have said come true." Luke 1:38 NLT*

July 12
A Sundial At Night

For a sundial to give you accurate time, you need sunlight. However, you can get a sundial to give you any time you want if you shine a flashlight on it at night.

Warnings like "It's later than you think" and "The end is near" used to be heard routinely. A sense of timing was derived from the mainstream culture being at least partially attuned to the message of God through his eternal Word. Now that society has ditched its allegiance to and reliance on the proclamation of God's Word they're like people shortly before sunrise using their flashlights and sundials to tell them that the sun has barely gone down. They now have all the time they need!

It's the same fuzzy logic that declares "I'm not really sure where I am and where I am going, but I just can't stop now for directions...I'm making really good time." We laugh at it in joke form but we should weep over its logic when it controls the destination of an entire culture.

Living among people who feel 'timeless' but who are quickly running out of it...sharing space with the crowd that continues going faster and faster toward an obscure destination ... watching people in the dark use the flashlight of 'consensus' to get an idea of the length of life...all of these give believers a huge agenda. It's an especially important job in the light of the fact that life really is short. In the oldest book of the Bible, Job reminds all of us of this when he says, *"My days come and go swifter than the click of knitting needles, and then the yarn runs out – an unfinished life." Job 7:6 The Message* Only the light of God's Son shining into our lives can give the proper sense of timing to our lives.

The other reason our task is so vital in this generation is that they desperately need an idea of which way to go. Speed is not the issue when you don't know where you're going. Jesus said *"The way to life – to God! – is vigorous and requires total attention." Matthew 7:14 The Message* There is a way that seems right to the undiscerning, but it leads to a place nobody really wants to go.

So I must look for gentle, yet firm ways of communicating God's love...love so amazing that it has already looked over every detail of our lives, including timing and destination. He wants us with Him throughout eternity.

July 13

Traveling Well

In just three short verses the Psalmist paints a picture of a spiritually-successful life that I would love engraved on my tombstone...if Jesus does not return before I'm ninety-seven.

> *"...How blessed all those in whom you live, whose lives become roads you travel; They wind through lonesome valleys, come upon brooks, discover cool springs and pools brimming with rain! God-traveled, these roads curve up the mountain, and at the last turn – Zion! God in full view!" Psalm 84:5-7 The Message*

My expectations and desires are beginning to simplify...not that you couldn't find some carnal yearnings still gnawing at the corners of my soul. But by and large I'm getting a clearer picture of the foundational ambitions of my life... those spawned by my love of God and orchestrated by the Holy Spirit.

How I desperately want to become a road on which God travels. Then when I walk through the lonesome valley I not only have companionship, but a Companion to share with those I meet who are also lonely. (And the road of life is crowded with lonely and disillusioned people.) When I come upon a brook, discover a cool spring and pools brimming with rain I can quickly acknowledge that these unparalleled blessings are mine because the Author of every 'good and perfect gift' is walking the roads of my life and sharing with me the serendipitous splendors of his heart.

Also pardon the spiritualizing here, but did you notice the roads curving up the mountain. A reminder that much of living is an uphill climb. You can only enjoy the descent when it's preceded by a trip up.

Today my goal is to present my life as a road upon which God can freely travel. I desire Him to be able to move as quickly or slowly as He desires. I will not fight the uphill portions of the trip when my emotional and spiritual mileage often slips a bit. I will accept his comfort when lonely and will constantly be on the lookout for other lonely travelers to whom I can introduce my Friend. And finally the day will come when I will crest the mountain…complete the journey…finish my course…and come fully face to face with the God of eternity who just happens to be my closest Friend.

And that give me great joy as I journey. May that joy be yours as well.

July 14

The Birds and the Bakery

Who doesn't enjoy a warm piece of fresh, homemade bread? One of our favorite early morning treats when in the Portland area is to stop by a bakery that offer a choice of several 'just-out-of-the-oven' pieces of buttered bread.

It's just one store in a line of many. On the sidewalk out front are a few metal tables for customers to use on nice days. To one side of the bakery was a clothing store … on the other a cell phone store. Actually, it was the only store serving food in the entire line of eight businesses.

And would you believe it … that's the very store where the birds hung out!

How fortuitous you say. What a coincidence you conclude. Neither. They're there because there is something to eat at that location.

Sometimes birds are more attuned to God's provision than we are. God lays out a great spiritual meal for us in our place of worship while we're on the couch at home watching football. He guides someone with a tasty spiritual morsel our way and we miss receiving it because we're hanging out in front of the cell phone store!

How intentional are we at finding spiritual nourishment for our lives? How tragic if the food I need today is in God's Word and I'm in the sports page. How stupid to wait for bread crumbs in front of the pet store.

Psalm 136:25 tells us that *"He gives food to every living thing."* *New Living Translation* David chronicled God's generous provision when he declared: *"Once I was young, and now I am old. Yet I have never seen the godly abandoned or their children begging for bread." Psalm 37:25 New Living Translation*

We just need to be smart enough and hungry enough to hang out at the bakery.

> *"He gives food to those who trust him; he always remembers his covenant." Psalm 111:5 NLT*

May you find joy (and nourishment) for your journey!

July 15
Breaking The Cycle

> *"Some of you wandered for years in the desert, looking but not finding a good place to live, Half-starved and parched with thirst, staggering and stumbling, on the*

brink of exhaustion. Then, in your desperate condition, you called out to God. He got you out in the nick of time; He put your feet on a wonderful road that took you straight to a good place to live. So thank God for his marvelous love, for his miracle mercy to the children he loves. He poured great draughts of water down parched throats; the starved and hungry got plenty to eat." Psalm 107:4-9 The Message

◆ It's like owning 1250 pair of exquisitely expensive shoes but still craving that pair of black, patent leather pumps from Payless Shoe Store.

◆ It's a guy with 37 priceless automobiles worth tens of millions who won't be satisfied until he owns his neighbor's Ford Fiesta.

◆ It's sitting down at the captain's table on a world-class cruise, able to order lobster, caviar, duck-under-glass and truffle infused red mashed potatoes oozing with butter, and griping because there's no tuna salad sandwiches offered.

It's called ingratitude and as a culture, we're getting very good at it. And it makes God sick to his stomach. It sets up a recurring nightmare of a time, in the very beginning, when He gave everything He could think of to Eden's first two residents.

Everything but one thing! And having 'almost everything' wasn't enough without that last thing. Ingrates!

And I'm afraid I've just labeled myself. Since our earliest relatives introduced this God-slapping sin, we've all come by it naturally. But it's an ugly sin that turns God from Benefactor to a cross between a 'wishing star' and a concierge in the hotel lobby.

I point … I want … my cravings take center stage and suddenly my mind goes blank. I forget the rose's fragrance, the giggle of a grandchild, the mystery of daybreak, the promise of spring. And ultimately, I even forget the Cross!

I want to see ingratitude broken for good in my life, the start of a well-spring of thanksgiving playing out moment by moment in my life. I want you to poke me and get a response of gratitude - to wake me up in the middle of the night and hear words of praise erupt instantly and instinctively from my lips.

I want to be thankful. (Because I really am ...)

> *"Let the redeemed of the Lord say so ..."* Psalm 107:2 *KJV*

July 16
Innocent Before God

I don't have any friends named Eliphaz, but if I did I'd probably 'de-friend' them on Facebook. Guilt by association.

Job had a friend by that name (Job 4) and he turned out to be a finger pointer, a denouncer, a fault finder where none existed. He specialized in criticism cloaked in false concern.

He revealed his theology in his first diatribe. He implies that Job's grievous condition must be the result of sin in his life. "After all," he postulates, "the righteous don't get this kind of treatment from God. But the wicked are going to get a full dose of God's judgment."

And where was this faulty theology revealed to Eliphaz? Listen to his own words here:

"A spirit swept past my face, and my hair stood on end. The spirit stopped, but I couldn't see its shape. There was a form before my eyes. In the silence I heard a voice say, 'Can a mortal be innocent before God? Can anyone be pure before the Creator?'" Job 4:15-17 *New Living Translation*

That sinister voice has been casting doubt about God's ability to wipe away sin and restore innocence since the Garden of Eden. That message robs us of hope. It casts mistrust over our Redeemer. It's a courage destroyer ... a confidence shaker. It's the voice of condemnation and it can discourage us as it did Job.

But there is another voice, and even when it corrects it dispenses hope. Even with a poor record and prior convictions, that voice offers an unclouded future. Listen to that voice as it states the truth that Satan doesn't want any of us to receive: *"But there is a great difference between Adam's sin and God's gracious gift. For the sin of this one man, Adam, brought death to many. But even greater is God's wonderful grace and his gift of forgiveness to many through this other man, Jesus Christ." Romans 5:15 New Living Translation*

Be very careful to whom you listen. It you receive a word that troubles your spirit, germinates hopelessness and raises a cloud over your future ... it's not God talking to you. Because greater than your sin and your past is God's wonderful grace and his unfathomable gift of forgiveness.

July 17
Hero Status

"The godly people in the land are my true heroes! I take pleasure in them!" Psalm 16:3 New Living Translation

Living in a culture that puts more emphasis on style than on substance, it's easy to get confused about who our heroes are.

♦ When we insist on artificial color added to our food and drinks so they 'look better' ...
♦ When we wear expensive designer sweat suits that we have no intention of sweating in ...

♦ When we prefer fruit in the supermarket that looks perfect at the expense of taste …

♦ When we save our adulation for the rich and famous whose character flaws are obvious, but they 'look striking' on the cover of the tabloids …

♦ When we'd rather be titillated at the risqué behavior of the foolish than to celebrate the accomplishments of the godly …

♦ When we overlook the accomplishments of good people who have worked hard for their contribution to their world because we're too busy 'oohing' and 'aahing' over contrived importance of those whose contribution to their world is synthetic and often illusionary …

Then we've got our priorities messed up. It's often difficult to pick out the 'godly' in the land for a number of reasons. They don't get the press. A magazine entitled "The Deeds of Decent People" probably wouldn't fly off the shelves. Second, they tend not to toot their own horn. And third, their motivation isn't to look good, but to leave something good behind as they move through life.

Take directions from the Psalmist and seek out the godly in the land. Pay attention to their input and realize that little by little they are making this world a bit more livable and are contributing to the moral fabric that holds a civilization together.

Honor them by giving them hero status.

July 18

Can't Stop The Joy

"Our hearts ache, but we always have joy. II Corinthians 6:10
New Living Translation

The norms in life dictate that when petroleum reserves go down, the price of gas goes up ... that we must trade age for strength. That you can't have more here if you don't give up something there. And that as difficulties come, joy must recede.

But that isn't true with joy! The 'joy of the Lord' is an outrageous commodity to say the least. When the Apostle Paul was raising money to help the Palestinian believers during tough times, he cited the Christians in Macedonia as models of generosity. Here is what he said about them:

> *"They are being tested by many troubles, and they are very poor. But they are also filled with abundant joy, which has overflowed in rich generosity." II Corinthians 8:2 New Living Translation*

Calamitous times do not require the cessation of joy. Jesus said that even when hated, mocked, excluded and cursed you are entitled to 'leaping joy'. (Luke 6:22)

From the words of James, does it appear that when the world falls apart around you that it has the power to mess with your joy? *"... when troubles come your way, consider it an opportunity for great joy." James 1:2 New Living Translation*

Make the decision that nothing coming into your life has the ability, the power, the permission or the authority to take away your joy. It's a very special gift from a very special Father and He has an inexhaustible supply for you.

> *"Even though the fig trees have no blossoms, and there are no grapes on the vines; even though the olive crop fails, and the fields lie empty and barren; even though the flocks die in the fields, and the cattle barns are empty, 18 yet I will rejoice in the Lord! I will be joyful in the God of my salvation! 19 The Sovereign Lord is my strength!" Habakkuk 3:17-19 New Living Translation*

May there be unspeakable, unquenchable joy for your journey!

My Way

There's a secular song written by Paul Anka entitled "My Way." It's a self-tribute to living life ego-centric. Mistakes made? Sure. Relationships broken? Possibly. Could I have done better and left a stronger legacy as I face life's final curtain? Certainly. But in spite of that, I leave with this bold statement: I did it all my way!

This classic song (recorded by no fewer than 140+ artists since 1968) traumatizes me at a very deep level.

I love the majestic sweep of the music and the resoluteness it conveys. But its message speaks to the darkest part of my being … it tugs at unholy ambition and God-defying self-sufficiency. It's the lie bought by my ancient ancestor Adam who purchased it from Satan, a snake oil salesman still selling the same product with great success in the markets of our culture.

Need God? Hardly. Why I don't even need help from friends. I am a self-contained package and regardless of my flaws, in-abilities or secret insecurities I will face that 'final curtain' with my jaw jutted, chest out and a hearty "I did it my way" as my life's final journal entry.

In his early days, the Apostle Paul would likely have been one of the 140 who recorded this song. But then he had an en-counter with One who offered him a 'better way' instead of the 'my way' he was pursuing. And here is what he later wrote to a nation that wished to make "My Way" their national anthem:

"So where does that leave our proud Jewish insider claims and coun-terclaims? Canceled? Yes, canceled. What we've learned is this: God does not respond to what we do; we respond to what God does. We've finally figured it out. Our lives get in step with God and all others by letting

him set the pace, not by proudly or anxiously trying to run the parade."
Romans 3:27,28 The Message

I don't know how much pride has accumulated in your life,
or how very sure you are of your own capabilities, but this would
be a good time to 'finally figure it out' as the Apostle said.
What wonderful freedom is found in pursuing God's way!

The song "My Way" is the song most frequently played at
British funeral services. But if I can put in an early request, let it
be known at my 'final curtain' that I chose the old Hymn "Have
Thine Own Way" as my quiet anthem.

May there be joy and humility on your journey!

July 20

What If …

We Christians have been losing our 'rights' for some time now.
Monuments of the Ten Commandments have been locked
out of public places … even the framed written text is not
allowed on the walls of our schools. The manger and wise
men are being replaced by Santa Claus and rotund snowmen.
Pictures of Jesus must come down unless flanked by pictures
of Mohammed, Buddha, the Pope, Confucius, Brigham Young
and Gandhi.

Even the wearing of religious jewelry is coming under fire.
The resilient and popular WWJD (What Would Jesus Do) bracelet could be next!

Many are frustrated by these seeming 'persecutions for
righteousness sake' and wish we could return to earlier years of
acceptance and tolerance. There are more than a few 'rankled
redeemed' crying "Unfair!"

But what if these diminished 'rights' were good, not only for
us, but more importantly, for the good of God's Kingdom itself?
Impossible? Then consider …

What if we didn't get to keep the picture of Jesus, but exhibited his power instead?

What if the crèche came down but we showed him radiantly alive in us?

What if a person left their WWJD bracelet at home but actually did what Jesus would do?

What if all the symbols, icons, pictures, monuments and statues that we have depended on to tell our story were taken away and we had to live the story instead?

What if God is not as concerned with these things being stripped from us as we are and He sees this time as history's finest hour to be the people that our artwork has only alluded to?

"For I am not ashamed of this Good News about Christ. It is God's powerful method of bringing all who believe it to heaven." Romans 1:16 Living Bible
"You are to live clean, innocent lives as children of God in a dark world full of people who are crooked and stubborn. Shine out among them like beacon lights, holding out to them the Word of Life." Philippians 2:15 Living Bible

July 21
Smile

"Jacob said, "Please. If you can find it in your heart to welcome me, accept these gifts. When I saw your face, it was as the face of God smiling on me." Genesis 33:10 The Message

The schemer was coming home. What he deserved he did not want. What he wanted he did not deserve. Years before he had brazenly stolen his older brother's coveted birthright and the important ceremonial blessing of his dying father.

Now it was time to face the music. It was time to 'fess up' and throw himself at his brother's feet in humility and remorse. How much anger had built up? How many ways could his brother make him pay? But running was no longer an option. Jacob had encountered God and felt his future warranted a reckoning with the past.

Oh the relief of a forgiving brother's welcome. Never had a hug felt so comforting. Never had tears told such a story of acceptance. Jacob put it in perspective when he said, "When I saw your face, it was as the face of God smiling at me!"

Today I'm sitting in a public place, watching the faces of people passing me by. How many of them are at odds with their father …their Heavenly Father? How many of them feel the perpetual weight of a fractured relationship in their past? Do they have any idea of the thoughts God is thinking about them right now?

Here's my agenda for this day. Hopefully you'll accept it as yours, too.

I get to look into the eyes of some of these disenfranchised fugitives, and on behalf of God, smile at them! Isn't that incredible? Not only do we become the hands and feet and the heart of the Father … we get to become his face to this world as well.

Don't frown … don't scowl … don't glare. Smile! Their Father has an important message for them and wants to use your face to convey it.

> *"I have loved you with an everlasting love; I have drawn you with unfailing kindness." Jeremiah 31:3 NIV*

July 22

On Being Selfless

It's an inherited trait, but it's easily honed over the years into a quality of perfection.

I did not acquire it with the arrival of my first grand child. Nor did it come to me upon the maturity of having my own children. My wedding did not usher it in, nor did my eighteen plus years of educational training. I had it long before any of those life experiences.

There were traces of it evident from my earliest years, and my parents first noticed it really come to the surface in me as a small baby. Though barely able to sit, they placed me on the floor with my cousin and three toys. Immediately I wanted and reached for all three toys even at the expense of my cousin's happiness. There it was…out in the open for any observant person to see…that part of the sin nature that is always ugly to behold: SELFISHNESS!

And we've all had lots of help with its development in our lives. As a young boy, the power of advertising constantly re-minded me that it was my right to own whatever it was that they were selling. Burger King was making a burger *my way*, not your way. L'Oreal hair products cost more, but we're told that we're worth it. McDonalds sang to me a few years back that "You… you're the one." Even the message that Jesus would have gone to the cross just for me, when interpreted through selfishness, puts the emphasis on me…not Him.

I'm not proud of my inherent selfishness. I need a powerful model in my life to bring about its demise. I need to see Jesus making his way to the cross. I am reflecting on the truth of Philippians 2:5-8 (The Message):

> *"Think of yourselves the way Christ Jesus thought of himself. He had equal status with God but didn't think so much of himself that he had to cling to the advantages of that status no matter what. Not at all. When the time came, he set aside the privileges of deity and took on the status of a slave, became human! Having become human, he stayed human. It was an incredibly humbling process. He didn't claim special privileges. Instead, he*

lived a selfless, obedient life and then died a selfless, obedient death—and the worst kind of death at that: a crucifixion."

Don't be surprised if the 'self-less-ness' of your actions makes some positive ripples across the pond of 'self-ish-ness' in someone's life. Remember, you're here to make a difference in this world.

July 23
Style or Substance?

Luke 21:1 "Just then he looked up and saw the rich people dropping offerings in the collection plate. Then he saw a poor widow put in two pennies. He said, 'The plain truth is that this widow has given by far the largest offering today. All these others made offerings that they'll never miss; she gave extravagantly what she couldn't afford— she gave her all!'" The Message

Style versus substance…we hear this phrase a lot during elections. The charges go back and forth. Should we be concerned about understanding the difference between these two? Only if we care about bringing Jesus up on the radar screens of peoples' lives. Otherwise, it makes little difference in the light of eternity.

- ◆ *Style* is about our relationship to our religion. *Substance* is how we relate to God.
- ◆ Style is what makes a church building attractive to people…substance is the presence of God once they get there.
- ◆ Style is making an obvious and sizable gift to charity … substance is an offering, possibly anonymous, that costs and originates in a heart of love.

♦ Style is having a defendable theology…substance is having a heart that pleases God.
♦ Style is having a bona fide answer to any possible question…substance is in trusting the Father no matter what.
♦ Style can make all men your friends…substance is telling the truth in love.

Style is beginning to absorb more and more of our time, attention and energy…substance often takes a back seat, and the world around us notices.

This is a culture that at one time worshipped at the altar of style. What impressed was what was seen on the surface. But matters of substance are coming back into vogue…especially with pre-Christians. There is a growing awareness that the most important issues in life can't be handled…can't be traded for… can't be trusted to tell the whole story.

Do a little soul searching. Are you mostly 'style' or is there substance to your life that's based on your knowledge of God's Word and your willingness to submit to it? There had better be more than leaves on the trees of our lives…others are hungry.

July 24
No Regrets

We were just about to cross from Arizona into Nevada, moving from Mountain Daylight Time to Pacific Daylight Time. I playfully asked Joanie what she would do differently since she was going to get to live the last hour over again.

Upon discussion we agreed that we wouldn't change a thing. We had been on the road for three weeks and were just hours away from home and our own bed. We'd do the last hour exactly the same.

That's not always the case. How many times in our lives would we gladly take the opportunity to 'try it again' ... to take a 'Mulligan' when our first shot hooked into the woods. But some things in life can't be replayed.

Like parenting your child ... remaining faithful to your marriage vows ... taking the high road in business. Unlike the main character in the movie "Ground Hog Day" we are not given the chance to keep working on a day until we have it right.

Because of the finality of many of our decisions we need to go into them with as much understanding and wisdom as possible ... but more often than not, it isn't enough.

So are we destined in life to blunder along, carrying an ever increasing burden of regrets?

The incredibly good news is that we have a Heavenly Father who can and wants to help. The Psalmist said: *"The steps of the godly are directed by the Lord. He delights in every detail of their lives." Psalm 37:23 New Living Translation* In James 1:5 we're told that God doesn't resent us asking for directions. And Solomon encourages us with these words: *"Trust God from the bottom of your heart; don't try to figure out everything on your own. Listen for God's voice in everything you do, everywhere you go; he's the one who will keep you on track." Proverbs 3:5,6 The Message*

So if you don't want to regret doing it wrong, do it right ... with God's help!

July 25

Broken Rules

"Jesus stood up and spoke to her. 'Woman, where are they? Does no one condemn you?'" 'No one, Master.' 'Neither do I,' said Jesus. 'Go on your way. From now on, don't sin.'" John 8:10,11 The Message

Her story has been raising eyebrows for 2,000 years. (*John 8:1-11*)

A woman of loose morals is caught in the act of indiscretion by 'men of rules.' And not just any men of rules … oh no! These are religious men who continually trapped the common man and woman in their rules so they could pronounce judgment on them while feeling good about themselves at the same time.

Never mind that these very men had 'worked the system' and bent the very rules they hoisted on others. They used finger-pointing to hide their own shadowy behavior. They had a victim and threw her at the feet of Jesus asking if He would agree with Moses that such a vile woman was good for only one thing …target practice.

The response of the Son of Man in this situation did a number of critical things. First, it showed that none of us is guiltless. All have sinned. No questions and no excuses. Sinners. All of us. But second, his contemplative delay in delivering his verdict does more to reveal the heart of the Father than almost any other words He spoke.

He finally speaks. "Anyone standing here who has never sinned may throw the first stone." As they weighed that challenge, beginning with the oldest in the group, they dropped their stones and left the woman alone, still cringing at the feet of Jesus. "Where are your accusers?" He asked her. Dumbfounded, she nervously glanced around for signs of the 'men of rules.' "Doesn't anyone condemn you?" she is asked.

"No one, Master" is her reply. And then comes words from heaven's most amazing theology: "You know the rules; now here's my heart. Neither do I condemn you. Go and don't keep sinning."

You may just need the One who not only knows the rules, and actually is responsible for them …but also the One who offers grace when a rule has been broken. Don't presume upon this exquisite forgiveness, but take it if needed.

Take his joy and pardon for your journey!

July 26
Mere Laymen

I don't know where I first heard the term 'mere laymen.'

It probably was in a sermon on Acts 4:13 when Peter and John were brought before the religious leaders in Jerusalem for violating religious protocol. That verse in the New International Version reads: *"When they saw the courage of Peter and John and realized that they were unschooled, ordinary men, they were astonished and they took note that these men had been with Jesus." NIV*

So possibly in the vernacular of a careless preacher, the words 'unschooled, ordinary men' came out as 'mere laymen.' God does not recognize the term nor the implications of it.

I grit my teeth now just as I did the first time I heard it. Religious elitists judging others on the basis of what they knew and the fact that they were not cut from the same cloth but were simply *'ordinary.'*

Not all of us get paid for ministry, but anyone following Jesus has been called into ministry. And how can anyone with the power of the Living God dwelling in them ... handpicked by the Creator to represent his heart, power and purposes on this planet ... how can that person be a 'mere' anything?

The apostles may not have had the credentials, but they had the relationship. The religious hierarchy recognized that they had been with Jesus. And the effect of that relationship was not lost on the Jewish leadership. The first question they posed to these unschooled, ordinary men was *"Who put you in charge here?" Acts 4:7 The Message*

Mere laymen indeed!

Spend some time with Jesus this week ...serious time ... more than your hour in church on Sunday. And as that relationship blossoms as Jesus wants it to, there will be an authentic power to your life that will enable you to be everything He wants you to be. No one will ever mistake you for ordinary.

July 27
No Other God

> *"I, even I, am the LORD, and apart from me there is no savior. I have revealed and saved and proclaimed— I, and not some foreign god among you. You are my witnesses," declares the LORD, "that I am God." Isaiah 43:11-12 NIV*

It's a shame for God to have to talk to his own people as some sort of 'outsider' or interloper. Imagine coming home from junior high one afternoon and being met at the door by your mother saying, "Good afternoon. I'd like to introduce myself. I'm your mother."

You'd think that after twelve or thirteen years of caring for, providing for, bandaging 'boo boos', serving meals to and generally interacting with every detail of our lives that we would have made that connection between ourselves and our mother's love.

But Israel's story so often mimics our own. We continually need for God to remind us that He is inextricably tied to each one of us in a relationship that defies description. For those who are unfamiliar with the word 'inextricable' it means: "hopelessly involved and impossible to untangle or undo."

And that's just the way God wants it. He would, however, like for us to have a bit longer memory about this unique relationship that we share. Rightfully He chides us for forgetting or minimizing this powerful family connection. After all, "You are my witnesses, that I am God."

Today you will rub shoulders with, will converse with, will influence some who are still unsure about who should take top honors of 'god' in their life. In many peoples' lives there is still tremendous competition between a variety of gods vying for preeminence. They need to know ... there's no contest. There is no god like our God. We need no Other than Him.

July 28

Sound of Heaven

In his book "Dreaming With God" author and pastor Bill Johnson makes this statement about Satan: "He walks about as a roaring lion, hoping to intimidate through noise. His noise, the constant report of bad news, is designed to give an illusion of greatness."

Who hasn't watched the national news on any night and failed to hear this 'noise.'

We're told it's bad ... it's hopeless ... it's even going to get worse! We're instructed to get used to it ... to prepare for it ... to accept it as it is and always will be. And I'm supposed to sleep after this assault?

But remember, the newscasters can only report on the seen. They have no insight into what is behind the obvious. For that reporting we need another source than ABC, CBS, NBC, Fox or CNN. We need the divine network.

The Apostle Paul said, " *So we don't look at the troubles we can see now; rather, we fix our gaze on things that cannot be seen. For the things we see now will soon be gone, but the things we cannot see will last forever." II Corinthians 4:18 New Living Translation*

The devil may be able to mess up our world for a time, but he has no right, power or authority to mess with our future in Christ! God's plans will prevail. His power is absolute. His schedule will be followed. His intentions cannot be dissuaded.

Weeping (and watching national news) may endure for the night, but glorious joy will explode at daybreak. You are a winner through relationship. You have chosen the right team (or more theologically correct, been chosen for the right team). The noise of the accuser will soon be replaced by the sounds of heaven!

You may need to turn down (or off) the noise of the news and strain to hear the rehearsal sounds of heaven's musicians. They're on next!

Ubiquitous Joy

> " ... *let the godly rejoice. Let them be glad in God's presence. Let them be filled with joy.*" *Psalm 68:3 New Living Translation*

> "*Our hearts ache, but we always have joy.*" *II Corinthians 6:10 New Living Translation*

> "*Dear brothers and sisters, when troubles come your way, consider it an opportunity for great joy.*" *James 1:2 New Living Translation*

OK ... so here's the phrase: *UBIQUITOUS JOY!*

Although I have difficulty pronouncing 'ubiquitous', I still love its meaning. *omnipresent ... world-wide ... in all places ... right and left ...hither and yon ...everywhere under the sun.*

I heard a pastor once say that in his last pastorate he made everyone joyful. Some when he came and the rest when he left. That's joy coming and going!

Joy cannot be a 'one way street.' It was meant to go both in and out. Forward and backward. Back and forth. You were meant to receive joy and to dispense it. However, you must find joy and receive joy or you will attempt the impossible ... give something away that you do not have.

And where is joy to be found? There are spigots of joy all around us. We receive joy from the grin of a child ... from an unsolicited affirmation from a friend ... from the welcomed sun on our face ... from the love of family. We find joy in serendipitous encounters with strangers who become friends ... from delayed hope that finally produces what we have patiently waited for ... and from the myriad blessings of God in hundreds of instances in our lives.

Many spigots ... but only one fountainhead. *"You have made known to me the path of life; you will fill me with joy in your presence, with eternal pleasures at your right hand." Psalm 16:11 NIV* The ultimate source of joy is never the people or things that appear to give us joy, but in knowing and responding to the One who authors joy. God is ultimately the fountainhead of our joy.

So take all the joy you can get from living under the provision and love of your Heavenly Father, then look for any way possible of passing on this 'ubiquitous joy' to the sad and disheartened around you.

May you find joy for your journey (and give it away)

July 30

An Aroma

I was on a prayer walk ... casually conversing with the Lord over the issues of life.

Coming toward me were seven young girls, obviously a high school cross country team on their afternoon run. None of them apparently went easy on perfume just because they were going to perspire (or maybe because they were going to perspire!)

But for quite a distance after they had passed me, I continued to walk in the fragrances they had been wearing and had left behind. The lingering aroma added joy to my walk for several minutes.

Some of you who are sharp can see where this is going!

The Apostle Paul said in *II Corinthians 2:15 "For we are to God the aroma of Christ among those who are being saved and those who are perishing." NIV* That means that those of us in whom Jesus resides convey a fragrance that is picked up by those we pass by in life.

I didn't have to converse with those girls for their aroma to impact me. And so it is with us as we move through life. Something of the aroma of Jesus in us should turn heads … should add joy to someone's journey … should remind others that there is more to life than the smell of decay and death.

As 'ambassadors of life' we have the joy and privilege of bringing the essence of our Lord into the streets, aisles and walking trails of our lives. You've got the fragrance … just don't cover it up with anything.

Your life is to be an epistle, read (and smelled) by all you come in contact with.

May you find fragrant joy for your journey that spreads to others

Backing Into Things

In more than 1.5 million miles driven, I've never hit anything or anybody while going forward … but I have backed into a couple of things!

Obviously we back into things that are behind us. That's why the Apostle Paul said, *"No, dear brothers and sisters, I have not achieved it, but I focus on this one thing: Forgetting the past and looking forward to what lies ahead, 14 I press on to reach the end of the race and receive the heavenly prize for which God, through Christ Jesus, is calling us." Philippians 3:13,14 New Living Translation*

There are things in all of our pasts that could either disqualify us or discourage us to the point of quitting.

*We hear a voice from the past telling us that we're too slow, too dim, too frivolous, too serious ... to amount to anything. That was then; this is now.

*We look with regret at a poor decision that affected the relationships in our lives and erroneously conclude that we're destined for a repeat. That was then; this is now.

*We look back at a time of disability and fear its return. It cripples us. That was then; this is now.

*Behind us are poor parenting techniques that left us with scars and memories and we wonder if the way we were raised will determine our success or failure as parents. That was then; this is now.

* We had a history of 'caving' on our spiritual commitments. We played Judas and Thomas and Peter in the courtyard denying his relationship with Jesus. With these on our resume, can we hope to be faithful? That was then; this is now.

You may have to really rest your case and your fears and submerge them in this spiritual reality: *"It doesn't matter whether we have been circumcised or not. What counts is whether we have been transformed into a new creation." Galatians 6:15 "This means that anyone who belongs to Christ has become a new person. The old life is gone; a new life has begun!" II Corinthians 5:17 (both passages from New Living Translation)*

Quit backing into things!

August 1
Are You Listening?

A company wanted their employees to contribute to the United Way fund. What they were looking for was 100% compliance. After several months of encouraging their employees to give ... even $1 per month out of their paycheck, there was one employee not cooperating. When memos and personal requests had no effect, the boss called the man into his office.

"Having 100% of our people on board with this project is so critical to us, that we're going to have to terminate you for not joining in," he told the recalcitrant man. "Oh, I'd be happy to give monthly," the man said. "Why now, after all our attempts at getting you to join us, do you make the decision to participate?"

"Well," the man replied, "I never had it explained this way to me before!"

The Psalmist said this to God: *"Now that you have made me listen, I finally understand." Psalm 40:6 New Living Translation*

Isn't it funny the positions we get ourselves in before our mouths stop and our ears work? Ken Taylor in the Living Bible has God saying this to us: *"My words are plain and clear to anyone with half a mind – if it is only open!" Proverbs 8:9* Most of us have at least half a mind, so the problem isn't always between the ears. Sometimes it is the ears themselves!

And of course we're talking about listening primarily with our spiritual hearing, although there are many times when God's voice to us comes via a person in our lives … their voice to our ears.

Today would be a good time to check your hearing. Make sure you get God's heart and his message clearly. Remember, He seldom shouts and can easily be drowned out by traffic noise, a television program or sometimes even Christian music! Don't require Him to 'make you listen.' Learn to listen just because you love the sound of his voice and because his instructions will make your life meaningful and satisfying.

August 2
Visibility Unlimited

We missed the 'Tule fog' by several hours. Our trip to the Fresno Air Terminal was made in clear weather. Not so for folks taking the same trip just hours later.

'Tule fog' is a specialty of the San Joaquin Valley in Central California. It's a winter fog formed from the ground up, usually after a rain and a quick change in temperature. It can reduce visibility to less than three feet! This week it brought over 100 vehicles together in a cacophony of squealing brakes, screeching metal, wailing sirens and at least two deaths.

It's nasty stuff.

It doesn't have to be very thick to be very deadly. But at the same time, it doesn't take much elevation to get on top of it! I have taken off from that same airport in dense fog, barely legal for a takeoff and within fifteen seconds had broken out above the fog. Fog so thick you could scarcely see your hand at the end of your arm at ground level was all below you by the fifth floor!

The spiritual implication is fairly obvious. It doesn't take very much to cloud my vision ... to reduce my visibility drastically. What was clear is now obscured. Certainty in direction now gives way to nagging doubts and troubling fears. Am I still going the way I intended? Are there things ahead that will stop my progress? Should I pull over and wait? Should I press on but at reduced speed?

I need GPS ... God's Protection Service.

My need is for someone bigger, taller, smarter and far more experienced to rescue me from the fog banks of my life. He needs to have greater visibility and see from a better vantage point. My request is that of the Psalmist: *"Lead me in the right path, O Lord ... tell me clearly what to do, and show me which way to turn." Psalm 5:8 New Living Translation*

August 3

Tsunami

"But as for me, I will sing about your power. Each morning I will sing with joy about your unfailing love. For you have been my refuge, a place of safety when I am in distress." Psalm 59:16 NLT

Ever been enjoying a soft breeze in your face from the west when you got 'tsunamied' from the east? You never thought to look over your shoulder and even if you had, you wouldn't have seen it coming anyway.

Life sometimes comes at us not as an easy mist, but as a downpour … not as tiny little snowflakes outlined by the streetlights, but as a howling blizzard obliterating all vision. The weatherman called for partly cloudy with possible sun breaks and we experienced the life-threatening landfall of a category 5 hurricane.

Can you identify? Has your life been shaken by an unexpected 7.2 richter-scaled earthquake? Are things shaking like never before?

If so, you are looking for a place of stability. A place that isn't being tossed around. A quiet in the midst of the tumult. There is a place like that and it's found in the presence of our Heavenly Father.

"So God has given both his promise and his oath. These two things are unchangeable because it is impossible for God to lie. Therefore, we who have fled to him for refuge can have great confidence as we hold to the hope that lies before us. 19 This hope is a strong and trustworthy anchor for our souls …" Hebrews 6:18,19 New Living Translation

Realize today that life can hit us from any direction, so the answer isn't in keeping a sharp lookout … it's being secured in the refuge of God's protecting arms and staying there until the weather improves and the storm moves out of the area!

August 4
Your Testimony

"I will bless the LORD at all times: his praise shall continually be in my mouth. My soul shall make her boast in the LORD: the humble shall hear thereof, and be glad. O magnify the LORD with me, and let us exalt his name together." Psalm 34:1-3 King James Version

Usually in Scripture when boasting and humility come in close contact, they are opposites repelling each other. In this verse, one is given to correct the other. The 'boaster' interacts with the 'humbled' or hurting and in the process hope comes alive.

First, the 'boaster.' Pride is not always wrong ... only if it centers on self. When God gets the total credit for the success, the healing, the business turnaround or the increase, it's called a testimony and it's a powerful antidote to all with broken hearts and shattered dreams. And there's an awfully good chance that you have a testimony that someone needs to hear.

As to the 'humbled' we get a better idea of who they are by checking out some other translations than the King James. In the New Living Translation we find humbled meaning 'helpless.' In the New International Version they are listed as 'afflicted' and Eugene Peterson's Message refers to them as those to whom 'things aren't going well.'

Not only do we know people presently in those dismal categories of life, but we, ourselves, have drunk from that polluted pond in times past. We know how it feels to wake to hopelessness day after day. But we've experienced a rescue! We've been reborn ... had a new and solid foundation placed under us. The dragons of the past have been dealt with decisively by our King.

Something exciting gets to take place wherever and whenever God leads the orchestra. Now filled with hope, we get to tell the hopeless about our God. We who have a future get to encourage the desperately despondent to put their hope in the One who has a glorious future planned for them.

So open your mouth and give the hopeless directions to their new future!

August 5

Moving

Not sure why I nailed them above the header in my garage ... but there they hang ... ten license plates spanning our life over the last 21 years.

In 1989 we traded in our Idaho plates for California's version. Then it was on and up to Oregon. At this point I'm missing the Colorado plates I wore on my car for three years while with Promise Keepers. From there we returned to Washington. From Washington back to California and now you'll find Washington plates back on my Honda ... but only temporarily. Now back on the desert the Washington plates will again be replaced by the California variety.

And to think that some of you haven't moved once in the last two decades. I'm a bit envious of you, yet have enjoyed every road that those cars and God's will have taken us.

I often end my Fresh Hearts with the phrase "May there be joy for your journey." I say that because we're all on one. You may not move your physical dwelling, but spiritually you are on your way somewhere else. In Second Corinthians 5:1 Paul said, *"For we know that when this earthly tent we live in is taken down (that is, when we die and leave this earthly body), we will have a house in heaven, an eternal body made for us by God himself and not by human hands." New Living Translation*

Remember, even the most move-resistant life has eternal movement in it. To a child of God there is a homing instinct very much alive in each of us. The wisest man to ever live said it this way, *"(God) ... has made everything beautiful in its time. He has also set eternity in the hearts of men." Ecclesiastes 3:11 NIV*

Trust your instincts ... hold lightly to things that aren't eternal ... and get ready to move!

May there be joy and anticipation for your journey!

August 6

Hope For Sure

> *"So be strong and courageous, all you who put your hope*
> *in the Lord!"*
> *Psalm 31:24 New Living Translation*

As I was reminded in a recent sermon, all hope is not the same. The difference between the 40 horsepower Smart Fortwo electric drive coupe and the 1200 horsepower Bugatti Veyron sports car seems almost inconsequential compared to the vast disparity between the faith mentioned above in Psalms and the kind most of us assume to be the real thing.

"I hope it doesn't rain this week-end" ... "Let's hope the economy turns around" ... "We hope you can come for a visit this year" ... these hopes are grounded in non-secure foundations. They are little more than "I wish I may, I wish I might have the wish I wish tonight." Assurances don't flood the heart speaking this wish toward the first star seen in a darkening sky.

Israel's prophet Isaiah lived in an era that mirrors our own in many ways. He echoed the wishful thinking of that dark time when he said, *"Therefore justice is far from us, and righteousness does not overtake us; we hope for light, but behold, darkness,"* Isaiah 59:9 *New American Standard* Inferior hope is not enough for times like this.

Contrast wishful thinking with this. *"Even when there was no reason for hope, Abraham kept hoping—believing that he would become the father of many nations. For God had said to him, 'That's how many descendants you will have!' 19 And Abraham's faith did not weaken ..."* Romans 4:18,19 *New American Standard*

What Abraham was hoping for was less than a million to one shot. Actually it was categorized as 'impossible.' What made it viable and active was the fact that he was hoping for something 'God had said to him.' You see, hope is different when the outcome is sure. A 50/50 chance of sunshine on Saturday or the winning numbers on a lottery ticket don't measure up to a sure word of God.

And so today let your hope be built on the things God has said and is currently saying to you. Immerse yourself in His Word. Let your heart say a hearty "Amen" to his promises. Then whether it rains or not, whether you win or not, whether or not the political climate swings in your direction, you will have the steadfast anchor that you need in times like these!

> *"I pray that God, the source of hope, will fill you completely with joy and peace because you trust in him. Then you will overflow with confident hope through the power of the Holy Spirit." Romans 15:13 New Living Translation*

May you have joy and confidence on your journey.

August 7

Little Foxes

> *"Catch for us the foxes, the little foxes that ruin the vineyards, our vineyards that are in bloom." Song of Solomon 2:15 NIV*

It wasn't huge … nothing to make me look like the Hunchback of Notre Dame … but it was a dark and slowly growing mark on my face. Thoughts of cancer hovered.

My opening words to the dermatologist was "The largest organ of my body (skin) is beginning to really bother me. I don't like a lot of the things it's doing. And this thing on my face has got to go."

He scarcely looked at it as his attention was drawn elsewhere on my face. "That growth you are concerned about it totally benign and of little consequence except cosmetically. These three areas here, however, are pre-cancerous and need to be burned off." As he pointed I squinted into his mirror and could see absolutely nothing of any consequence at all. But to him, they were potentially dangerous to my health.

I left his office with four facial blemishes having been introduced to liquid nitrogen. The removal of the three were covered by insurance; the biggest and most noticeable I had to pay for personally. I left his office with a reminder as well.

As I pondered the experience it helped me understand a Biblical principle. It's not just the 200 pound wolves that pose the destructive danger but the small foxes that often spoil the vineyard. It's the little sins that often knock the wheels off our wagons.

While guarding the front door judiciously, we forget that we've left the back screen door open just a crack. In taking care to keep immorality at bay, we allow the sin of fear to creep in. In safeguarding our theology to keep it pure, we let pride in.

Don't overlook the little foxes. Although possessing the power to destroy, our diligence will keep them at bay.

August 8
Taken For Granted

It was Ralph Waldo Emerson who pondered what we'd do if the stars only came out every thousand years. His response? "*No one would sleep that night, of course. The world would become religious overnight. We would be ecstatic, delirious, made rapturous by the glory of God.*"

But alas, someone has observed, stars come out every night and we stay inside and watch television! So while the heavens are declaring the power and majesty and creativity of God we yawn and watch a rerun of a sitcom accompanied by a fake laugh track!

It's disconcerting how we take significant things for granted just because they are routine ... the kiss of a spouse at bedtime ... the dependability of a car over years of driving ... the comradarie of a friend through decades ... the tight grasp of our hand by our child in a crowd ... and the astounding faithfulness of God

Consider:

♦ He promised to never leave us (Hebrews 13:5) ... and He hasn't - not once.
♦ He said we could count on Him to bear our burdens (Psalm 68:19)... and He has - faithfully.
♦ He said He'd accompany us through deep sorrows (Psalm 34:18)... and He's done just that.
♦ He said the waters wouldn't overflow us (Isaiah 43:2) ... and they haven't.
♦ He told us that our foundation would be his everlasting arms beneath us (Deuteronomy 33:27) ... and they've been there for us.
♦ He promised us rest in troubling times (Hebrews 4:1) ... and it's always been available.
♦ He has given us 'great and precious promises' (II Peter 1:4) to sustain us in life's storms ... and they haven't been rescinded.
♦ He said He'd take care us, drawing from his great riches (Philippians 4:19) ... and they're still available to us.
♦ He has plans for our future that are good, giving us a future and a hope (Jeremiah 29:11) ... and those plans are still in place!

Wouldn't this be a good day to reflect on the faithfulness of God in your life? And maybe start by turning off the TV and sitting outside tonight gazing at God's exquisite handiwork as it silently, yet powerfully testifies of his greatness.

He's the last One you ever want to take for granted.

August 9

New Destination

> " ... *speak unto the children of Israel, that they go forward:"* Exodus 14:15 KJV

Evangelist Mike Murdock has stated: "*You will never leave where you are until you decide where you would rather be.*" Think about it for a minute and you will see the irrefutable logic in it. So I have decided where I'd rather be and that decision brings about another irrefutable corollary: *I can't get to where I'd rather be unless I'm willing to leave where I am!*

The old song says that breaking up is hard to do and I'm here to tell you that getting ready to leave is no picnic either.

In the past weeks we have literally fingered every old letter, greeting card and post card... we have foraged through long-forgotten boxes of memorabilia...we have pondered the value of nick-knacks and mementos. Few decisions about what to take and what to leave have come easy.

But it's the price we pay to move ahead. Do you think that Abraham glibly and mindlessly threw everything he owned onto the back of the caravan animals and slipped out of town? Can you conceive of young John Mark simply throwing a couple of extra sets of underwear in a backpack before joining the Apostle Paul and friend Barnabas on their missionary journey? Think that Jesus mindlessly gathered up a few things before making his journey from glory to the manger? No. Getting ready to follow God into any new endeavor...any new dream...any obedient response... requires the traveler to count the cost and pay the price to move out.

So what destination has God chosen for you today? Is it a new relationship or one that must be renewed? Is there a new plan for an old problem that He has placed in your heart and mind? Is there a career change that you know is the right thing for you, but the transitional cost seems too overwhelming? Or is God simply calling you to move into a more personal relationship with Him at the expense of other things in your life? Any of these moves to a new destination will require a breaking free of your present circumstances.

Are you ready for the trip? If God is pointing, the trip is worth taking!

A Private Party

Picture this...four lepers huddle outside the walls of their city. It's a city under siege from an enemy army. All this attacking force need do to win is wait...until food and provision run out and the gates are thrown open in surrender. But God is at work here. The besieged people are His people and He routes the enemy troops by causing them to hear the sounds of a vast army marching against them.

The only sound heard are the cautious footsteps of the four lepers who will die if they stay where they are and will die if they re-enter the city. Their only hope is to walk into the camp of the enemy and plead for mercy and food.

They arrive to find tent after tent empty...the cocky and well-provisioned soldiers gone in an instant. At first the four eat and plunder, going from tent to tent. They cannot believe their good fortune. For a time they don't have enough hands to grasp what is now theirs... gold, silver and clothing unlike anything they have ever owned. And then, a moment of divine insight... a spiritual shunt to unclog arteries choked with selfishness...a true word from the heart of God that is still needed in our day. *"We shouldn't be doing this!"* they said. *"This is a day of good news and we're making it into a private party!" II Kings 7:9 The Message*

The Apostle Paul was quoting from Psalm 68 when he wrote: *"Out of the generosity of Christ, each of us is given his own gift. The text for this is, He climbed the high mountain, He captured the enemy and seized the booty, He handed it all out in gifts to the people." Ephesians 4:7,8 The Message*

So what are you doing with God's gifts in your life? How inclusive is the party you are throwing? Are you keeping eternal life, freedom from sin, good health, an exciting testimony and a personal relationship with the Eternal Father to yourself? Who have you invited to your party? Never in history has a generation needed your good news like today. Move your party to a bigger venue…buy a thousand colored balloons…pay for billboards throughout the city…send invitations to family, friend and even foe. The Gospel is literally a party to those with no hope, and it must not be kept private.

August 11

The Power of the Cross

A young, rebellious youth out sowing his wild oats is tragically killed in a rollover accident. His friends immediately place a cross at the place of his death.

A well-known rapper whose filthy lyrics are barely superceded by his utterly immoral life-style holds his frenzied audience in his diabolical charisma. As he strides across the stage the top of his shirt opens revealing a large gold cross hanging on a chain.

A man with no religious leanings throws his weight behind a group trying to protect a cross located at a regional park … giving both time and money to fight the godless attempt by the American Civil Liberties Union.

What makes the cross a symbol that seems to speak to the issues, desires and fears in the human heart? How could people never touched by the power of the cross of Jesus have such a primal, spiritual hunger to have it in their lives or on their person?

Or ... have they been touched by its power? Could there be lingering affects of the cross woven into the fabric of our culture? Might its effects still be felt even by an alienated culture who claim no holdings to the message of redemption that the cross made possible?

The very real possibility is that those of us whose lives have been radicalized and reoriented and rescued by Christ's death on that cross leave traces of it wherever we go. And it doesn't take much of a trace of that cross's incredible power to make a difference in the lives of those it touches. And so, spiritual hungers are ignited ... fears sense a potential end to their tyrannies ... hopelessness recognizes the fountainhead of renewed hope. For the truth is, the cross makes a difference in the lives of everyone everywhere.

The tragedy is that most people won't allow its power and potential to do more than provide them with a talisman, a lucky charm or a symbol of a friend no longer with them.

The cross speaks most powerfully about a Friend who longs to come into their lives to rescue them and never leave them.

> *"As for me, may I never boast about anything except the cross of our Lord Jesus Christ. Because of that cross, my interest in this world has been crucified, and the world's interest in me has also died." Galatians 6:14 New Living Translation*

August 12

Your Own God

> *"I am the Lord, and there is none else, there is no God beside me." Isaiah 45:5 KJV*

"I am God, the one God there is. Besides me there are no real gods." Isaiah 45:5 The Message
"I am the Lord, and I do not change." Malachi 3.6 New Living Translation

Nobody needs to remind God to be God. He has always been ... is currently ... and will be into the farthest reaches of eternity, God. He never veers the slightest from his God-ness. Nothing and no one can change Him.

You don't need to leave Him a note reminding Him to be faithful to you. He doesn't need to be nudged toward mercy or compassion. Justice and love never accidentally slip from his personality traits. These are bedrock theological certainties that millions of us have made a safe harbor for our storm tossed lives.

But sometimes theology isn't personal enough for me. The dusty tomes that line my bookcases may contain truth, but at times it's someone else's truth. God may be love, mercy or com-passion on page 379 of some book, but I need something more.

My heart's cry is that of the Psalmist in Psalm 71:3 where his request was simply "Be *to me* a protecting rock of safety." *New Living Translation* I'm glad that God is faithful, loving and pa-tient with others ... and I'm glad that He is those things to you. But I desperately need a 'personalized God' who brings who He is and what He does into my life.

Selfish? Hardly ... for a distant God is not who He claims to be. Read these words of God through his prophet Isaiah for his people. *"When you're in over your head, I'll be there with you. When you're in rough waters, you will not go down. When you're between a rock and a hard place, it won't be a dead end – Because I am God, your personal God ... I paid a huge price for you ... that's how much you mean to me! That's how much I love you!" Isaiah 43:2-4 The Message*

Now relish the relationship you have with such a personal God!

August 13
Spiritual Perception

It's sometimes called 'situational awareness.' In the business world it's a tremendous tool. To an NFL running back it's the difference between being stopped in the backfield and finding a hole for a six yard run. To a soldier on the battlefield it can be the difference between living and dying.

With or without a spiritual connotation it is a valuable asset in anyone's life.

But coupled with the living, breathing Spirit of God living in and through a believer, this sometimes-innate natural ability becomes electrifying in its potential. Spiritual perception moves a believer from someone simply strolling through life on his journey to heaven into a vital partner with God in redeeming this world.

Note: *"Now while Paul waited for them at Athens, his spirit was provoked within him when he saw that the city was given over to idols." Acts 17:16 NKJV*

Spiritual perception blows the fog away from what we are seeing and lets us see what is really going on in the spiritual dimension. Make no mistake about it … we Christians are living in two worlds at the same time. The people God can really use are those capable of seeing through the obvious to the real.

This spiritual awareness will help you find that person who at this exact moment needs your testimony or your love or your comfort. It will make you aware of where spiritual battles need to be fought and won. As in the Apostle Paul's situation above, God's Spirit moved him from the tourist mode into the evangelist mode. He saw things in his spirit that weren't on any Grey Line bus tour brochure.

God wants you to be situationally and spiritually aware of your world. Let his awareness challenge your conventional view of life. And then move obediently into service at his direction. It's going to be exciting!

"See, I am doing a new thing! Now it springs up; do you not perceive it!" Isaiah 43:19

August 14
Ungrateful

As I sat in our Monday morning prayer group, coffee cup in hand … a question crossed my mind.

We assemble weekly to pray for the requests of our congregation and to rejoice in their praise reports of answered prayers. Actually, it's the answers to prayer which provide fresh stimulus and faith to keep us faithfully praying for the requests.

As others prayed … I counted. There were 36 requests and 4 praises. Even early in the morning I can do the math. That would amount to a 1 to 9 ratio. Which produced the question that I hesitatingly raised to God.

"Um …" I began, not entirely sure how to continue. "Is this a typical ratio for You as far as prayers being answered?" I queried.

I felt more than a little awkward even hinting that God's batting average (.111) would send any major league player back to the minors for more training! And then I remembered a story from the New Testament.

It's found in Luke 17 and tells the story of Jesus healing ten men with leprosy. After their healings only one came back to give thanks. Just one. It's a ratio of 1 to 9 which you'll notice is the ratio found in that early morning prayer meeting.

Could it be that God's average is much higher, but that we, like the ungrateful cleansed lepers are not very good at 'praise reports?' I must concur with the writer of I Chronicles when he says emphatically, *"Great is the Lord! He is most worthy of praise!" I Chronicles 16:5 New Living Translation*

The next time you conclude a prayer with the words "And I'll be careful to give you the praise" ... remember to do it!

May there be joy (and much praise) in your journey!

August 15

Love Like This

I heard someone make this challenge: *Love like you've never been hurt.*

Yeah ... sure! Like that's possible.

But it sounded like something Jesus would have said. So I asked Him, "Jesus, did you make that statement? Because I've been hurt so many times. People have slandered me, ignored me, taken my intentions all wrong. If You only knew how hard it was for me to forgive them."

He smiled as He replied "No. Those aren't my exact words, but they pretty much sum up the way I lived my life. If I were to have offered 'pain-free' love, there wouldn't have been much to give. I was hurt by a lot of people as well and it culminated at the cross. The physical pain wasn't as bad as the pain of rejection by people I loved."

"But Lord," I countered, my mind buzzing with the implications of His words, "forgiving them is hard enough to do? Do I have to love them, too?"

"No" He answered. "You don't have to love ... only if you want to obey Me and be like Me. Love refined through the crucible of pain is the kind of love strong enough to heal and build. Anything less is simply an emotion with short shelf life."

He continued "'Love like you've never been hurt' is not the way I stated this valued principle. Here is how I said it: *"You're familiar with the old written law, 'Love your friend,' and its unwritten companion, 'Hate your enemy.' I'm challenging that. I'm telling you to love your enemies. Let them bring out the best in you, not the worst." Matthew 5:43,44 The Message*

May there be joy and genuine love toward others as you journey!

August 16
God In The Storm

The writer of Ecclesiastes makes it abundantly clear ... there are seasons in life.

- ◆ some are just coming on stage ... some are just exiting.
- ◆ some are putting seeds into the ground ... others are gathering the harvest
- ◆ some are crying while others are filled with happiness
- ◆ for some it's time to speak up ... others are to be quiet
- ◆ there's war for some and luxurious peace for others

If we were allowed to vote on which side of the ledger we'd rather live on, it would be an easy vote to cast and count. How about these choices: *Young, life overflowing with joy, with enough for contentment, seeds in the ground with a simultaneous harvest going on, nothing to cry about with peace internally and coming from every direction around us.*

But we don't get to choose. Oh, we can make choices that somewhat mitigate the negative and emphasize the positive. However, we live in a wicked world where our own poor choices and the poor choices of others make living difficult. We never seem to be able to eliminate the sad and difficult side of life. Nor should we ...

For God is Master at not only making something out of nothing, but of turning the terrifically terrible into mountainous mounds of blessing. What begins as a curse becomes blessing, as in Joseph's experience. What his conniving brothers instituted as a 'low blow' meant to cripple and destroy came back years later as the ultimate positive, not only in the life of their victim brother, but in their own lives as well.

So remind yourself of this. God is God when the tide is in and the ship sits majestically in the harbor with flags of victory flying from the mast. But He's also God when the ship appears to be in mortal danger and we stand wiping the salt spray from our eyes as they mingle with the salt of our own tears of sadness as we plow through storms unlike we've experienced before.

Wickedness and disaster, disillusionment and tears, crumpled dreams and shattered hope ... God can orchestrate them all to produce breath-taking music. He can play the intended instruments of wickedness like a virtuoso. Whether the tide's in or out, through either tears or shining sunlight, good times or not so good times ... let Him be God. He's very good at it!

> *"And we know that for those who love God all things work together for good, for those who are called according to his purpose." Romans 8:28 ESV*

May you hang on and find joy for your journey!

August 17
Game Of His Life

A speaker recently told of his high school football experiences. As a 125 pound running back he was clearly 'bench material.' Early in a very important league game, their renowned, cunning and powerful running back split his pants from back to front. Our 'running back wannabe' was summoned by the coach. He assumed he was going into the game.

Instead, as teammates formed a human dressing room, he traded jersey pants with the star. And in his own words that star "went on to play the game of his life … in my pants!"

I can't help but think that God is waiting to play "the game of His life" wearing my pants and my gifts and my talents and my obedience. We have heard it said that God has no hands or feet but ours and probably gloss over the incredible implications of that statement. It's not that He couldn't sidestep us and do what needs to be done on His own. He has all the equipment needed to accomplish what His great heart longs to do.

But He chooses to work through us!

As Augustine said, "Without God we cannot; without us, God will not."

On this day don't wait around until you can figure out why God made this choice. Instead, throw yourself with abandon into the game of life. Let God's power, wisdom and compassion be played out using your pants, hands, feet and heart.

Don't let your hesitancy, fear or disobedience keep God on the bench!

"The person who trusts me will not only do what I'm doing but even greater things, because I, on my way to the Father, am giving you the same work to do that I've been doing. You can count on it." John 14:12 The Message

August 18

Hope With A Long Shelf Life

"You intended to harm me, but God intended it for good to accomplish what is now being done, the saving of many lives." Genesis 50:20 NIV

In one of the most emotionally charged scenes in the entire Bible, we become the 'fly on the wall' and witness it firsthand.

Joseph, now the second in command in all Egypt, confronts his brothers with their treachery against him years before when they sold him into slavery.

The pathos and irony of this moment are not lost on us as we watch awareness dawn in the eyes of Joseph's siblings and they struggle to equate this man of immense power over their lives with the idealistic young brother they hated so many years before. The tables are now turned and justice is about to be played out.

They stand terrified in fear and confusion.

Then with emotions no longer containable, Joseph shares with them the breathtaking news that their despicable actions had teamed up with God's loving design and was actually going to bless them. Justice hasn't just been postponed, it's been swallowed in the immensity of God's loving plan.

But here's a question I have about this core belief of Joseph … that God turned potential harm into life-changing good. When did he acquire it? Did it just dawn on him at that moment in a burst of spiritual insight?

Or did he nurture it in the pit awaiting his possible execution? Did he consider it when unjustly going to prison for something he didn't do? Was his theology being formed during those long years of incarceration when any hope of the promise of leadership given him as a young boy seemed further and further from fulfillment?

When God says that the check is in the mail, and it doesn't come for weeks or months or even years … must that destroy hope? Or can hope survive depressive delay? Faith that is dismantled in the face of obstacles and disappointments is not really faith at all.

Ask God for the hope that outlasts all competitors. Ask Him for faith that sees the promise clear through to the glorious fulfillment. Ask for an increase in the size of your 'trust capacitor.'

God did get Joseph from the pit to the throne, but it was the intensity of the journey that made him fit to rule.

August 19

You're Not That Good

" He who did not spare his own Son, but gave him up for us all—how will he not also, along with him, graciously give us all things?" Romans 8:32 NIV

Sometimes we're so busy slapping ourselves on the back and 'high fiving' our peers that we forget there's somebody else who deserves the credit.

In Deuteronomy chapter eight, God is giving Israel some last minute instructions on living in their new homeland. He wants to establish a relationship principle with them. He wants them to look back and see his interaction in their lives.

"Remember the long trip from Egypt to here? I guided you. Remember the hot breath of the angry Egyptians coming after you at the Red Sea? I saved you. Remember the manna and quail in the middle of nowhere? I fed you. Remember indestructible clothes and un-blistered feet? I protected you. Every time you put your foot down I was totally integrated in your life.

"Now you're about to take up residence in the land I pre-pared for you and you're going to like the springs of pure water, fields of crops with unfathomable harvests awaiting, the most succulent fruit ... a land where everything has been given to you in mind-shattering abundance."

"But as you are enjoying, be sure to stop and praise me for what you have. Because down the other path from praise is pride. Be careful! It will be easy to assume, nestled down in your fine home and surrounded by the best life can give ... that you pulled this off by yourself."

And the beat goes on:

♦ At retirement we enjoy a comfortable income. Smart planning on our part, we say to ourselves. God reminds, "It was me."

♦ We move through life with health intact and credit it with wise living and bottles of vitamins. God reminds, "It is me."

♦ We enjoy an extended cruise with family and believe that our foresight, creativity and diligence made it all happen. God says, "It's my blessing."

Obviously we have a part to play, but without God doing his part, we'd have nothing … the mind to conceive it, the strength to bring it about. Satan loves to eat away at that truth because to do so chips away from our reliance and gratitude for the Father's love and care in our lives.

Every good and perfect gift in our lives came to us vertically, from above. (James 1:17) Look around you carefully. Carefully take note of the abundance you enjoy. And then remember … you may be good, but nobody is that good!

August 20
Seriously Underestimating God

"Don't be intimidated in any way by your enemies. This will be a sign to them that they are going to be destroyed, but that you are going to be saved, even by God himself."
Philippians 1:28 New Living Translation

They tend to seriously underestimate our God!

Wicked king Ben-Hadad (First Kings 20) represents the evil intentions of Satan against God's people. His pushy intimidation and threats are meant to frighten us out of our inheritance, rob us of God's peace and cast a serious cloud over our future.

After sending his sizable army to surround Samaria, the nation's capital, he demanded: "Give me your silver and gold and the pick of your women and children." When Israel's king agreed the demands only increased. If they'll do that, they will most likely give me even more, Ben-Hadad reasoned. "I want everything you have," he next insisted.

But this time, after consulting with his advisors and his people, Ahab, king of Israel said an emphatic "No." The threat factor increased as the voice of intimidation was ratcheted up a notch. "There won't be enough dust left of your city to give each of my men a handful," Ben-Hadad sneered.

However, he seriously underestimated God!

With God's intervention and his army soundly crushed, Ben-Hadad escaped by the skin of his teeth ... only to plot revenge. A year later he assembled his troops to draw Israel into a battle in the plains. Since their defeat had come in the mountains they assumed that the gods of Israel were 'mountain gods.' "Let's engage them on the plains" he was advised.

However, they all seriously underestimated God!

And so the story continues. Satan demands all that we have ... our finances, our homes, our kids, our peace ... all of it. He struts and pretends that he has a right to it. And if not a right, at least the power to take it from us.

However, he continues to seriously underestimate our God.

Today you need to remind yourself who you belong to, and by extension, all that you have. It's God's. Every bit of it. The Book of James tells us that every perfect gift in our lives comes from above – from a Heavenly Father who loves us. And if Satan thinks he can take that away, well ... he is seriously underestimating our God.

"But the Lord is faithful; he will strengthen you and guard you from the evil one." II Thessalonians 3:3 New Living Translation

August 21

The Waiting Room

*"Hope deferred makes the heart sick, but a dream fulfilled
is a tree of life." Romans 13:12 New Living Translation*

You arrive at your doctor's appointment 20 minutes early (just
in case they're running ahead and can get to you sooner!) … it
is now 45 minutes past the appointed time and you're hoping
that if the doctor has retired, eventually someone will come out
and let you know.

So, how well do you wait?

We do an enormous amount of it in our short lives. We wait
at red lights, for the kids to get out of school, for a gas pump to
become available, for the movie to begin, for the microwave to
finish reheating our coffee.

The calculated average is between 57 and 62 minutes per
day … we wait. But what we can't calculate is **how we wait**.
Particularly if we are waiting on God!

The microwave shows 28 seconds left. The automated voice
on the phone tells us that someone will be with us in less than
4 minutes. The calendar shows that we have 93 more days until
vacation. But God? He keeps his timetable to Himself. When
Jesus had ascended after promising a restoration of His kingdom, the disciples wanted to know when. The angel said, *"You
don't get to know the time. Timing is the Father's business." Acts 1:7 The
Message*

That's frustrating to us. We are left in the dark with only
God's promise that the 'check is in the mail' and with our faith.
Is that enough? Can we possibly get by with just a promise and
our faith? Obviously we can. It's been heaven's method since
the beginning of time. God promises … we wait and believe …
God's answer arrives. It's in the patient waiting that faith flour-
ishes and God becomes trustworthy in our experiences.

For faith isn't just waiting. It's waiting, knowing that while you wait something is happening!

God's word to his people through the prophet Habakkuk offers us these instructions for the waiting room: *"This vision is for a future time. It describes the end, and it will be fulfilled. If it seems slow in coming, wait patiently, for it will surely take place. It will not be delayed." Habakkuk 2:3 New Living Translation*

May there be joy on your journey and, when necessary, a determination to wait patiently!

August 22

Hanging With Celebrities

I have known friends who almost weekly bump into famous people. A well known politician is behind them in line at the grocery store. Or a camouflaged Hollywood personality is seated at a nearby restaurant table. If a paparazzi was snapping pictures, you'd see my friend right there.

Racking my brain I've been able to remember 'bumping into' two famous people … Marlin Perkins and Don James. (Don't remember either? That's how pathetic I am at this whole 'let-me-impress-you-with-who-I've-seen' game.)

Marline Perkins was the star in Mutual of Omaha's Wild Kingdom television show 50 years ago. We both sat inside the same airplane into Columbia, South Carolina. And Don James? He coached the University of Washington Huskies from 1975 to 1992 winning four Rose Bowl and one Orange Bowl games. He and I hung on to the same pole in a crowded bus on the way back to the Park and Ride lot.

Pretty heady stuff, right?

All right. I haven't impressed you and in truth, I'm not very impressed by those 'sightings' either. But here's one of my real goals in life … to be seen in proximity to Jesus.

I'd love for the spiritual paparazzi to see me hangin' with Him. If snapshots are being taken of me in various aspects of living, I'd love for Jesus to show up in all of them. There's Jesus and me having lunch. There we are hanging out at the park, or down at the river. "Look … there's Paul working in his yard, and isn't that Jesus there next to him?"

However, He won't show up in the viewfinder of anyone's camera … digital or otherwise. But if I let Him, His presence will not only accompany me, but will be discerned by anyone hungry and hoping to see Him.

Who you hang with can make a powerful and lasting impression!

> *"His purpose was for the nations to seek after God and perhaps feel their way toward him and find him—though he is not far from any one of us." Acts 17:27 New Living Translation*

August 23

You Have … I Have

> *"David replied to the Philistine, "You come to me with sword, spear, and javelin, but I come to you in the name of the Lord of Heaven's Armies—the God of the armies of Israel, whom you have defied." I Samuel 17:45 New Living Translation*

We constantly evaluate and compare what we have with what 'they' have. We do it in most arenas of life. The problem we face is that without divine perspective we often end up with an incorrect sum at the bottom of each list.

Young David (the man after God's heart even as a teen) did the math as he stood in front of the wildly intimidating warrior named Goliath. With a voice that could shake rocks, a sneer of contempt on his face and an armor bearer equally amused at this one-sided contest with so much in the balance, Goliath's ledger was impressive.

"Let's see," David thought as he analyzed the situation. "He's got a sword, a spear and a javelin and years of experience using each of them with decidedly deadly force. I've got the Name of the Lord of Heaven's Armies. This is hardly fair … and if he wasn't the sworn enemy I could almost feel sorry for him!"

With victory just a stone's throw away he advanced toward the giant having studied the odds with the assurance that for all practical purposes he had already won the battle.

We too evaluate our enemies:

- ♦ "You come to me with layoffs, piled up bills and a recession."
- ♦ "You come to me with a diagnosis, poor medical history and a prescription."
- ♦ "You come to me with depression, fear and some Zanax."

And on the other side of the ledger? The same thing David had … the help and might of Almighty God! This week we come to the same conclusion David reached: I'm a winner and this victory is in the bag!

August 24

Eggnog and Ben Gay

> *"So we're not giving up. How could we! Even though on the outside it often looks like things are falling apart on us, on the inside, where God is making new life, not a day goes by without his unfolding grace." II Corinthians 4:16 The Message*

My Dad was a simple man of faith. He taught me to trust God implicitly and wholeheartedly. But he relied on two things to get you through those rather minor problems that as yet didn't need divine intervention. Eggnog and Ben Gay.

He believed that most internal afflictions could be cured with a cup of homemade hot eggnog. Making it was an art that he excelled in. But with external aches and pains, he looked no further through the medicine cabinet than for a tube of Ben Gay.

If I had the misfortune of accumulating both the flu and the muscle soreness that often accompanied it, you could find me slathered in Ben Gay with a cup of eggnog beside my bed. But you'd have to say that when putting a spiritual spin on these two 'wonder drugs' … the internal would deserve the most attention.

For it's not the aches and pains in our spiritual life that can be life threatening, but the far weightier issues of the heart and soul. The Apostle Paul went on in the above passage to say that if we can see it (the external), it's basically here today and gone tomorrow. But the inside stuff … that's another matter entirely.

Separating the major from the minor is a challenge. Knowing what could kill you rather than simply annoy you is crucial. Taking care of the inner man or woman has a far greater spiritual weight than membership at the local health club.

Ask yourself what you're doing to 'beef up' the inner, eternal part of your being. For instance, you gain two totally different views of yourself by studying yourself in a mirror or studying yourself while looking into God's Word.

The part of you that will live forever is begging for attention … a little spiritual 'eggnog' if you will. Let's recognize that there are some things that Ben Gay just won't touch.

August 25

A Broken Heart

> *"Even now," declares the Lord, "return to Me with all*
> *your heart, with fasting and weeping and mourning.*
> *Rend your heart and not your garments." Joel 2:12 NIV*

It's frightening how quickly we take refuge in the external ...
finding security in the things we can see, hear, smell, taste and
feel with our fingers.

There is probably no greater sign of our humanity than our
attraction to the visible. At some level spiritually we agree that
we are not physical beings attempting to be spiritual, but in
reality spiritual beings living in physical shells.

"Return to you Lord? Institute a fast? Show our sorrow with
tears? We can do that!" we tell Him. "We'll even shred our
clothes to show you how serious we are about the whole matter."

But God wants our returning to be more than theatrics ...
to move us past the point where the saltiness of our tears is the
indication that something real has occurred.

It is a heart issue far more than it is a head issue. The head
can make decisions that the heart won't follow through on. And
it isn't even just about any old kind of heart. "It's the broken
heart that matters more," He seems to be saying.

God is always taking us beyond the seen and into the unseen. We get good at the outside stuff, hoping it will make its
way inward. His emphasis has always been change from the
inside making its way to the outside world.

It's not just our repentance that requires the right origin,
but everything we do. The work of our hands must always
proceed from the work going on in our hearts. Otherwise
is becomes just 'play acting' and does neither of us much
good.

August 26
If I Had Been There

If I had been there …

If I had been on the streets that day would there have been a palm branch in my hand and Hosannas on my lips … or would I have stayed in the shadows needing still more proof of the validity of the Messiah?

If I had been in the temple that day would I have fought alongside Jesus to maintain the integrity of worship … or would I have sided with those who made a living capitalizing on the religious fervor of others?

If I had been inside the temple courts that day would I have smiled with delight at the exuberant declaration of the young children shouting "Praise God for the Son of David!" … or would I have become agitated, anxious and jealous over the popularity of Jesus at my expense?

It's an interesting spiritual exercise to attempt to insert ourselves into the events of the last days of Jesus' life. The garden, the upper room, the public area outside the courtroom, even the foot of the blood-drenched cross … all became places of decisions for those who followed Jesus.

And many of those same 'decision places' still are with us. In our daily lives we all play out the ramifications of these critical choices. Do we speak up or hide out? Do we allow Jesus to be preeminent at our expense? Do we recognize pure praise in those around us and does it bring a smile to our faces and joy to our hearts? Do we join unabashedly in the celebration whenever and wherever Jesus arrives in our midst?

Today realize the honor it is to replay the events of the Passion Week. And although still half a year away from Easter, thank God that you can and do script your own part on a daily basis. The central issue isn't "If I had been there

..." but "I am here today and I choose to honor, love and respond to the Lordship of Jesus Christ right here and right now."

"For to me, living means living for Christ, and dying is even better." Philippians 1:21 New Living Translation

August 27

A Compelling Force

"Whatever we do, it is because Christ's love controls us ..." II Corinthians 5:14 New Living Translation "For the love of Christ controls and urges and impels us ..." II Corinthians 5:14 Amplified Bible

Why do Christians donate lavishly to people in need? Why do they build hospitals and orphanages overseas for people they will never know? Why do they go out of their way to minister to the poor ... the AIDS patient ... the disadvantaged? Why go overseas with a missions group and help dig a well in a third world village? Why get so worked up over the spiritual condition of someone that they will actually lose sleep in prayer for that person?

There is one easy answer for all those questions. Christ's love in our lives compels us to act. There is a torrent of love that comes from God through his Son that not only washes our sins away, but carries us along in its current into the lives of those who also need that love.

As the Amplified Bible puts it "... the love of Christ controls, urges and impels us" through life. The old King James Version uses the word 'constrain' to get this point across. Synonyms for this word include: coerce, force, drive, press, pressure, hustle and railroad. It's a divine irritant to a selfish lifestyle. But that only happens when you willingly move into that flow. Stand on the shore and you only get to watch it happening to and through others.

However, that Greek word is also used in other passages in the New Testament to mean: "hem in, curb or limit." And there is significance for us there as well. The powerful effusion of God's love into our lives that moves us into ministry, also will hem us in from drifting out of the white water of service and into the still, brackish water of non-involvement.

So don't fight the current. Let his love flow unimpeded into and then through your life. It's his love for you that provides the impetus; not your love for him. Your love can be fickle and inconsistent, but his love is constant and immense. Carry and deliver that love with a sense of divine destiny.

August 28
Does God Sing Bass?

I've got some questions for you.

Does God sing bass? Is He a Republican? Is He more masculine than feminine? Does He prefer the color white over brown, black, yellow or red? Does He choose hymns over choruses? If given the choice would He pick a pipe organ over a band of guitars, drums and electronic keyboard?

If it was easy for you to answer those questions, you just might be majoring on the wrong issues. The only obvious answer is the one pertaining to colors. God is color blind... He has no favorites! (Sorry skinheads, racists and purveyors of prejudice.)

The favored responses to the rest of the questions come from our individual preferences and traditions. We may be comfortable feeling that God is 'in our box' but the reality is, you can't fence Him in. He's the God of the valleys as well as the mountains. His favorite instrument is a heart of worship and adoration and the accompaniment can be anything. He leans politically in no direction but throws his entire weight behind justice, righteousness and mercy. The male species gets no special attention; instead He looks through external flesh right into the heart. He possesses both a father's heart and a mother's love.

As far as the sound of his voice (aside from Hollywood's dramatic renderings) how do you describe a voice so full of power and majesty that it breaks cedars, divides the flames of fire and shakes the wilderness? (Psalm 29) Do you think you can assign a particular timbre to that voice? Let's quit feeling smug about having God and his operating systems all figured out and begin, with awe and reverence, to view Him as the One exalted above the heavens. Beware of trying to package God into a bundle that you can carry. Instead, let your testimony be *"Take a good look at God's wonders – they'll take your breath away." Psalm 66:5 The Message*

Don't major in minors. As soon as we have fitted God with all of the components that we understand and relate to, we have stripped Him of his ability to be to us the God which we desperately need and long for.

August 29

I Want To Scream

"Friends, when life gets really difficult, don't jump to the conclusion that God isn't on the job. Instead, be glad that you are in the very thick of what Christ experienced. This is a spiritual refining process, with glory just around the corner." I Peter 4:12,13 Message

Don't assume you are too spiritual to ever feel like God isn't on the job!

We've all 'been there – done that' and more than once if truth be known. It's part of the human condition that goes right along with blaming others, making excuses, blaming ourselves and any other mindset we use to try to figure out how the wheels have all fallen off our wagons.

The Psalmist asked, " *Has the Lord rejected me forever? Will he never again be kind to me? Is his unfailing love gone forever? Have his promises permanently failed? Has God forgotten to be gracious? Has he slammed the door on his compassion?" Psalm 77:7-9 New Living Translation* King David, a man close to God's heart asked, *"My God, my God, why have you forsaken me? Why are you so far from saving me ..."* Psalm 22:1 NIV We know that these are the same words Jesus uttered in agony from the cross. Even He felt momentarily estranged from His Heavenly Father.

A close friend of mine recently made this observation of his own life during just such a 'down time': "I want to scream and He wants me silent. I want to run and He wants me to sit. I want to talk and He wants me to listen. I want to be angry and He wants me to be thankful. I want to feel sorry for myself and He wants me to think of others. I want to fight and he wants me to surrender. I want to doubt and He wants me to believe. It is a wonder I can get anything done!"

With 'glory just around the corner' wouldn't it be tragic to give in to the lie that God doesn't care ... that He is absent ... that you've somehow fallen off his radar screen? And wouldn't it be wonderful to be so sure that He is aware and involved that we take joy in our journeys knowing that it's only refining us, and not ruining us; it's only for a short time and not forever; it's meant to build me, not destroy me.

Take heart and keep moving toward the glory!

August 30

Don't Sneer At The Promises

GOD: *"For I know the plans I have for you," says the Lord. "They are plans for good and not for disaster, to give you a future and a hope." Jeremiah 29:11*

MAN: "Thanks, but I've put a lot of thought into my future. My plans have been in place since I was in high school."

GOD: *"Come to me, all you who are weary and burdened, and I will give you rest. Take my yoke upon you and learn from me, for I am gentle and humble in heart, and you will find rest for your souls." Matthew 11:28-29*

MAN: "I'm sure that's a heartfelt offer, but in my industry rest is not a commodity to be chosen. It's the tension of the battle that keeps me going. I'm sure there are some low-producers or elderly who'd appreciate that offer."

GOD: *"But if any of you lacks wisdom, let him ask of God, who gives to all liberally and without reproach; and it will be given to him." James 1:5*

MAN: "I don't wish to sound ungrateful here, but 'ancient wisdom' won't cut it in my line of work. There is so much new data coming in all the time that staying current is my only hope to stay on top of my game."

GOD: *"For He shall give His angels charge over you, To keep you in all your ways." Psalm 91:11*

MAN: "Angels, huh? Just not sure any of them could keep up with my lifestyle. And besides, everything I own is either under warranty or heavily insured … I'd say I'm already covered."

GOD: *"And this same God who takes care of me will supply all your needs from his glorious riches, which have been given to us in Christ Jesus." Philippians 4:19*

MAN: "That's awfully kind, but right now my needs are being met, but if the economy goes sour in my later years I may need some help from you. In the meantime my IRAs are doing quite well, my investments have the 'Midas Touch' on them and my financial acumen seems to be serving me quite well."

Those foolish enough to shine God's promises on would most likely respond to his offer of salvation with these words: "Thanks for the offer God, but I'm a pretty good person and hopefully the good I've done far outweighs the bad. I have this one covered, but thanks anyway!"

Receive his promises with gratitude and humility.

August 31
Read, Heed, Proceed

"The Kingdom of God is not just talking; it is living by God's power." I Corinthians 4:20 The Living Bible

I'm not at Starbucks every day, but often enough to see something that brings joy and encouragement to my heart. As I sit, ponder and pontificate via my computer, I also do a lot of watching and listening.

There is a lady working on a Bible study. By the front window are two young men vigorously working their way through a passage of Scripture together. Often there will be a larger gathering of men or women engaged in systematic study of God's Word. This is happening in coffee shops, restaurants, parks and gathering places all across our land. And it's all being done out in the open, in full sight of a watching world!

But the world isn't interested in watching us study and talk the Christian life, they're waiting for us to live it. Because talking like a Christian and not living like one actually destroys the Message. It takes the Kingdom backwards, not forward.

What really smashes through anti-Christian bias and skepticism is the life of someone living out the powerful truths of the Book we are studying. God's Word is to be studied and memorized, but then it must be lived out. The easy parts and the hard parts!

The love it talks about must be shared. The compassion spoken of must become actions that alleviate suffering and sorrow. The truth it promotes must counter the cultural lies that confuse and enslave. The Bible is not just a textbook to study, but a pattern for living.

To read and not heed and proceed is to shortchange our world. It needs to see the powerful application of obedient response to our study of God's Word. Today would be a good time to turn our 'study hall' into a traveling 'show and tell' experience that will show our world just how serious God is about performing his Word through our lives.

May you find great joy for your journey!

September 1

Graffiti

"The Sovereign Lord has given me a well-instructed tongue, to know the word that sustains the weary." Isaiah 50:4 NIV

Once, in a moment of divine inspiration (I think) I asked God to use me as a fence in the neighborhood of life and then spray paint his graffiti all over me.

Consider this: If God had us scattered all over the landscape of life…in strategic places where lots of traffic goes by…what messages might He spray paint on us? If He were the ultimate 'graffitist' with millions of us placed within sight of the masses shuffling along the pathways of living…what would He like to say to them through us?

To be sure, our lives have been message boards. But I'm not so sure that they are the messages that God would like conveyed. After all, we are to represent his heart and his story. We've all come across Christians bearing messages like:

"Do as I say, not as I do"

"Turn or burn"

"God's kinda ticked"

"Our way or the highway"

Hardly winsome and wooing expressions. On the other hand, the messages that have drawn me into closer relationship with Him are messages like:

"Come to me all who are weary" (Matthew 11:28)

"I have loved you with an everlasting love"
(Jeremiah 31:3)

"Cast all your cares on Me because I care for you"
(I Peter 5:7)

Check the reader board of your life…the one that people see whenever they see you. What messages are looping there for all to see? Are they words that draw or words that repel? Does God come out looking like someone people would like to get to know better or someone they'd best keep out of the way of?

Let God spray paint the right words on your life this day. And enjoy the journey as He does.

September 2

Trusting His Timing

"Is this the time?" Acts 1:6

Have you ever felt like God 'missed his cue?'

We struggle at times trusting God's intentions and his ability. But our confidence in Him can also be shaken when He doesn't respond when we expect Him to respond. It's amazing how quick we are to assume that the Almighty should adapt to our timetable, even though we possess but a fraction of the background information He has at his disposal.

The disciples thought that immediately after the resurrection of their Lord would be an opportune time to restore the kingdom to Israel We feel their hurt and indignation when Jesus replies, "*You don't get to know the time. Timing is the Father's business.*" *Acts 2 The Message* What a blow to our egos and our sense of control! And what a resounding blessing that God doesn't let us mess up his wonderful plans by taking control of timing issues.

We read the story of Moses and discover that *he "...was taught all the wisdom of the Egyptians, and he became mighty in both speech and action." Acts 7:22 New Living Translation* "He's ready," we inform God. "He'll never suit your purposes any better than he does right now." But we're off in our timing by 40 years. We think he's ready, but God knows he's not.

Have you been trying to get God 'on stage' in your life using your script? There is a master script that calls for God to arrive in what the Bible calls the 'fullness of time.' And that simply means that exactly where and when you need God to be there...He'll show up and He'll bring with Him just what you need.

Learn to relax in the fact that God cares...He is more than able...and his arrival will be right 'on time.' Find great comfort in that as you enjoy the journey.

September 3

Your Mission

> *(Jesus speaking) "As the Father has sent me, I am sending you."*
> *John 20:21 NIV*

Jesus didn't come all the way from heaven to earth just to attend church!

True, He did attend the Jewish equivalent of church and did so regularly. He is our example in all things. But the primary item on his divine 'to do' list was not to show us how to do church.

He came on a mission.

On one occasion that mission focused on a notorious crooked tax collector from the town of Jericho. The man's name was Zacchaeus. Jesus found this short but influential resident of Jericho beside the city's main thoroughfare, hanging onto the branches of a sycamore tree. Zacchaeus only wanted to get a look at this popular holy man. Jesus' interaction with him changed his life forever. He was profoundly and foundationally reoriented. To demonstrate his changed life he offered full restitution to all he had cheated.

And of that experience we read in Luke 19:9,10 *"Jesus responded, 'Salvation has come to this home today, for this man has shown himself to be a son of Abraham. 10 And I, the Son of Man, have come* to seek and save those like him who are lost. '" *New Living Translation*

That's the mission in a nutshell: To seek and save those, who like Zacchaeus, are lost. And just as Jesus didn't find the tax man in the synagogue on the Sabbath, you are unlikely to find today's Zacchaeus in church on Sunday. These people who need the message of God's love are what give your life meaning and direction between Sundays!

Your mission is pretty straightforward. Find someone who has lost his way spiritually and introduce him to your friend Jesus. Never forsake the fellowship that waits for you in church…but never assume that by simply attending church you have fulfilled your mission.

September 4
Got A Need?

What I need … He is!

I was told there was absolutely no hope. *"O Lord, you alone are my hope. I've trusted you, O Lord, from childhood." Psalm 71:5 New Living Translation*

It appeared to be a 'dead end.' *"Your road led through the sea, your pathway through the mighty waters – a pathway no one knew was there!" Psalm 77:19 New Living Translation*

My enemies had me in their sights! *"I wait quietly before God, for my salvation comes from him. He alone is my rock and my salvation, my fortress where I will never be shaken." Psalm 62:1,2 New Living Translation*

The bottom fell out of my life. *"The eternal God is your refuge, and his everlasting arms are under you …" Deuteronomy 33:27 New Living Translation*

I felt assaulted from all sides! *"He has hidden me in the shadow of his hand." Isaiah 49:2 New Living Translation*

I have never been this lonely. *"Don't be afraid, for I am with you. Do not be dismayed, for I am your God. I will strengthen you. I will help you. I will uphold you with my victorious right hand." Isaiah 41:10 New Living Translation*

I feel totally outnumbered and out-gunned. *"He may have a great army, but they are just men. We have the Lord our God to help us and to fight our battles for us!" II Chronicles 32:8 New Living Translation*

All my resources are gone! *"He who did not spare his own Son, but gave him up for us all – how will he not also, along with him, graciously give us all things?" Romans 8:32 NIV*

Got a need? God has a promise to meet that need.

September 5

Who Sets Your Agenda?

How do you prioritize your life? Or do you?

Does the 'tyranny of the urgent' keep you running at full speed in several directions at the same time? Do you have a filter that holds on to the critical and lets the rest sift through? How does a person get to the end of their life and say to God as Jesus did, *"I brought glory to you here on earth by completing the work you gave me to do." John 17:4 New Living Translation*

Who or what sets your agenda?

How can you be assured that what you do today has a shelf-life of value that goes beyond today? How do we press the eternal into earthly? Can we?

I've got a suggestion. Instead of going through life asking "What would Jesus do?" how about asking "What is Jesus doing … right now … around me?" As Henry Blackaby encourages in his powerful study 'Experiencing God', seek out where God is at work and then join Him there. And how do you know you've found such an opportunity? Look for the signs!

A troubled heart that appears open to spiritual light … a question that opens a door for your testimony … a disturbing event that leads you into intercessory prayer … the sudden awareness of the emptiness of a current activity … and the learned response of recognizing God's voice and where his finger is pointing. Isaiah 30:21 says, *"Your own ears will hear him. Right behind you a voice will say, "This is the way you should go, "whether to the right or to the left." New Living Translation*

Read and study Peter's response to his environment in Acts chapter three. Watch him as he follows God's script, reading God's teleprompter as it scrolled at a breathtaking speed. And then ask, "If Peter, why not me?" Make sure today that what you do has the touch of eternity in it.

September 6
Pay Attention

We must pay more careful attention, therefore, to what we have heard, so that we do not drift away. Hebrews 2:1 NIV

So here's the picture that came to mind after reading this verse. I'm in a boat drifting on the swift currents of a river. I lost my paddle upstream and am not at all sure what's around the next bend, but I do hear a growing noise that is making me very nervous.

My cries for help have alerted some campers and they rush ahead with a rope, ready to throw it to me as I drift by. The moment of truth arrives ... the rope is thrown accurately ... it lands across my lap and the future should have brightened considerably.

However, my attention is drawn to a duck skimming across the water. My inattention allows the rope to slide past me and into the water. As I disappear around the bend the future has suddenly turned very uncertain.

A bit melodramatic? Probably. But that's the way my overactive imagination works at time. There is truth, however, in that far-fetched story.

We are all recipients of enough truth to get us through life/trials/disappointments and set backs successfully. The Handbook's been thrown to us and it provides the Father's security and blueprint. But if we fall into the category of 'hearers and not doers' as described in James chapter one, we let the rope slip through our hands and not only put ourselves in danger, but short-circuit God's best intentions for our lives.

So we need to pay attention ... to the Word ... to the advice of people in our lives who love us ... to the still small voice of the Holy Spirit. There are plenty of ropes being thrown our way to keep us from what's around the bend in the river. We best not get distracted!

September 7

Just A Yellow Leaf

"I tell you the truth, unless a kernel of wheat falls to the ground and dies, it remains only a single seed. But if it dies, it produces many seeds." John 12:24 NIV

I picked up a yellow leaf today while on my prayer walk. I felt I had no choice ... it fell directly in front of me as if on assignment from God to get my attention.

So I held its stem between my fingers and began talking to it. (At least my wife talks to living plants around our house!) "Well," I began "your cycle is almost complete. Just months ago you were an emerging bud who soon turned into part of a breathtaking wall of green against the backdrop of our bright, blue Seattle summer days. And now you're about to play another role."

I feel a bit silly even now talking about my 'leaf talk' but the spiritual parallel was too obvious to not comment on ... even to a falling leaf.

This single yellow leaf is now destined to give itself as nutrient for next spring's newly forming foliage. And as such it played a part in a much larger picture. In the same way ... we are to be constantly giving ourselves away in acts of love and service to nourish those who come after us.

We are always profiting from someone else's gift. And although they don't die in the process as the leaf does, they are spending themselves ... giving away time, resources and strength. We all grow, prosper and mature because others invest themselves in our lives and futures.

Thank God for those who have gone before you and watered and fertilized your life in so many ways. And then feel good about your opportunity of investing in those who follow you through life.

September 8
Waiting For The Shoe To Fall

" I pray that God, the source of hope, will fill you completely with joy and peace because you trust in him. Then you will overflow with confident hope through the power of the Holy Spirit." Romans 15:13 New Living Translation

When our first-born came to our home, so did the prognosticators. These pseudo-clairvoyants claimed to know the future of the relationship we'd have with our son Wes.

"Oh, he's cute now, but just wait. The 'Terrible Twos' will soon be here!"

"Well, you missed the bullet on the twos, but the 'Turbulent Threes' are next."

We were forewarned about the 'Frightening Fours' and the 'Formidable Five" and on to the 'Seismic Sevens.' We could have lived waiting for the shoe to fall, but we were waiting for something far better ... God's promised blessing on our family.

Decades later we've never heard the shoe hit the floor or witnessed the devastation it was forecasted to bring. Instead, we've been chased continuously through life with goodness and mercy. (Psalm 23:6)

It's not just your kids who provide fodder for negativity, but the weather ("Expect far more killer tornadoes this year."), the economy ("Better start looking for cheap apartments because you won't be able to keep your home.") to politics ("It's no use fighting it, we're going down!").

In a time when news means 'bad news' ... when the doom and gloom prophets haunt the airwaves ... when waiting for the sun to break through is considered an exercise in futility, we need to look in another direction. We need to get our information from a different Source!

So often with downcast eyes and furrowed foreheads we fail to see God standing off to the side with a slight smile on his face and in his hands the answers to our most terrifying nightmares. We must ask ourselves if the One who promised to never leave our sides, to supply all of our needs according to his full-to-the-rafters storehouse, to guide and protect us and grant us his unmerited favor throughout our lives ... is He no longer trustworthy? Has the world turned into a puzzle He can no longer find the pieces to?

Of course not. If He is the same yesterday, today and forever, (Hebrews 13:8) then the trust that used to work will still provide security and peace of mind today. Get into his Word and pull out those promises that speak to you and sleep on those ... not the last words of the naysayers.

September 9
Why Flee?

> *"For the wicked have strung their bows, drawn their arrows tight against the bowstrings, and aimed from ambush at the people of God. 'Law and order have collapsed,' we are told. 'What can the righteous do but flee?'"* Psalm 11:2,3 *Living Bible*

This is a description of persecution gone viral.

They're not just slandering ... they're trying to destroy us! They're not just snide, but vicious. They don't just want us put down, but taken out.

Never underestimate the intentions of Satan. Scripture makes it clear that he moves about seeking anyone he can devour. And his objective puts a bulls eyes on the back of anyone who doesn't follow him. Make no mistake; this is not a friendly picnic tug-of-war where the winners and losers will all share potato salad and ribs when the contest is over. This is serious.

What is one to do who has had war declared against him? King David's advisors had looked at the looming conflict and had come up with the only option they felt he had.

Flee. Run from the threat. At least put your head in the sand so you won't see what's coming!

But they were addressing the warrior king, the one who in fighting a lion, bear and Goliath knew there was never just one option. Not as long as he had a God in heaven ... a Friend in the highest place!

"How dare you tell me, 'Flee to the mountains for safety,' when I am trusting in the Lord?" he thunders. Listen to the rest of his impassioned rebuttal: " *...the Lord is still in his holy temple; he still rules*

from heaven. He closely watches everything that happens here on earth. He puts the righteous and the wicked to the test; he hates those loving violence. He will rain down fire and brimstone on the wicked and scorch them with his burning wind. For God is good, and he loves goodness; the godly shall see his face." Psalm 11:1-7 Living Bible

Remember this ... when the enemy comes in like a flood (he will and does), God will raise up a standard against him. (Isaiah 59:19). Ultimately this is not your war. You are called to bear arms and stand your ground and fling your stone at the enemy. But it's God's battle and He will win it and we will have all of eternity to celebrate the victory.

So don't think about fleeing ... think about trusting.

September 10

Waiting With A Purpose

"I waited patiently for the Lord ..." Psalm 40:1 KJV

Waiting.

As much as we all must do it, few are very good at it. In the doctor's office there are old magazines to read. At stop lights we can watch other drivers singing along with their radios, putting on their mascara or talking on their cell phones. In the super market line we can read the tabloid headlines about the human cannonball shot into the air who never came back down or about the couple in Tulsa with the bi-lingual, two headed parrot.

But what do you do when you're waiting on God? Especially when the scenario is best described by Eugene Petersons rendering of the verse above in The Message: *"I waited and waited and waited for God."* Waiting with patience for God's answer in the middle of a culture worshiping at the altar of immediate gratification, whose mantra is: Why wait when you can have it now? ... is hard work.

How did Abraham fill his time waiting for God's promise of a son? What did David do between being anointed king and actually getting the throne? What did elderly Simeon (Luke 2) do after being told he would live to see the Messiah, and the time he actually held the baby in his arms? And how did Joseph survive years in prison, serving time for a crime he did not commit, and still keep his dream and God's promise alive in his heart?

Scripture says that Joseph was abused and hurt while incarcerated. And what was God doing during all this time? Note Psalm 105:19 *"Until the time came to fulfill his word, the Lord tested Joseph's character." New Living Translation*

So while you're waiting, your options are often limited, but oh, so important. First, keep your faith alive. Revisit the promise or instructions you've been given. Turn a deaf ear to those who say to you that it's not faith but misguided assumptions and that you're apt to go down in flames. And settle it in your soul that God is shaping something very special in your life during this interminable time of waiting.

And take heart from someone who wrote from his own experience: *"For when your faith is tested, your endurance has a chance to grow. So let it grow, for when your endurance is fully developed, you will be strong in character and ready for anything." James 1:3,4 New Living Translation*

September 11
Blackberries

"Blessed be the Lord, who daily loadeth us with benefits … " Psalm 68:19 KJV

Blackberries tell the story quite well.

In the great Northwest, you can walk up to a blackberry patch, stand in one spot and pick enough berries to last a third of a lifetime. Honest! God is incredibly liberal in His provision of this succulent fruit of the rose family. (genus *Rubus* for you intellectual types).

I have often pondered the extent to which God appears to waste his resources. When He plants a hillside in spring wildflowers He goes way overboard. When painting a sunset, He uses the color palette way too extravagantly. When He expresses love, it exceeds the depths of the ocean and clears the tallest mountain ranges. Everything He gives, He gives in abundance. He super-sizes all his gifts.

We on the other hand, often take giving to new lows. Our generosity to each other can be miniscule. Look what we do with the blackberries. God provides at least a billion trillion berries for each person on earth, and unless they're located on private property, they're free. We box them up in pint boxes of about 25 lonely berries and sell them in the supermarket for about $4.00 a box.

We've been freely forgiven … we hold on to grudges and anger until forced to let go. We live in a limitless sea of mercy … yet we withhold it from others for the most obscure reasons. If the dynamic inflow of God's goodness into our lives isn't given a larger opening to flow out to others, some of us are in danger of blowing up sometime this year.

I'd love to plant a measureless blackberry patch in the lives of people I meet. I want them to find the blackberries of love, acceptance and forgiveness from me that they haven't found in other places. Just a pint of berries is a poor representation of God's lavish love in my heart.

September 12

The Tide of Battle

> *"The very day I call for help, the tide of battle turns.*
> *My enemies flee! This one thing I know; God is for me!"*
> *Psalm 56:9 Living Bible*

The battle may not be over until the last bullet has been fired … the last soldier has given up … or until the ink dries on the document of surrender.

But the outcome has often been determined long before. Historians tell us that in every major battle in the history of the world, there was a deciding point when the outcome was assured. The tide of the battle had turned.

It may have been in an obscure location, far from the war's major players. Possibly on a remote island where a small band of men held valiantly to their position and against all odds defended it until reinforcements arrive.

In other cases it was the death of a strategic general whose passing keeps an important element from occurring, thereby sealing victory for the opposition … the turning point of the whole conflict.

There is such a moment for any child of God, and according to the Psalmist, it's the very day we decide to call out for help to our Heavenly Father. We're told that from that time until the victory is seen and fully experienced … it is a done deal!

Although not an end to the struggle … not an immediate cessation of opposition … not a white flag waving over the enemy's encampment, nonetheless the outcome is sealed.

And when we ask King David how he could know such a thing, he smiles and with confidence replies, "It's because I know that God is for me!"

It may not mark the end of the fighting, but it is the end of the discussion.

September 13

Are You Laughing?

> *"Then Abraham bowed down to the ground, but he laughed to himself in disbelief. 'How could I become a father at the age of 100?' he thought." Genesis 17:17 New Living Translation*

It's called 'spiritual posturing' and can hide serious doubts.

Abraham had received a promise from God. It was over the edge to be sure, but then God operates clearly out of the box at times. But a promise from God, no matter how patently impossible it seems on the surface, will always arrive on time and intact.

So Abraham did what religious people do … he bowed down in an outward sign of pious agreement, but inwardly he laughed in a state of 'is-this-really-gonna-happen?' Abraham's wife Sarah also heard the promise. Her response? "*…she laughed silently to herself and said, 'How could a worn-out woman like me enjoy such pleasure, especially when my master—my husband—is also so old?'" Genesis 18:12 New Living Translation*

The Lord (one of the three visitors at Abraham's home) asked, "Why did Sarah laugh at this information? Is anything too hard for the Lord?" This is the question that, if answered correctly, changes everything in our lives.

Because we face this fight over and over again … the continual conflict between what is and what can be … between what we see and what we hope for … between what we'd really like and what we think we're going to get …between cautious pessimism and a total abandonment to faith's challenge.

However, when we arrive in the book of Hebrews and walk down the long corridor of God's "Hall of Faith Fame" we find this ancient couple there. The Apostle Paul said that Abraham arrived at a place in his walk with God where he was " … *fully persuaded that God had power to do what he had promised." Romans 4:21 New Living Translation*

You may be struggling with one or more of God's promises in your life. The encouragement you need to hear is that the fulfillment of the promise isn't dependent on your perfect faith. God bears the full responsibility of performing His own Word. Your faith will grow each time you witness the faithfulness of God.

September 14
New Hope Road

It's called the King's Highway, the Narrow Way, the Pathway to Heaven and the Glory Road ... but I like to refer to it as New Hope Road.

Sometimes it winds through the desert, but then next to flowing streams of unsurpassed beauty. It winds up steep hills and then down while bordering fragrant flowers. Sometimes it leads through urban jungles, but at other times it seems almost like walking on air. There is variety of the broadest sort on this Road, but every step is anchored in hope. We know where it is going and we know that God is a constant companion throughout the journey.

Our trip through life finds us crossing many intersections ... with street names like Heartbreak Ridge Court ...Despondency Drive ... Burden Boulevard ... Fearful Valley Road and Sin Sick Street.

I met Webster this morning at the corner of New Hope Road and Dismay Way. We were physically at Starbucks, but our paths crossed at the junction of those two spiritual roads.

"When did things turn south for you?" I asked him. "Fifty years ago," was his response. "What happened then?" was my next question. "I was born," he said softly. So began his life and so it continued. Life had started hard and hadn't gotten any easier for Webster.

So we talked and prayed and drank our coffee. My prayer for him is that he'll make the turn onto New Hope Road. There is no future in the direction he's going nor in following Dismay Way any longer. Today I'm grateful to be on the right road, but I'm on the lookout for travelers who got poor directions in life and are hurrying on their way to no where.

I want to be ready, because ministry takes place at the intersections.

"But thank God! He has made us his captives and continues to lead us along in Christ's triumphal procession. Now he uses us to spread the knowledge of Christ everywhere, like a sweet perfume." II Corinthians 2:14 New Living Translation

September 15

A New Adjective

"This means that anyone who belongs to Christ has become a new person. The old life is gone; a new life has begun!" II Corinthians 5:17 New Living Translation

It's frightening how an adjective placed before our name can both label us and shackle us throughout our lives. Some grew up being called "lazy" or "good for nothing." Others received the adjectives of "slow", "rotten" or "dumb." The wrong adjective can put a lid on life for a lifetime. Many are trying to escape the implications of a bad label.

But God changes adjectives as easily as He changes lives.

Childless Abraham becomes the father of many nations.

Stammering Moses masterfully leads God's people to their inheritance.

Little David proves big enough to bring the giant down and then become Israel's king.

Uncouth John the Baptist is used as the PR man for Son of God.

Unstable Peter becomes a foundational part of God's proclamation to the whole world.

Frightened Gideon gallantly leads his army against 400 to 1 odds … and wins!

Doubting Thomas has enough faith to lead him to a martyr's death in India.

Persecutor Paul becomes the best friend the Church ever had.

The list is endless and the implications are staggering
and empowering. God is not impressed nor dismayed by any
adjective-enhanced name you may carry. Your destiny is not in
your history but in your present and future relationship with
Almighty God.

If you need one, today would be a good time for God to affect
a name change for you. What the enemy would use to label and
limit you can be replaced by a God who knows why you are here
and has a specific, captivating and astonishing plan for your life.

> *"Now you're dressed in a new wardrobe. Every item of*
> *your new way of life is custom-made by the Creator, with*
> *his label on it. All the old fashions are now obsolete."*
> *Colossians 3:10 The Message*

September 16
Diversity

> *"(God) has made many parts for our bodies and has put*
> *each part just where he wants it. What a strange thing*
> *a body would be if it had only one part! So he has made*
> *many parts, but still there is only one body." I Corinthians*
> *12:18-20 Living Bible*

We celebrate diversity yet illogically insist on uniformity. God
created diversity but shuns uniformity. He looks for unity!

How short-sighted to believe everyone should be just like us
… same outlook on life, same personality quirks, same likes and
dislikes. The Apostle Paul helps us with this unrealistic view of
life by painting some absurd pictures in our minds. If the body
were one big nose, it might be located in Kansas and able to
smell garlic growing in Central California … but so what? And
if the entire body were one large ear and could hear a pin drop
clear across town, what good would it do?

The analogy goes further. A full head of stunning hair may be more comely to look at than a kidney, but which is more important? The 'beautiful people' may assume that they're what make the world go around, but without a lot of others their world would quit turning. We need each other more than we realize.

According to the teaching of First Corinthians, there are some precautions laid out for me. I must not assume my gift is the best (gift exaltation)... or that yours is (gift envy). I am not allowed to look with suspicion, jealousy, disdain or even disinterest at the gifts of others. I am not allowed to ignore my unique gifts to try to gain yours. I must conclude that God needs every gift He created to make the whole He desires.

Let's happily put our gifts to work alongside those with differing abilities. Let's celebrate the diversity that God has placed in his Body while trying our very hardest to do it with unity and understanding. It's an honor to be a part of the Body of Christ and to play that part with skill and dedication.

September 17
Software Update

I'm typing this on my MacBook Pro (operating system version 10.7.4). The software being used is Word:Mac (version 14.2.2). While these words are finding their places on this blank document ... in the background ... the computer has found and is updating software for iPhoto, Java and several other 'outdated' programs and apps.

Most likely only God and several big wigs at Apple and Microsoft understand just how important these continual updates really are. Being a fairly low tech person (didn't discover my belly button until I was twelve!) I don't understand it fully, but have been made to realize that my world as I know it would cease to operate without them.

There's a price to be paid to keep current. Some days I get very little work done just trying to download all the updates. I am desperately afraid that without version 9.3 for iPhone suddenly pictures of my backyard would start to morph with pictures of Uncle Seymor and Aunt Frances at their anniversary party.

Without Facebook 4.1.1 operating at full capacity my friends may not hear that I had a second cookie before brushing my teeth and heading for bed. And I'm quite sure that 10.6.3 is necessary for iTunes to keep Michael W. Smith from sounding like Lady Gaga.

With any version older than 2.3.0 those conniving pigs would never pay for stealing eggs, no matter how angry the birds became!

There is, however, one critical component of my life that never requires an update. Years ago I installed God 0.0 in my life's operational system and I've never been advised that I need to upgrade anything. He boldly proclaims that He is "the First and the Last" (Isaiah 44:6). My responsibility is to just keep the plug in.

With God 0.0 comes an amazing instructional manual covering every possible operational issue imaginable. He's also very fast. For instance, a 2GHz processor can complete 2,000,000,000 processes per second, but for God 0.0 that's a walk in the park. He looks after the personal affairs and needs of over 6.8 billion people on a 24/7 basis, year in and year out.

And the greatest thing about God 0.0 is that while I never need to update Him, He is continually and lovingly updating me. He's actually 'updating me' as I type, with technology is so profound that it starts feeling like a relationship!

"The Lord protects and preserves them— they are counted among the blessed in the land— he does not give them over to the desire of their foes." Psalm 41:2 NIV

Enjoy the journey and the relationship and stay plugged in!

September 18
Where You Live

Where you live will affect how you live.

- ♦ Live in the desert and you'll live with suntan lotion, tumbleweed and sand.
- ♦ Live in the Northwest and you'll live with umbrellas, verdant flowers and rain.
- ♦ Live in the Arctic and you'll live with parkas, whiteouts and snow.
- ♦ Live in the past and you'll live with regrets, stagnation and boredom.
- ♦ Live in the fast lane and you'll live with tension, excitement and pressure.

But how about this one: *"He who dwells in the shelter of the Most High will rest in the shadow of the Almighty." Psalm 91:1 NIV* I'm not sure there is another more sought after commodity in today's world than rest ... real, satisfying, life-renewing rest. And where you live will determine if you have it or not.

The perpetually weary just need to move.

The rest spoken of here is not the lemonade and hammock variety. And the craving for it is not satisfied with a five-day trip to the tropics. (Nothing wrong with either of these, but they only scratch a surface itch.) What we really quest is the kind of soul solace that works in any environment ... at any time ... regardless of the tumult around us.

It's the rest that enabled Jesus to sleep in a storm-ravaged boat. It's the inner confidence in God's plan that allowed Daniel to make it through a long night with lions prowling his bedroom. It's the absolute certainty in God's trustworthiness that kept Job's faith strong when his entire world was collapsing around him.

After losing his four year old son in 1871, Horatio Spafford experienced the great Chicago fire which ruined him financially. Two years later his wife and four daughters travelled ahead of him to Europe while he stayed in Chicago, delayed on business. While crossing the Atlantic the ship struck another vessel and rapidly sank. His wife survived and sent him a telegraph message of two life-shattering words: "Saved alone."

But Horatio Spafford lived in a special place ... within the 'secret place of the Most High'. The remarkable inner tranquility came through as he penned these famous lyrics:

> *When peace like a river, attendeth my way, When sorrows like sea billows roll;*
> *Whatever my lot, Thou hast taught me to say, It is well, it is well, with my soul.*

Don't expect a world with no noise, no storms and no strife. Instead, move into the 'Most High Shelter'. The amenities of this gated community will offer you not only protection, but deep and satisfying peace for your soul.

September 19
There's Hope

The assassination of hope is easy to spot.

The light in the eye is extinguished. The shoulders slump. The walk becomes laborious and plodding. The future dims in the bright glare of reality. Quitting becomes the only apparent option.

Scripture says that hope deferred or delayed is enough to make the heart sick. But what happens when it dies completely? It's not a pretty sight and that sight surrounds us today. Millions upon millions who walk the various corridors of living are doing so with disintegrated hope ... hope gone for so long it can scarcely be remembered.

How can there be hope when so much is wrong. How can hope possibly survive the onslaught of crime, greed, broken promises and missed opportunities? What will we do if the day ever arrives when finally all hope is gone?

Ah, there's not a chance of that occurring. With over one half billion believers worldwide and that number growing ... that means that there are that many receptacles of hope, since God resides in each of them in power and presence. Note the Apostle Paul's words:

> *"May the God of hope fill you with all joy and peace as you trust in him, so that you may overflow with hope by the power of the Holy Spirit." Romans 15:13, NIV*

So here's the way this whole thing works. We are comforted by God so when the time comes, we can turn around and offer comfort to someone else who needs is just as we did. The same thing happens with hope. God adds massive amounts of hope, coupled with joy and peace and from that abundance, we offer hope to others.

There's no way our world will run out of hope as long as God has us here. We're called to be 'overflow-ers!' So be quick to share some of your hope with someone who may be lacking. You won't lose it by giving it away! Shared hope somehow grows in the donor.

September 20
Light In A Dark World

"You are the light of the world." Matthew 5:15 NIV

Notice ... we don't just have 'light potential', nor while hosting the Living God within us do we have the ability to turn that light on or off. There is no Off/On switch on a believer who carries God's Light of the world within them! Our only choices according to the verse that follows is to either climb a hill for maximum radiating purposes or crawl under a big bowl to hide that light.

Jesus simply says, "You are this world's light!" Now we know theologically that the light being spoken of is God Himself, who James calls "the Father of lights" ... light's Creator. But so thoroughly and completely has God moved into our lives by His Spirit, that the Ultimate Light of the World is now part of our spiritual makeup.

The word picture given by Jesus in this passage is that this cold and dark world has no light whatsoever aside from that coming from the people of God. And that's why it is so vital to live open and holy lives that let us climb hills, instead of unholy lives that seal us under bowls of sin and guilt and for all practical purposes keep the world around us in the dark night of hopelessness. Holiness and integrity showcase that light in marvelous ways.

So it's time to climb the highest hill and let the light out. It may also be time to break that bowl that has been covering the light. *"Let your light shine before men, that they may see your good deeds and praise your Father in heaven."* (Matthew 5:16 NIV)

Who knows ... you may be the light at the end of someone's very long tunnel!

September 21
Full Plates

> *"But Moses told the people, "Don't be afraid. Just stand where you are and watch the Lord rescue you. The Egyptians that you see today will never be seen again." Exodus 14:13 New Living Translation*

Packing and moving! Ah, what fun...what discoveries...what exercise...what perspectives. During the last couple of weeks a recurring theme has been vocalized by my wife. Dog tired and a bit overwhelmed...surrounded by box lids, packing tape and black marker pens, Joanie will say (with a cheerfulness I am not feeling) "Just think; we'll never have to pack this stuff again!"

Last Thursday, well into our fourteenth straight hour of driving, with the front seat permanently attached to my body and my eyes beginning to glaze over, she spoke profundity from the same source of wisdom. "Just think; these are miles we won't ever have to drive again."

And it's true. Other miles, for sure. But these miles belonging to this particular segment of our lives...never again.

It got me thinking about the stuff that moves onto and off of our plates. Life is a lot of things, but it's always a transition. If there's any movement to your life, some things are coming while others are in the process of leaving. I like to think of it as God's way of helping us keep our plates from overflowing. Like the excess in our garages and lives, moving ahead demands that some things be left behind.

And they're not all bad. Some, like the Egyptians above, would fall into the 'bad' category. And to them we say, "Good riddance!" But we often leave friends, the familiar and that which we've thoroughly enjoyed. Our wise Heavenly Father knows what we don't...that there are experiences and new friends and brand new opportunities ahead of us that would find no room in our lives if something weren't left behind.

So as you are pondering what stays and what goes, thank God for the wonderful memories of good things left behind and thank Him also for his help in releasing you from those things that have held you back and impeded his best plans for the next stage of your life. And may you find incredible joy for your journey!

September 22
Jesus or Barabbas?

"So if the Son sets you free, you are truly free."
John 8:36 New Living Translation

When I call Jesus "Lord and Master" of my life, it denotes the outcome of a battle that rages within every individual on this earth.

It's a battle that makes the Battles of Britain, Waterloo, Iwo Jima, Normandy and Viet Nam pale in comparison. It is the battle exemplified by Pilate as he placed Jesus and Barabbas before the people and asked who they chose to be set free.

On one hand is Jesus, the Way ("kind of exclusionary, aren't You?") the Truth ("what is truth and what makes You think you have the corner on it?") and the Life ("way too restrictive, Man...I want to really live!"). Beside Him on the balcony stands Barabbas, who represents the lawlessness that makes going out at night such a danger.

The crowd does what the majority of the crowd continues to do. It chooses the scoundrel over the Savior...the risky over the Sure Thing...the path of least resistance over the choice of conscience. After all, the alternative to releasing Barabbas is always having "that Man rule over us." And the thought of having the righteous rule and authority of Jesus over our lives seems to frighten us more than the downward spiral of moral and physical degradation that running from Him always brings.

But doesn't having "that Man" rule my life bring with it bags of "No-don't do that!" and a hemmed in feeling of claustrophobic restrictions and layers of guilt and shame? Just the opposite. "That Man's rule" brings the most incredible freedom money can't buy. Nobody has truly lived until they've had their less-than-adequate blue prints overlaid by those of the Master Planner. There's no thrill quite like having your puny plans take on new life and vitality when modified by heaven's agenda. And the elation at having your endless purposelessness transformed by the thunderbolts of divine direction is something that can only be explained by experiencing it.

Quit fighting against the plan and the Plan Maker that you were destined to embrace. Don't worry about losing your freedom or anything else you think is important to your future and your ultimate satisfaction with life. "That Man" is the only One who has the power to really set you free and move you into an arena big enough to allow you to be the person you were intended to be.

September 23
But It Works!

You strap yourself into a narrow seat in a confined aluminum tube and then hurtle through the air six miles above the earth at over 500 miles per hour. It's insane … but it works.

You pay monthly for a company to deliver electricity from a distant location, which enters your house, moves through wires into every room and waits for you to flip a switch to illuminate your world. It's incredulous … but it works.

You climb behind the wheel of your car and with a destination in mind, turn the key. Unseen by you, modern technology stands ready, as well as more computer power than took early astronauts into space and back. The engine comes to life and you move toward your destination. It's mind-boggling … but it works.

With your world broken into enough pieces to make a 1000 piece puzzle look like a pre-schooler's quest, you read the words *"And we know that all things work together for good to them that love God, to them who are the called according to his purpose." Romans 8:28 KJV* From this verse you determine to rest and let God work the problem to its conclusion. It appears a preposterous response … but it works.

Your sins run deep enough to drown you. You deserve only the worst. Then you read: *"But you are a God of forgiveness, gracious and merciful, slow to become angry, and rich in unfailing love." Nehemiah 9:17 New Living Translation* You decide to throw yourself on this God's mercy. It's both irrational and outrageous … but it works.

We seldom have even a fifty-fifty chance of making the right choice, because usually there are more than two choices on our test sheet to choose between. There are multitudes of possibilities, and you don't have a clue as to which one will take you where you need to go. The Scripture says this about God: *""The Lord directs the steps of the godly. He delights in every detail of their lives." Psalm 37:23 New Living Translation* Allowing Someone you have never seen with your own eyes, or ever heard with your own ears to call the shots in your life could seem unthinkable and absurd … but it works.

So take all the insane, incredulous, mind-boggling, preposterous, irrational, outrageous, unthinkable and absurd reasons why you can't really trust God and get rid of every one of them … permanently.

September 24
Fork In The Road

I believe it was Yogi Berra who once said, "When you come to the fork in the road ... take it." What made it a "Yogi-ism" is that it sounded all right until you tried to do it. The truth is, every fork in the road requires a choice.

People who can't or won't decide simply stay at the fork in the road. You can't move forward until you choose. There are so many opportunities to choose in our lives that it can become wearying. Maybe the lure of big and invasive government control in our lives is that we're sometimes willing to relinquish decision making to someone else. However, we're seldom happy with someone else making life's choices for us.

Some 'forks in the road' aren't worth losing sleep over. They simply add a couple of miles of scenery to a journey and re-connect with the main highway just up the road. But there are much more serious consequences to some choices.

Here is what a very good friend told me the other day: "I have everything to gain and nothing to lose by maintaining a simple heart of faith. I have everything to lose and nothing to gain by embracing fear, doubt and unbelief."

Go ahead and read it again several times until it settles in your spirit. Life gives us ample opportunities to jettison our faith and cave into fear, doubt and unbelief. Difficulties linger ... life does not turn out 'our way' ... the news is terrifying again ... faith appears to lie dead in the doorway. But in every situation where fear, doubt and unbelief appear to be your only road into the future ... you are standing at a fork in the road. Look carefully ... there is another route! Down the other path is the maintaining of a simple heart of faith.

It may be the road less traveled in our world of constant upheaval, but today you'll find it to be the road that leads to this promise: *"My people will live in peaceful dwelling places, in secure homes, in undisturbed places of rest." Isaiah 32:18 NIV*

Remember, it's always safe to trust God … always!

September 25
God Can't … Be We Can

A little girl was sitting on her grandpa's lap as he read her a bedtime story. From time to time she would take her eyes off the book, look up at him and then touch his wrinkled cheek. Then she would stroke her own cheek. Then his.

Finally, she asked, "Grandpa, did God make you?"

"He sure did sweetheart … a long time ago."

"Did He make me, too?" she then asked.

"Yes He did. He made you just a while ago."

Feeling their respective cheeks one more time, she said, "He's getting better at it, isn't He?"

From a four year olds perspective that was the apparent truth, but theologically we know that God isn't getting better at anything. He is, was and will forever be the epitome of perfection. There is no "New and Improved" model.

But we can be getting better! Actually that's God's goal for each of us and He diligently works in our lives to bring about positive change. II Corinthians 3:18 says, " *… as the Spirit of the Lord works within us, we become more and more like Him and reflect his glory even more." New Living Translation*

So today, celebrate God's ongoing work in your life. Look for additional ways to expedite that work through your daily disciplines of Bible reading and prayer. Find and cultivate friends who will sharpen the steel of your soul and help you reach the potential God sees for you.

There will always be plenty of room to grow but take the initiative by giving God access to every part of who you are. Ask Him specifically to allow His glory to shine through the 'growth spurts' of your spiritual life.

May there be joy (and significant growth) on your journey!

September 26
Just Let Go

"How old are you, grandma?" asked her six year old grandson. "Thirty-nine and holding," was her reply. After a moment of thoughtful silence the boy asked, "How old would you be if you let go?"

Great question!

There are spiritual parallels to the little guy's question, because all of us tend to hold on to some things that become anchors, holding us in place. We're tied to what we've become comfortable with. But the question asked above is a good one for us to ponder as we are prompted to ask additional questions ... like:

> How much spiritual growth would take place if we'd let go and let God?
>
> How much further down the road would we be if we'd let go of the past?
>
> How much more trust would occupy our hearts if we'd let go of our questions?
>
> How much more peace would we enjoy if we'd let go of our fears?
>
> How many roads would straighten out and destinations reached if we'd let go of both the steering wheel and control of the accelerator and brake pedal?
>
> How much of our spiritual maturing creeps along at snail pace because we don't have the guts and gumption to let go and give the control of our lives to God?

The prophet Isaiah made this bold declaration about the origin of his confidence when he said, *"See, God has come to save me. I will trust in him and not be afraid. The Lord God is my strength and my song: he has become my salvation." Isaiah 12:2 New Living Translation.*

This would be a good day to assess our level of trust and agree with God that our constant fidgeting with life usually messes with his plans for us and fills us with little satisfaction. The trick for all of us is to recognize the hand of God at work in our lives and let Him do what He does best ... be God!

September 27
Options

They should have known better, those close advisors to this king whose faith in God was big enough to send a small stone at a large giant.

The counselors were only doing their job. They looked around, made assessments on what they saw and then advised accordingly. And what they saw was shocking indeed:

> *"the evil bows are bent, the wicked arrows aimed to shoot under cover of darkness at every heart open to God. The bottom's dropped out of the country; good people don't have a chance" Psalm 11:2,3 The Message*

"David," they say, "You have only one option. Run, escape, get out of town, try to find somewhere where you'll be safe."

But David had long before determined that he would trust his future and his safety to Jehovah. He responds to these who have his best interests at heart, but have no assurance in his God. "Why should I flee to the mountains when I am trusting God?" he asks.

He was not down to one option as they assumed as long as God was still in control.

And what about our parallel today? Ever feel like there's an arrow behind every bush, behind every wall ... aimed directly at you? Ever feel like the dark is getting darker and the light is all but extinguished? Ever feel like every new law and judicial ruling favors wickedness and is pushing righteousness over the brink to free-fall into extinction?

If we're not careful our hearts begin to believe in the opposite direction of where belief should take us. We see no hope, we ignore what we've heard and learned about God's faithfulness. We sense his strong arm shriveling into impotency.

Our hearts implode with fear and a nighttime stealthy flight to the mountains sounds better and better. It appears to be our only option. Because if God can't turn things around, what hope is there?

But take heart. The one in you is *"greater than the one who is in the world."* *I John 4:4* The One who set limits on the sea is the One who will not allow wickedness to win. *"The God of peace will soon crush Satan under your feet."* *Romans 16:20 NIV* And again, *"The Lord brings the counsel of the nations to nothing; he frustrates the plans of the peoples. The counsel of the Lord stands forever, the plans of his heart to all generations."* *Psalm 33:10,11 English Standard Version*

Remember … without faith in a great God, fleeing becomes your only option. But with faith come options! *"Weeping may endure for a night, but JOY WILL COME IN THE MORNING!"* *Psalm 30:5 KJV*

September 28
Insignificant In Whose Eyes?

"When the angel of the Lord appeared to Gideon, he said, 'The Lord is with you, mighty warrior.'" Judges 6:12 NIV

When God declared that Gideon was a 'mighty warrior' He wasn't writing a commentary on his past. Hardly. He was not complimenting him on an extraordinary faith-filled life. He was speaking these words to someone we would call timid.

You can't fault Gideon for looking in back of him to see if the Lord was saying this to someone else! It's one of those times when God says something to us and we either reply "Huh?" or

'Ha!" There are moments when believing God takes a great deal of….well, faith.

God saw in Gideon the potential to be the savior of his people from the feared Midianites.

What indeed. When Scripture tells us that God doesn't look at us from the outside perspective, but at what's inside, it implies that He sees things that we often miss entirely. Gideon saw himself quite differently from the 'hero of Israel' role spoken over him.

"Of all tribes in Israel, " he told the angel of the Lord "ours is the least significant. And of all the clans and families in our tribe, mine is at the bottom of the pecking order. What do you see in me?"

Don't ever ask God what He sees in you if you're not ready to be swept off your feet, away from your preconceptions and toward an explosive future. As the old saying goes, God doesn't make junk. You were fashioned into a work of extraordinary potential. You have been primed and prepared for such a time as this.

Insignificant? Hardly!

September 29
Hemmed In

No one likes to feel hemmed in.

Remember that crowded elevator? Remember the department store at 4:30 p.m. on Christmas Eve? Remember the crushing walk to your car after the stadium released 43,000 of you all at once? None are good memories.

Having just moved from a beautiful home in the Northwest whose surrounding vistas were obscured by thousands of trees, bushes and plants…and having moved to the wide open spaces of the Mojave Desert where mountains 60 miles away feel close enough to touch…I have gained a new appreciation for the

Apostle Paul's words in Romans chapter five. From Eugene Peterson's The Message we read: *"We throw open our doors to God and discover at the same moment that he has already thrown open his door to us. We find ourselves standing where we always hoped we might stand – out in the wide open spaces of God's grace and glory, standing tall and shouting our praise."* Romans 5:2,3 The Message

But the 'open country' of which the Apostle speaks is not a geographical location. It has nothing to do with what's out your window. It is a place in the soul. It's the kind of openness and freedom that you carry within you. It's a peaceful place in the middle of craziness and chaos. It's the very real sense that nothing coming at you can ever get inside you to steal the peace and assurance that God's grace provides and his glory illuminates.

Today realize that the place you are standing in Him is the destination that your heart and soul have always longed for. Nothing and no one can 'hem you in' when you're roaming the 'wide open spaces' of God's incredible care and provision. Stand tall and shout praise to the One who has set us free.

And have joy for the journey.

September 30
The Pipe, Not the Pump

Have you ever done something that would have exhausted another person, yet it energized you? Or on the other hand, have you ever had a job to do that turned you into a soggy pile of absolute weariness?

In the first, you were operating in the strength of your God-endowed giftedness. In the second, you were (in the words of Max Lucado) 'living out of someone else's suitcase.' As in all of our histories, we've been there and done that. Or at least we gave it a good try.

Shepherd boy David operated in his 'sweet spot' while dealing with the rigors of the wild ... caring for the family's sheep. It was relatively easy to use the tools that God had equipped him with to accomplish rather spectacular deeds. Yet when facing Goliath and offered the king's armor, he attempted to use another man's tools to do what was in his heart to execute (pardon the play on words here); it de-energized him before he had begun.

Have you discovered not only why God made you, but how He made you? Have you experimented with various tasks until you know for sure what outfits you with strength and enthusiasm and what saps your natural resources? In response to the question "How can I know God's will for my life?" someone once said this: God's will for your life is where your great joy and the world's deep need meets!

That's a vitally important intersection for you to find. That becomes your 'sweet spot' of ministry. Begin to look for a task that accomplishes both criteria. Find a job that brings great joy to your soul and adds passion to your outlook. Then look to see if that venture is in some way impacting our world by extending God's Kingdom.

Do you know where both the motivation and joy of ministry came from for Jesus? Here is the answer: *"My nourishment comes from doing the will of God, who sent me, and from finishing his work."* *John 4:34 New Living Translation*

When you are in sync with God's plan for your life, the pressure of performance is lifted, for you are simply the pipe through which ministry flows. God is the pump.

October 1
Credit Due

Give credit where credit is due. Sounds reasonable, doesn't it? But did you know that basic human nature has a hard time with that one?

The Psalmist David said, *"You are my Master! All the good things I have are from you."* Psalm 16:2 New Living Translation Yet when we take stock of those things that surround us and attempt to trace their origins to God, we somehow end up on a detour.

♦ "I know God is good, but that quad was bought by me with last year's bonus check."
♦ "I'm enjoying a carefree retirement, but paid dearly for it over 42 hard years of work."
♦ "Our family cabin in the mountains? Got it with a second on our home."

God knew our propensity for hogging the spotlight. He also knew the danger of us assuming that we are the architects of our own successes and blessings. He warned Israel before they got into their promised land that they would find *"a land with large flourishing cities you did not build, houses filled with all kinds of good things you did not provide, wells you did not dig, and vineyards and olive groves you did not plant."*

He continued *"When you eat and are satisfied* (when you're enjoying your mountain cabin, when you're traveling on your retirement income, when life is good with paid up bills and health for everyone in your household) *...be careful that you do not forget the Lord!" Deuteronomy 6:10-12 NIV*

One of God's amazing abilities is to provide blessings in our lives without taking away our sense of worth or our dignity. And we don't have to apologize nor make up some crazy story about how we made it happen!

Resurrect the old Doxology from long ago and in song remind yourself to praise God, from whom all blessings flow!

October 2
Letting Loose

"With that, Peter, (full of the Holy Spirit) let loose ... "
Acts 4:8 The Message

Peter was torqued!

As the prominent spokesman for new found freedom in Jesus, and a whole new way of relating to God the Father, the Apostle Peter stood before the sanctimonious Sanhedrin who demanded to know who gave him permission to mess with their religious hierarchy and suffocating rules … and actually bring healing to a lame man right in front of the temple!

So Peter let loose. Read the full account for yourself to discover Peter's defense. It's quite a read.

Peter reminds me a lot of myself. I, too, often let loose. Unfortunately seldom while 'full of the Holy Spirit.' And can you believe, the results are mostly dismal and counterproductive to what God had in mind for the situation.

I believe it was George Jessel who stated, "The human brain starts working the moment you are born and never stops until you stand up to speak …" By the way, the effect he speaks of also happens when you speak sitting down.

How about a little less 'letting loose' and a lot more seeking the words and timing prompted by the Holy Spirit? The wisest man to have ever lived (Solomon) had something to say on this subject: *"Those who control their tongue will have a long life; opening your mouth can ruin everything."* Proverbs 13:3 New Living Translation

On your journey may there be joy and a bit of caution when you speak!

October 3

God's Route

On a trip I like a clearly defined route. I like my freeways to have several uncluttered lanes. I like frequent road signs with a lot of helpful information … like how far it is to my destination and what amenities are available at the next off ramp. I don't like questions or ambiguity. Don't make me guess, just give me clear and concise information.

And then there's life.

It's like traveling on a cow path under heavy cloud cover making it impossible to even determine the direction I'm heading. Throw in some low-lying fog for effect. There are no signs ... no indicators of distance traveled or distance to the destination. And speaking of destination, there's often the feeling that I don't even know what that destination is!

Hungry? Low in fuel? Need a bathroom break? There's no way of knowing if any of it is even available, let alone close.

We wonder if we are even showing up on God's radar screen.

Ah, but we are. Not only are we under Divine Direction, but on a route carefully engineered by God to get us precisely where we are to go. It's just often well-camouflaged.

Israel had the same perception problem. They were being divinely led, but on a road they couldn't see. It was only later, once they had arrived at their intended destination that they looked back with a degree of understanding. Their prayer of thanksgiving made this statement: *"Your road led through the sea, your pathway through the mighty waters – a pathway no one knew was there!" Psalm 77:19 New Living Translation*

It's easy to see how you got there after you're there! But it takes faith to acknowledge the road when you can't see it. That's what trust is all about. Take away outward signs and you're either left floundering in a sea of questions, or holding on confidently to a God who promises a safe arrival.

Stop worrying about gas stations and your next fast food rest stop and begin enjoying the adventure that faith often requires. If your confidence is authentically anchored in a faithful God, then let Him handle the trip ... the whole trip.

According to Scriptures He takes great delight in leading his flock and getting them safely to his green pastures.

October 4
Goodness and Mercy

"…surely goodness and mercy shall follow me all the days of my life…"
Psalm 23 KJV

We seldom think about being pursued through life by God's goodness and mercy. But both are dogged in their determination to catch up with us and overwhelm us. The problem is, we often outrun them both!

The fact that they're after us…even the further distinction of having been put into the 'chase mode' by God Himself, doesn't necessarily guarantee their successful intercept. The unfortunate reality is that some of us run faster than they do!

God and his marvelous gifts travel at a pre-determined pace. God hardly ever hurries. As the saying goes, He's seldom early but He's never late. We on the other hand, run our lives on 'spurts and sudden stops'. And there are more spurts than stops in most of our lives. As a result we get going faster and faster. And as we rush along, before our pulse rate gets into the 'critical' zone and our energy level plummets…take some time to stop and look behind you. See them, out there just coming over the horizon? Those are two companions worth waiting for.

God has sent good things with them. They're gifts with your name on them. He longs to be good to you in ways you can't even begin to imagine. His goodness is meant to overwhelm you with love and care. His mercy has the miraculous ability to cover over your recent mistakes, harsh words, broken promises and fractured relationships. It's designed to do those very things.

The Apostle Paul cautions us to flee from certain things, but never outrun God's incredible gifts of goodness and mercy. There's nothing in life important enough to gain at their expense. Enjoy God's goodness, mercy and joy as you journey.

October 5
Don't Yell

To anyone on a quest to be more like Jesus, any Scripture that describes him or his characteristics should grab our attention. That happened to me this morning. In Matthew 12, the author speaks about Jesus quoting from the book of Isaiah:

> *"He does not fight nor shout; He does not raise his voice!*
> *He does not crush the weak, or quench the smallest hope;"*
> *Matthew 12:18-20 Living Bible*

Eugene Peterson in The Message translation says it this way: *"…He won't yell, won't raise his voice; there'll be no commotion in the streets. He won't walk over anyone's feelings, won't push you into a corner. Before you know it, his justice will triumph; the mere sound of his name will signal hope."*

We seem to have a lot to learn about interacting with pre-Christians. We pride ourselves in being 'right' (meaning that everyone who doesn't think like us is wrong?). We wade into the battle between right and wrong, between good and evil, between His way or the highway with our chests out, fists clenched and 'setting everyone straight' as our agenda.

Oh, there is a time and place for boisterous and unyielding stands, even as Jesus dealt with the money-changers in the temple. But remember, they were part of the religious community. They were players in the system. But to those they took advantage of, there was an entirely different side of Jesus. Three chapters earlier in Matthew we're told that Jesus felt pity for the crowds that surrounded him, *"because their problems were so great and they didn't know what to do or where to go for help. They were like sheep without a shepherd." Matthew 9:36 Living Bible*

Today you may rub shoulders with, share meals with, casually converse with and possibly live with people with problems so great that they are overwhelmed. Can I be so bold as to say that they don't need the shrill, strident voice of the righteous… not the finger pointing to their failures…not even a theological treatise on right versus wrong. Those things will more than likely crush whatever fragile hope they may still have about their lives. But in quiet, confident and respectful tones, we need to introduce them to our closest friend Jesus. Because if done correctly, the *"the mere sound of his name will signal hope."*

October 6

More Than Enough

> *"Honor God with everything you own; give him the first and the best. Your barns will burst, your wine vats will brim over." Proverbs 3:9 The Message*

How incredible it would be to have and be able to offer more than people expect.

- ♦ More time from you than they were expecting.
- ♦ More patience than the circumstances would have called for.
- ♦ More energy than the tough job even required.
- ♦ More resources than what was needed.
- ♦ More spiritual insight than anyone could have imagined.
- ♦ More knowledge and background information than the situation demanded.

Having not 'just enough', but 'more than enough' is unusual today. 'Not near enough' is pretty common in the lives of most of us. The exceptional ones seem to be those who possess just enough. But oh the luxury and surprise of meeting someone who has more than is required.

There was a crippled man we find next to the Jerusalem temple gate back in the first weeks of the newly-birthed Church.

He did what every maimed and short-changed person of that period did...he begged. He apparently didn't pay Peter and John any special attention, for after all a crowd is a crowd and very seldom did a person materialize, notice him and drop something into his cup. But Peter noticed him.

"Look at us!" Peter said. And he did. As he looked up his cup automatically moved forward. His was a life of 'never enough' and maybe this kind man would raise him to the level of 'just-enough-to-get-by.' But Peter had way more than just enough. What he held title to and was about to give away would forever change the entire future of this special needs person.

Peter said, *"I don't have a nickel to my name, but what I do have,* (way more than enough!) *I give you: In the name of Jesus Christ of Nazareth, walk!"* Acts 3:6 *The Message* We could discuss the implications for the man now healed and the new direction his life is headed. But I want to concentrate on what a thrill it is to carry a surplus around in life. Go to the list at the beginning of this devotional and see if you might ask God to give you an abundance of those things that people around you are in desperate need of.

And then, as a 'more-than-enough' person, spend some time equalizing the playing field. Surprise someone today with a special gift taken right from your abundance. Savor the experience as you joy in the journey.

October 7

Kingdom Extenders

All you have made will praise you, O Lord; your saints will extol you. They will tell of the glory of your kingdom and speak of your might, so that all men may know of your mighty acts and the glorious splendor of your kingdom. Your kingdom is an everlasting kingdom, and your dominion endures through all generations. Psalm 145:10-13 NIV

God's Kingdom is often misrepresented. We assume it's heaven … or the body of believers. We recite the words "Thy Kingdom come" and assume that it's locked in the vault of the future. To be sure, God's Kingdom does have a breathtaking hereafter, but it is at the same time an 'everlasting Kingdom' so it's a current happening as well.

Want to define it simply and make the theologians crazy? (I have a hunch that they sometimes loath the uncomplicated and lucid!) I believe that God's Kingdom comes to any situation, place or person whenever God is honored as King. It's that simple.

In other words, at every point of obedience to God and his Word, there is a new outpost of the Kingdom established. Each time we respond positively to the prompting of God's Spirit in our hearts and step out in obedience, (maybe coupled with a bit of apprehension), we've extended God's Kingdom through that yielding. In any situation where the choice is between what we want and what God wants and we side with Him, his Kingdom has just come.

Today begin seeing yourself as a 'Kingdom extender' … someone who looks to set up branches of the Kingdom throughout your daily routine. The Kingdom of God has powerfully broken in on our lives, freeing us from the tyranny of selfishness and greed. It has broken the back of sin's death grip on our lives and given us a riotously optimistic view of our future. It has transported us from the old kingdom of darkness and despondency and taken us ashore in a new land of unlimited possibilities and awesome light.

Why not share the glory of that Kingdom to anyone willing to listen! And may you experience joy on your journey.

October 8

A Pile of Stones

6 We will use these stones to build a memorial. In the future your children will ask you, 'What do these stones mean?' 7 Then you can tell them, 'They remind us that the Jordan River stopped flowing when the Ark of the Lord's Covenant went across.' These stones will stand as a memorial among the people of Israel forever.'" Joshua 4:6, 7 New Living Translation

A young bride made a ham dinner for the second time. Her husband hesitatingly asked why she cut off both ends of the ham before baking it. She said she honestly didn't know, but her mother always cooked ham that way. Several months later, eating a ham dinner at his in-laws, he brought up the question again ... this time to his mother-in-law.

She had the same look in her eyes as her daughter had. She said, "I'm not sure. But it's the way my mother always did it." All eyes turned to grandma, who happened to be at this particular meal. "Mom," she asked, "why did you cut the ends off the ham?"

"I never had a pan big enough," was the simple answer.

Tradition isn't valuable just because it's old, but because it has meaning. We don't revere the old simply because it's old, but because of the lessons it has for us.

When Israel finally crossed the Jordan River and entered the Promised Land, Joshua commanded one man from each of the twelve tribes to pick up a large rock from the river bottom and carry it ashore and pile them on each other.

It was a memorial.

There would come a day when little ones too young to remember Israel's miraculous crossing would look at the pile of rocks and say, "What's that all about?" And the rocks would cease being just rocks and would convey an important story that must never be forgotten.

How about you? Do you have any traditions that have lost meaning? Got anything with meaning that lacks some kind of memorial? Don't leave piles of rocks around that tell no story and don't ever have a significant spiritual story without a pile of rocks that prompts the telling of that story.

October 9
Breakthrough

The shout is coming.

Any victory or breakthrough in our lives comes at personal cost to us. God gives the victory, but we must fight. He eventually conquers but we must persevere. The battle is ultimately the Lord's, yet we often play pivotal roles in its outcome.

Some of you, like the Israelites of old, have been circling your 'city of Jericho' for some time. Your city could be debilitating circumstances in life…a weakening relationship that means the world to you…a physical ailment that you just can't shake. To some of you the city represents financial stability that seems impossible to attain. Yet you've been doing as you've been instructed. You've been silently walking, but inwardly wondering. And outwardly trying to smile like everything is fine.

Meanwhile the people on the wall are laughing. The delay isn't bothering them one bit. It's amusing to them to watch you circle the city with your head held high in faith even as you begin to doubt on the inside. I can identify. "Been there…done that!"

But this message is one of tremendous hope. It's true that hope deferred or put off makes the heart sick, but it's equally true that our hope in God always pays huge dividends. So my word to you today?

Simple. The shout is coming! And when it does, you'll walk where God intended you to walk. You will have the answer that you've longed for. The enemy won't be snickering from the top of any wall, for the wall will be gone!

> *"Shout. For the Lord has given you the city!" Joshua 6:16 The Message*

October 10

Just A Gardener

> *"She, thinking that he was the gardener, said, "Mister, if you took him, tell me where you put him so I can care for him." John 20:15 The Message*

We often make the same mistake as Mary Magdalene at the tomb of Jesus, when in her deep sorrow...and her eyes filled with tears, she almost bumps into the risen Savior and doesn't even recognize Him.

There was nothing wrong with Mary's heart. It was devoted to Jesus. She was at that place at that time for no other purpose than to minister to her Lord. And yet she almost missed him.

Have you ever been so troubled and tormented by a circumstance of life that you mistook Jesus for just another warm body? Ever been so busy that you assumed that his hand reaching out to help or comfort you was simply the hand at the end of the arm of somebody wanting something from you? Ever been so overpowered by the noise of life around you that you failed to hear his quiet voice saying, *"Come to me, all of you who are weary and carry heavy burdens, and I will give you rest." Matthew 11:28 New Living Translation*

None of us can afford to assume that Jesus is anyone or anything but who He truly is...the Son of God who showed up in our turbulent world to set things right between the Father and our sin-prone hearts and who longs to be our closest Friend through every circumstance of life.

Many of your friends and work associates have distorted ideas of who Jesus is and why He seems to be hanging around. But by your intentional invitation of Him into every arena of your life, show them his real intentions. Don't let anyone think that He is simply the gardener!

October 11
Microwave Christians

Ever get frustrated over the speed at which God works sometimes? We, on the other hand, attempt to live each moment at warp speed. We tap our foot with impatience in front of the microwave … we continually pass up the scenic routes because they would add another twenty minutes to our trip … we pride ourselves over our ability to do three things at once. What a combination we make.

Microwave Christians and a Crock Pot God!

But while we glance over our shoulders for this God 'who won't keep up' it might be a good idea to consider some things. First, God never needs to hurry because everything in his world is pre-planned and carefully thought-through. God doesn't relate to the phrase "spur of the moment." A second thing to remember in our moments of distress over God's seeming lack of break-neck speed is that most things in life take more time than we are willing to give.

Things that would fall into perfect place under God's direction are artlessly, thoughtlessly and hastily thrown down to become piles of unrecognizable junk with little earthly value. Sometimes we've already attached our names to these piles … much to our embarrassment!

But the third reason why we should temper our impatience is that God knows precisely when the breakthrough should occur in our specific circumstances. In Psalm 18, the Psalmist was overcome with an incredibly hostile set of events. He could feel the hangman's noose around his neck. The waters of the drowning pool had reached his trembling lower lip. But in the 'fullness of time' God broke in on his desperation. The light of God's coming was far brighter because of the darkness of the trial.

The rescue is all the more awesome because we come to the realization that God had to have been at work all the time to come through at the exact, appropriate moment. Take heart and learn to trust completely.

> *"Wait patiently for the Lord. Be brave and courageous.*
> *Yes, wait patiently for the Lord."*
> *Psalm 27:14 New Living Translation*

October 12
Well Placed Trust

What do you do when your leader fails?

Many have been traumatized by this question. But to a Christian, it's a superfluous question.

We have only one Leader and He the Lord, God Almighty. He never fails. Ever.

People we look up to can let us down ... folks we depend on can prove undependable. They drop their guard, turn south morally, renege on their word or fall apart under pressure. If we transfer allegiance to them, walk lockstep in their shadow, follow their words as if divine ... we set ourselves up for a sucker punch somewhere down the line.

But our real Leader produces what's promised. He follows His intentions with all the 'carry through' required. To Him we're more important than our last donation. He'll keep His word even if He must bear the entire cost.

He's never lied ... doesn't need the approval of the masses ... means 'yes' when He says 'yes' and 'no' when He says 'no.' His integrity is matchless ... His word absolute truth. You never have to wonder what He's really thinking when He says something.

Are you getting the picture? Our trust in God is safe every time and in every circumstance.

Trusting people in our lives is good and can provide a measure of confidence and security. But ultimately everyone of us is fully capable of failing. Everyone but the One about whom the Psalmist said, *"The Lord is my strength and shield. I trust him with all my heart. He helps me, and my heart is filled with joy. I burst out in songs of thanksgiving." Psalm 28:7 New Living Translation*

May you experience joy and well placed confidence on your journey!

October 13
Kryptonite and the Human Soul

Kryptonite was a fictional radioactive ore from Superman's home planet of Krypton. When he was exposed to it he lost his super powers while mere humans suddenly became 'superhuman.' Not a good turn of events for the good citizens of Metropolis!

Is there a 'kryptonite' of the soul ... something that weakens us while strengthening our enemies? ... something that takes away our strength and gives it to another?

What turns "I can do all things through Christ which strengthens me" into "I'm powerless to deal with what life is bringing me?" How do we move from awesome potential to wasted years and opportunities? Why do great spiritual intentions dissolve into useless apathy?

Might the word 'neglect' define the spiritual kryptonite that transfers our spiritual power, potential and promise to another? When God rebuked his people in the Old Testament it was for neglecting his words to them. They abandoned the relationship ... disregarded his instructions ... were careless and inattentive to his directives.

Proverbs warns us: *"My child, listen when your father corrects you. Don't neglect your mother's instruction." Proverbs 1:8 New Living Translation* Jesus told the religious people that while being careful to adhere to the externals of religion, they had *'neglected the more important issues of justice, mercy and faith.' Matthew 23:23 NIV*

The Apostle Paul cautioned young Timothy not to neglect his spiritual calling and gifts but to *"give your complete attention to them." I Timothy 4:14 NIV* And we're all challenged to keep in fellowship with other believers and *"not neglect our meeting together, as some people do, but encourage one another, especially now that the day of his return is drawing near." Hebrews 10:25 New Living Translation*

Pay attention to the basics of your faith. Guard your heart. Listen for and to God's voice. Stay faithfully in the Word. Celebrate your spiritual heritage. Brag on the good things of God in your life. Stay open to counsel. Don't close your spirit to the Spirit of God. Be obedient and faithful to everything God has asked you to do.

And be exceedingly joyful that kryptonite is powerless against the power of the One who lives in you!

October 14

We're Different

"It happens so regularly that it's predictable. The moment I decide to do good, sin is there to trip me up. I truly delight in God's commands, but it's pretty obvious that

not all of me joins in that delight." Romans 7:21,22 The Message

It's a part of the human condition and unless you're trying to please God with your life, it's no big deal. Someone was once described as having a strong will, but a weak won't. That could be the cover letter for each of our lives, at least at certain points.

A big part of the fight the Apostle Paul said he was constantly fighting was that of his strong will. Every time he got the 'sanctified' side of his life nodding in agreement with God, the 'not-yet-but-working-toward-being-sanctified' part of him went the other direction.

What's a person to do when her strong will says a resounding "No" to the One who is to be Lord? What course of action should we take when our determination to stay clean … to take the high road … to not respond to the temptation, isn't functioning? When our 'won't' isn't working?

And don't take these questions carelessly. The ability to control the will when it sets itself against God's direction is one of the most significant jobs we have. And the ability to turn that spiritual belligerence into an ally in our stand against poor behavior and sub-par obedience is critical … because if we lose this battle we also lose our identity as followers of Jesus!

Unless we win this fight we end up just like everyone around us. Us and them look and act identically. We may occasionally spend an hour in church on a Sunday morning, but that's the only noticeable difference. We watch the same movies and TV shows, we laugh at the same jokes, we are wooed by the same materialism, we succumb to the same fears. The 'salt' has lost its flavor and the 'light' has left the building!

Today fight the good fight. Take that strong will back to the cross and remind it who is boss and why. Affirm your determination to say "No", not to the Lord, but to the very things that his death gave us victory over. It's time to rise up in obedience and bring about the distinction that Godly living calls for. Because we're not like everybody else. We're called to live a better life.

October 15

Upon Further Review

It's the final two minutes of the fourth quarter and we're down by two points. We've moved the ball down the field with skill and determination. Hope is soaring; the expectation of a 'come-from-behind win' is palpable.

It's 'gasp or go' time. On fourth and long a sideline pass to the tight end is caught at the 16 yard line. In the waning seconds, a quick time out and an easy field goal will hand us the victory.

But wait.

The line judge said our receiver's foot was out of bounds as he made the catch. Our coaches and players right in front of the play disagree … obviously. But there is enough of a question in the call, that the officials stop the game to review many different camera angles of the play.

After an interminable wait, the ref steps back onto the field, activates his mic and says, "After further review both of the receiver's feet were in bounds. First down."

♦ With mounting disappointments layered on top of each other, the verdict is rendered: life is meaningless and futile. *But after further review* comes the perspective we didn't have on the field of life. *"The ways of right-living people glow with light; the longer they live, the brighter they shine." Proverbs 4:18 The Message*

♦ Just moving through life has left you weary beyond description. There is scarcely strength to draw the next breath. The ruling on the field: the end is near. I can't make it another day. *But after further review* the ruling changes. *"He gives power to the weak and strength to the power-less." Isaiah 40:29 New Living Translation*

♦ Money isn't tight … it's non existent! The line judge's ruling? Bankruptcy and disgrace. *But after further review* things change. *"And my God will meet all your needs according to the riches of his glory in Christ Jesus." Philippians 4:19 NIV*

♦ The diagnosis is shared: nothing medical science can do can stop the disease. The ruling? This very possibly is the end for you. *But after further review* another viewpoint is presented: *"I am the Lord, the God of all the peoples of the world. Is anything too hard for me? Jeremiah 32:27 New Living Translation* *"He sent his word and healed them." Psalm 107:20 KJV*

Make sure you understand this: anytime the ruling on the field portends defeat, discouragement and dismay let the One who has a far better vantage point (He sees from eternity past to eternity future … sees what we cannot possibly see) change the conclusion you were given.

October 16

Good and Faithful

Several of us were discussing Matthew 25:21 where the Master commends his servant for his handling of his five talents … having doubled them in value.

> *"His master replied, 'Well done, good and faithful servant! You have been faithful with a few things; I will put you in charge of many things. Come and share your master's happiness!'" NIV*

Good and faithful … both are important.

It's pretty hard to celebrate someone who is faithful but unproductive. Nor do we tend to raise a flag for a person loaded with talent who doesn't' happen to show up very much. The teamwork between 'good' and 'faithful' closely parallels the passage that says that God is both 'willing' and 'able.'

Again, a God who wants to but can't, isn't all that much help in our time of need. Nor would it be helpful to be under the care of a God who can, but doesn't really care to! I am thankful that the two go hand in hand in my life.

And so it must be with 'good' and 'faithful.' The kind of life that is apt to make a difference in any circumstance is one that has a lock on both qualities. I want the work of both my hands and my heart to be beneficial to God's Kingdom and available 24/7.

We may know people who were heavily blessed with great talents and wonderful gifts of ministry, but they don't stay with the project to see it through to completion. The gifts appear wasted. God looks for this strong combination of coupling our abilities with a life of faithful commitment in using those gifts.

When my Master greets me, I want more than "Welcome servant. Come in." I want his words to reflect the fact that who He made me, and the gifts that He placed in my life … were thoroughly used consistently and joyfully.

"Well done, good and faithful servant!"

October 17
The Church

> *"For husbands, this means love your wives, just as Christ loved the church. He gave up his life for her to make her holy and clean, washed by the cleansing of God's word. He did this to present her to himself as a glorious church without a spot or wrinkle or any other blemish. Instead, she will be holy and without fault." Ephesians 5:25-27 New Living Translation*

I have always loved the Church.

My love of her first came through Godly grandparents and then passed on by my own parents. They were a vital part of her and represented her well. Then I made my personal commitment to Jesus, joined his incredible family called The Church and began to look around.

I now had brothers and sisters scattered all over the world speaking a myriad of languages. The Church that I was now a part of stretched across geo-political boundaries made its way into places it wasn't welcome. Wherever it grew it made a profound impact on the culture. Every place the Church went peoples' lives were made better. The intentions of man's enemy, Satan, were thwarted and hope came alive in the lives of even those who were not yet a part of her.

There are times I get frustrated and confused over the way we 'do church.' Some of the trappings of our institutional packaging often tend to take something away from the core values and even mission of The Church ... but The Church itself is endearing as it is eternal.

You can't have a fondness for Jesus without loving his Bride. The two are inseparable.

This week as I'm sitting in church, I'll remember that behind the local congregation with both its strengths and weaknesses, dizzying potential and occasional shortcomings, its glory and at times lack of perfection ... is the beautiful Bride of Christ. He lavishes his love and attention on her and day-by-day is bringing out her breathtaking beauty.

He loves his Bride and so do I.

October 18
The Still Small Voice

"Go out and stand before me on the mountain," the Lord told him. And as Elijah stood there, the Lord passed by, and a mighty windstorm hit the mountain. It was such a

terrible blast that the rocks were torn loose, but the Lord was
not in the wind. After the wind there was an earthquake,
but the Lord was not in the earthquake. 12 And after the
earthquake there was a fire, but the Lord was not in the fire.
And after the fire there was the sound of a gentle whisper." I
Kings 19:11-12 New Living Translation

And that's the voice of God that Elijah heard.

There's a Serbian proverb that simply states: 'Solitude is full of God.' Our problem is that solitude is hard to find in a world that so highly values wind, earthquakes and fire. And I'm afraid that we often seek after God in just such noisy and boisterous arenas.

We are becoming a culture that says, "Give me my life hot, heavy and loud. Make it so dramatic that it blocks out everything but the main stuff." The obvious difficulty with that is that God usually isn't in the main stuff. Please don't mistake noise for news...wind for direction...or a raging inferno for your life's passion.

Don't be like God's people Israel when God said to her in Isaiah 30:15 *"The Sovereign Lord, the Holy One of Israel, says, 'Only in returning to me and waiting for me will you be saved. In quietness and confidence is your strength. But you would have none of it'." New Living Translation*

Always expect that God has something of import to say to you, and then carve out a quiet corner for that dialogue to take place. May the wind cease, the earthquakes stop and the fires of living be extinguished as you listen for His still, small voice.

October 19

Working At Our Play

"The apostles returned to Jesus from their ministry tour·
and told him all they had done and what they had taught.
31 Then Jesus said, "Let's get away from the crowds for a

while and rest." There were so many people coming and going that Jesus and his apostles didn't even have time to eat. 32 They left by boat for a quieter spot." Mark 6:30 New Living Translation

With six grandchildren within hailing range (and a seventh on the way!) it's a 'no-brainer' for Paul and Joan Walterman to have passes to Disneyland. At this moment we are now in our ninth hour in the park and I'm taking a break to reflect, rest and contemplate this devotional...and doing a lot of people watching as well. Many of those I see are working very hard to have fun!

Last week a quote from Chuck Missler was given to me. "We worship our work...work at our play...and often play at our worship." Let me comment on the integrity of our playtime. Should we play? Yes. Should our times of relaxation and refreshment come regularly and often? Absolutely.

Those questions aren't the pertinent ones, however. How about these?

1. Am I searching for relaxation or entertainment? In my life, rest and relaxation leaves me satisfied...entertainment leaves me panting for more. There is a legitimate place for entertainment...for chasing the next thrill ride or 'sense-defying' experience. Just don't confuse it with relaxation. They both offer you something quite different.

2. Shouldn't relaxation be more easy to come by and cheaper than entertainment? I should be able to find a hammock...a cool path in a dark forest...a shaded rest area on the interstate...an evening walk among my neighbors and the neighborhood...all offering a recharge of my battery. And it shouldn't cost an arm and a leg. Actually, if you have to pay for it, there's a chance that it won't satisfy your craving for rest!

3. Do I have regularly scheduled times, as well as spontaneous ones when I 'get in a boat and get away to a quieter
place'? You owe it to yourself emotionally, mentally and
spiritually to periodically find an 'oasis' where the voices
of this world lose their shrillness and urgency.

Disneyland just may not count as a real 'oasis!'

October 20
Stereotypes

*"Be ready to speak up and tell anyone who asks why
you're living the way you are, and always with the utmost
courtesy." I Peter 3:15 The Message*

While working with Promise Keepers we were actively striving
toward racial reconciliation. And along that journey came face-
to-face encounters with various stereotypes that we have of each
other. A stereotype is an assumption we make based sometimes
on facts, but mostly on misconceptions and fear. (I'm sitting in
my favorite coffee shop as I write this, listening to three men
seated near me stereotyping teen drivers!)

Much to our consternation this culture stereotypes
Christians. They assume that we're boring – irrelevant – narrow
minded – homophobic – hypocritical … well, you're getting the
picture. Unfortunately, some of their assumptions can be traced
to reality and that is both tragic and too big of an issue to be
covered here.

For the Gospel to gain a hearing and our culture's respect,
we need a generation of 'stereotype busters.' Would you like to
be one? It's not rocket science to accomplish and it's actually
kind of fun. First, choose an obvious label that has been hung
around our necks. Second, ask God to give you both wisdom

and opportunity. Third, spend a day 'debunking' the attitude or action that people say belong to us.

For instance, for the accusation of 'narrow-mindedness' sow some seeds of polite listening, with a side dish of understanding. Forget your answers for a while and concentrate on the questions actually being asked. It doesn't mean that your answers are wrong or that the narrow way still isn't the only way… but it just might allow you to retain an audience and find them eventually open to the truth.

Take the label of 'hypocrite' as another theme. How do we combat this nomenclature? Easy…don't be one. Simply say what you mean and then live like you say. There's no excuse for anyone to be able to pin this stereotype on any serious believer. Walk your talk, even though it's costly. End of stereotype!

Let's take a small bite out of a gigantic problem. Will you sway everyone you meet? No. How about the majority? Again, highly unlikely. But how about one person? Is it possible to break down one or two stereotypical assumptions by your prayerful and careful actions and words? Absolutely.

And in so doing, you have just improved the quality of the soil of that person's life, so that as the Gospel presentation comes, the seed will have good ground in which to grow.

October 21
The Nick of Time

Do you ever ponder who it is who controls the 'nick of time?' Who is it that sends in the cavalry just as the circled wagon train is about to be overrun? Who anticipates the 'last gasp'… the 'letting go of the rope'…the final "I can't take this anymore?"

Why it's the same Someone who controls how far the sea is allowed to encroach the land…the One who puts the ultimate limit on wickedness...who will never allow evil to win in the end.

Though not a very deep theologian, I often ponder these issues of how far and how long and there is seldom a really good answer from my limited human perspective. I am aware of the Psalmist saying, *"My troubles turned out all for the best – they forced me to learn from your textbook." Psalm 119:71 The Message* And that knowledge encourages me at the time of victory (when our testimonies are the loudest and most exuberant) but also while in the trouble.

And that's what faith is all about...simply believing that what has been said to us by God, will actually turn out just as He declared. White knuckles? Often. Fast-beating heart? Regularly. Bewilderment over timing and the question of why sin appears to be winning at time? Almost constantly.

Yet we keep winning. Our destiny is assured. Our passage has been paid. The destination is more than worth the wait and struggles of 'now.' The One who began a good work in us will finish it, to his suiting and for our benefit. He will never leave us...ever. Looking back over his shoulder the Psalmist exulted, *"Your pathway led through the Sea...a pathway no one knew was there!" Psalm 77:19 The Living Bible* That's part of the mystery and the excitement of the journey we're on.

So keep the faith. If you've reached the end of your rope, tie a knot and hang on. The Master still controls wind and wave and still operates in that breathtaking zone called 'the fullness of time.' Just remember, it's his time...He has a perspective you couldn't gain standing on earth's highest mountain. You're the object of his affection and He promises that 'all things work together for good' in your life.

That's just who He is and what He does best! And that should give you incredible joy!

October 22

Wanting

"As Jesus and the disciples left the town of Jericho, a large crowd followed behind. Two blind men were sitting beside the road. When they heard that Jesus was coming that way, they began shouting, "Lord, Son of David, have mercy on us!" "Be quiet!" the crowd yelled at them. But they only shouted louder, "Lord, Son of David, have mercy on us!" When Jesus heard them, he stopped and called, "What do you want me to do for you?" "Lord," they said, "we want to see!" Matthew 20:29-33 New Living Translation
"Then, calling the crowd to join his disciples, he said, "If any of you wants to be my follower, you must turn from your selfish ways, take up your cross, and follow me." Mark 8:34 New Living Translation

We spend considerable time discussing the 'haves' and 'have nots.' But what about the 'wants' and 'want nots?'

Scripture says that we have not because we ask not. It would not surprise me at all to find that many times we 'ask not' because we 'want not.' On a number of occasions when Jesus met someone, He arrowed straight past the "How're you doing?" and "How's it going?" questions and asked directly, "What do you want from Me?"

Our nonchalance about our deepest longings may not be killing us, but it is robbing us. It's time to take account of what we are settling for and ferret out those heart desires that are truly meaningful. We might ask ourselves:

Am I willing to lay down something nice for something necessary?

Am I willing to give up the gaudy for the gratifying?
Would I trade in the stale for the satisfying?
Could I lay down the temporary for the transcendent?
Would I relinquish the mundane for the truly miraculous?

Are there some significant wants that if expressed and asked
for would rock my world? Bail out on the 'want not' crowd
and join those whose hunger and thirst can't be easily satisfied by anything other than what comes from the hand of God
Himself.

October 23
Self Sufficiency

*Sufficiency: enough to meet the needs of a situation or a
proposed end Merriam Webster Dictionary*

Sometimes events in life leave us feeling powerful, adequate
and prepared for anything. Not often, but sometimes.

Then time and circumstances change and our tune changes
right along with it. Suddenly we're helpless, hopeless, powerless, clueless and defenseless. At those times we're amazed that
anything worthwhile is coming from our lives. From thinking
and believing we can ... to being positive that we can't. What do
we believe?

What is the bottom line in our quest for self-affirmation and
a sense of self-sufficiency? Get ready ... this next part is hard
on our self esteem and our pride. This verse, written by a once
very proud Jew explains it pretty well: *"It is not that we think we
are qualified to do anything on our own. Our qualification comes from
God." II Corinthians 3:5 New Living Translation*

Did you notice the word 'self' three times in the last para-
graph? That's our basic problem ... a preoccupation with self.
We can sing "I Did It My Way" and sound somewhat convincing.

The only problem is that the 'it' that I did on my own typically didn't amount to much of anything.

And that's where God comes in. When we're helpless, hopeless, powerless, clueless and defenseless He says to us, "Good. Now we're ready to get something done. *My grace is sufficient for you, for my power is made perfect in weakness." II Corinthians 12:9 NIV*

So remind yourself that it's not about you … it's about Him. It's not dependent on your help, your hope, your power, your clues or your defenses. It's all dependent on Him. That may mess with your pride, but it sure takes the pressure off!

October 24
Just Stop It

> " … *they were alarmed. And he said to them, 'do not be alarmed.'" Mark 16:5,6 ESV*

We live in alarming times. Every night the newscaster begins by saying "Good evening" and then proceeds to spend the next half hour telling us why it isn't!

Our financial situation is alarming … the crime scene is alarming … our weather is becoming alarming … the number of broken relationships is alarming. We all seem to be getting better at being alarmed, frightened and anxiety-filled. And it's not a new phenomenon.

A cursory glance through Scripture tells the story: *"I was afraid …she was afraid … then Jacob was greatly afraid … the men were afraid … Moab was sore afraid … Saul was afraid … they all made us afraid … then were the men exceedingly afraid." (various passages)*

And the truth is, you'd have to be a little strange to see what we see, hear what we hear and sense what we sense without it affecting our emotional and spiritual equilibrium. That is, unless

Someone who knows more of the story than we do tells us that it's going to be just fine and that we don't need to worry.

And Someone has!

The message given to the frightened women coming to the tomb of Jesus on Resurrection morning is a message that God, through his Son, the Holy Spirit and His Word, has been giving since the earliest days of mankind. It almost seems preposterous that the antidote to worry is to stop worrying, but that's God's challenge to us today.

This might be a good time to memorize the following prescription for worry: *"Don't worry about anything; instead, pray about everything. Tell God what you need, and thank him for all he has done. Then you will experience God's peace, which exceeds anything we can understand. His peace will guard your hearts and minds as you live in Christ Jesus." Philippians 4:6,7 New Living Translation*

May there be joy (and an elimination of alarm) on your journey!

October 25

Whispered Power

Job and his friends have been deep into their interchange. Job has lost it all and his comforters/tormentors have been looking for right answers, but in all the wrong places. Job maintains his innocence, but the conclusion of the matter is still up in the air.

But one thing comes through all of their observations … God is above all. His power is absolute. His omnipotence is beyond doubt. His omniscience is unquestionable. The question that stumps is … why? At some time or another we all join in that discussion.

But this devotional isn't about what we don't know about the 'why.' It's about what we do know about the Who. Thanks to the Word of God, we can know far more about God than we can imagine. There are no shortages of powerful descriptions of his omnipotence. In the 26th chapter of Job some of God's accomplishments are listed, including 'stretching the northern sky over empty space' and 'hanging the earth on nothing.'

Think for a moment of the staggering word picture this statement gives. And get ready for what comes next ... this remarkable statement: *"These are just the beginning of all that he does, merely a whisper of his power. Who, then, can comprehend the thunder of his power?" Job 26:14 New Living Translation*

If hanging the earth on nothing takes just a whisper, I'm not sure there's anything in my life that requires His thunder!

I'll gladly let Him whisper to my inadequacies ... my shortages ... my enemies. This plays well with the Apostle Paul's exuberant declaration in Ephesians 3:20 when he said, *"Now all glory to God, who is able, through his mighty power at work within us, to accomplish infinitely more than we might ask or think." New Living Translation*

Your needs today may require infinitely more than you can imagine, but a mere whisper of his power will be more than enough!

October 26
Don't Believe Everything You See

"We now have this light shining in our hearts, but we ourselves are like fragile clay jars containing this great treasure. This makes it clear that our great power is from God, not from ourselves." II Corinthians 4:7 New Living Translation

Things are seldom as they appear.

It's what's going on inside that should be in the news ... not what is being observed on the outside.

♦ outwardly we're being pressed on every side by troubles; inwardly we're not being crushed.

- ♦ outwardly we are perplexed and confused; inwardly there's no despair.
- ♦ outwardly we're being hunted down, inwardly God is closer than our next breath.
- ♦ outwardly we get knocked down; inwardly we get back up, having taken no real damage.
- ♦ outwardly we suffer; inwardly it's the privilege we feel of getting to share in the life of our Lord, both the good times and the tough.

The body you see may get old, slow down and sometimes hurt. But inside there is more life and vitality than this world can handle. The bottom line is this: we aren't really made for this present environment ... it's not our native soil. We're made for a better place. A place where we'll not have to contend with time and its consequences over our lives.

This truth ... this perspective ... must become more and more the hope we foster. The Apostle Paul wasn't confused about this. Although his outward persona told one story, it wasn't the real script of his life. Listen to his conclusion:

> *"So we're not giving up. How could we! Even though on the outside it often looks like things are falling apart on us, on the inside, where God is making new life, not a day goes by without his unfolding grace. These hard times are small potatoes compared to the coming good times, the lavish celebration prepared for us. There's far more here than meets the eye. The things we see now are here today, gone tomorrow. But the things we can't see now will last forever." II Corinthians 4:16-18 The Message*

For the believer, things on the outside are never the real story about what is going on in the inside. These 'fragile clay pots' aren't going to be able to keep the inside in for much longer!

October 27
Do-Overs

"Thou hast turned my mourning into dancing."
Psalm 30:11 KJV

I'm a windshield guy more than a rear view mirror guy. It's important at times to look behind you, but that's not where I'm going. That's where I've been. In the same vein, I don't do a lot of soul searching over decisions made, clothes bought or miles traveled. That was then and this is now.

Having said that, I did attempt to play that little game called "If-I-Could-Go-Back-And-Have-'Do-Overs'-What-Would-I-Do-Differently?" So I mentally went way back and reviewed the major decisions of my life … and concluded there's not a whole lot I would have changed.

I'd marry the same cute eighteen year old. I'd want the same incredible sons and their sweet wives. I would change little about where full-time ministry has taken me for 48 years. I'd choose the same eight grandchildren. By and large I'd reorder my life with few changes.

Except I would have danced.

I didn't say 'dance more' … I said I would have danced.

Some who know me would say, "But we saw you dancing at a wedding reception or two." No, I was standing still, holding on to Joanie while she danced. My feet were pretty much glued to the floor.

And it's not that I'm unwilling. It's that while growing up I was instructed that dancing was wrong … by the same people who intoned that going to a movie was a sin. Christianity has fought the Pharisaical mindset for a long, long time. We were judged by the length of our skirts, hair and scowl, not by the joy and freedom of salvation in our hearts.

God's directions and instructions are plain and relatively simple. But they don't include things like:

♦ which translation of the Bible gets a God nod 'seal of approval' and which don't pass muster
♦ that Sunday School must begin at 9:45 a.m.
♦ that 1611 English must be spoken in ecclesiastical gatherings
♦ and a myriad of other addendums we've added to God's original counsel.

Every time we add our own rules or our interpretations to his rules, we add layers of heaviness that extracts a bit of life that God intended us to enjoy. Freedom in Christ is replaced by only 'duty to Christ' and while I have the privilege of following Him I wish to do it with gusto, not guilt.

I wish I would have danced.

October 28
Deception

Are you an easy mark? Is the wool pulled over your eyes to the point you think you are a sheep? Have you participated in not just one, but several snipe hunts? Is your gullibility the talk of every prankster who knows you?

The serious side to these questions is that there's not much distance between being fooled by a jokester and being taken by a dangerous con man. The difference between safe and dangerous, between good and bad, between right and wrong seems to get more and more blurred in today's world.

When Israel entered Canaan and began eliminating enemies, the Gibeonites hoodwinked them. Although the people of Gibeon lived close enough to feel the ground shake when Israel's army marched, they set up an elaborate deception. They came to Joshua and his leaders with worn out dusty clothing … with moldy bread and brittle, cracked wineskins. They claimed they had come from a far distant land and sought a peace treaty with Israel.

They were met with some hesitancy and suspicion, as they should have been. They lied convincingly and consistently while pointing to the wineskins, clothes and hard bread. And here is today's verse to remind us of a vital truth: *"The men of Israel looked them over and accepted the evidence. But they didn't ask God about it." Joshua 9:14 The Message*

This world is full of con men and damning deceptions devised to separate you from truth, health, peace of mind and your future. Through inventive advertising and by the constant bombardment of their 'evidence', our only hope is to inquire of the Lord.

Don't be taken by lies and false reports. The truth is as close as the One who claims to 'be Truth.' Scripture says that if you know the truth, it will make you free. And it will keep you that way, too.

October 29

The Question

God had just snatched an unparalleled victory from the grip of almost certain defeat. With their hearts still pounding after a harrowing flight on dry sand between mountainous walls of water, the Israelites turned in time to see the entire Egyptian army drowned as the waters collapsed back into the seabed.

Once unbelieving eyes and terrified hearts had partially processed what they had seen and what it now meant to their freedom, a wonderful song was sung … led by Moses himself. You can find this unusual temporary 'national anthem' in Exodus fifteen.

After singing about their God's awesome might and recounting in stunning detail the entire Red Sea saga, there is a question posed: *"Who among the gods is like you, O Lord? Who is like you – majestic in holiness, awesome in glory, working wonders?" Exodus 15:11 NIV* The answer by implication is simple. There is no God like the One who just delivered them

Israel had lived in a multi-god culture for over 400 years.

I've been living in a multi-god culture for several decades. It must be my question, too.

The 'god of materialism' lives close to me. The 'god of greed' is his next door neighbor. The 'god of pride,' the 'god of anarchy,' the 'god of rebellion,' the 'god of dishonesty' ... they and many more are part of my world and each wants my worship and allegiance. And so every day in my personal devotional life I stand or kneel before my God and ask the question: "Who among the gods is like you, O Lord?"

The answer is always the same. After comparisons are made, memories of stunning deliverances are recalled, the claims and fulfilled promises of each is analyzed, the answer never changes. There is no one like You, O Lord ... no one.

> *"Then I heard the sound of massed choirs, the sound of a mighty cataract, the sound of strong thunder: Hallelujah! The Master reigns, our God, the Sovereign-Strong! Let us celebrate, let us rejoice, let us give him the glory!" Revelation 19:6,7 The Message*

October 30
God's Fences

No one likes to feel hemmed in.

God doesn't want anyone or anything bullying us...badgering us...cornering us...putting lids on our lives. He doesn't want us hemmed in, except...by Himself!

There are some wonderful ways in which our loving Heavenly Father wishes to 'wrap us up in Himself.' Note Psalm 5:12 *"For you bless the godly, O Lord, surrounding them with your shield of love."* New Living Translation And in Psalm 30:11 we read, *"You have turned my mourning into joyful dancing. You have taken away my clothes of mourning and clothed me with joy."* New Living Translation

Two chapters later in Psalm 32:7 the Psalmist boldly declares, *"For you are my hiding place; you protect me from trouble. You surround me with songs of victory."* New Living Translation In Psalm 103:4 we read, *"He ransoms me from death and surrounds me with love and tender mercies."* New Living Translation Now add God's assurances in Deuteronomy 33:27 that *"underneath are the everlasting arms"* NIV and you begin to get the picture that God has placed some incredible fences around us.

There are instructions that God has made very clear regarding the living of life. We often wrongly assume them to be restrictive and burdensome. Like a rebellious teen who takes the advice of parents who love him and desire to protect him, and considers those instructions and rules to be unfair and stifling.

When we take God's loving concern as intrusive and abusive, it overlooks the fact that we have his words because of his love. They are signs of his tender mercies. Jump God's fences and consequences await that He desperately wants us to escape.

Thank God that previously hemmed you in and tied you up and addict you and enslave you have been taken away. In its place are the encouraging fences of God's love and tender mercies. May they produce in you a feeling of wonderful security and through them may you sense God's strong and loving arms around you.

That should add joy to your journey!

October 31

Living In God's House

"How happy are those who can live in your house, always singing your praises." Psalm 84:4 New Living Translation

This fascinating verse falls in the middle of an exuberant yearning for God's House and what takes place there. Yet the implementation of such a goal would present us with insurmountable problems.

For us all to live in God's House would require an enormous building program with accompanying financial pleas. Secondly, a non-stop worship service would wear out our Ministers of Music as fast as we could hire them.

No…what David longs for is most assuredly difficult if not impossible to attain. Or is it? Is it conceivable that what means the most to us about attending God's House could be enjoyed even after the lights have been turned off and the front doors locked? Might the fellowship, the heart-felt singing, the thrill of the entry of God's Word into our hearts and lives, the closeness of God's very presence…might they all be a part of our 'non church-time' lives?

The answer must be a very obvious "Yes" simply because God cannot be confined to any particular building or period of time. He inhabits eternity, so He must inhabit (or at least be available) all 168 hours of my week. So while you are committed to weekly fellowship with a corporate body of believers, never assume that that's the only place and time that God will show up.

Always be on the lookout for fellowship Monday through Saturday. Find an excuse to spend some time with another member of God's great and growing family. Make room in your schedule and heart for a personal exploration of God's Word.

Let the song of God's Spirit find release from your heart, even if you don't vocalize it so others will hear.

Remember, a church service makes it easy to be with other believers and to sense the reality of God's presence, but the church service shouldn't be the only chance that God has to meet powerfully with his people.

November 1

The Unfriendly Skies

It was a beautiful fall day...October 18th to be exact...and I was making the short flight across Lake Michigan from Chicago's O'Hare airport to Detroit. Blue skies and little puffy white clouds completely disguised the treacherous winds that were waiting for us.

Seated in an aisle seat about two thirds of the way back in a DC10 aircraft (which I have never liked) I was ready for the lemonade the flight attendant said they would bring around as soon as they were allowed to leave their seats. Suddenly the bottom seemed to drop out of the sky. Without warning we dropped several hundred feet and then roller-coastered back up past our original altitude. At that point in my life I had flown the equivalent of 37 times around the earth...been in a wide variety of aviation experiences, some good and some very bad. But I had never been exposed to what we 'drove through' during the following twenty minutes.

That giant plane did things that I never dreamed it could. We not only bucked up and down, but would be blasted from side to side during the elevator movements. And then the winds would literally corkscrew the plane when you could feel the plane twisting down its entire length. The lady next to me gripped my arm in a death-like hold and frantically asked me if we were going to die. I felt like a liar when I said, "No, this plane has been built to take this."

Obviously we came out the other end of those wicked winds and hellish frontal system, and I'm not sure if the aircraft came through it in better shape than those of us confined to its long aluminum shell. But what kept us safe during that episode was the fact that the "Fasten Seat Belt" sign had been on when the chaos began. So all the important stuff on that flight (like us) had been secured. Loose passengers during that ride would have fared rather poorly, if they had survived at all.

And just what is it that serves as our spiritual 'seat belt'? How is it possible to fly in and out of deadly storms and come through with no spiritual injury? Listen to what the Psalmist says. "*Say this: 'God, you're my refuge. I trust in you and I'm safe!' That's right – he rescues you from hidden traps, shields you from deadly hazards. His huge outstretched arms protect you – under them you're perfectly safe; his arms fend off all harm.*" Psalm 91:2-4 *The Message* "*On the day when I was weakest, they attacked. But the Lord held me steady. He led me to a place of safety; for he delights in me.*" Psalm 18:18,19 *The Message*

Today I'm going to fly with my seat belt firmly tightened. This powerful relationship with my Protector (who also is my closest Friend) will keep me safe and secure in spite of any weather that comes my way.

November 2
Satisfaction

"Why spend money on what is not bread, and your labor on what does not satisfy?" Isaiah 55:2 NIV

As a teen from a pastor's home, my secular music tastes ran more to Pat Boone and the Everley Brothers ...definitely not the Stones. So much of the music in the early sixties was centered around anger, disenchantment and anarchy. But behind the strutting and screaming and rebellious gestures were signs that all was not well in the souls of the singers and their audiences.

That 'lostness' doesn't come through any more clearly than in the Rolling Stone's "Satisfaction." Nineteen times in that driving, bass-powered song Mick Jaggers testifies that he 'can't get no satisfaction.' The English was lousy, but the message was clear.

In those free-love, mind-altering drug days the same search was going on as goes on today. Men, women, teens and even our kids are looking and desperately hoping to find something that satisfies. An obituary list from performers at the first Woodstock festival reminds us that many go into eternity having never found that for which they searched for.

How satisfied are you? Where do you find satisfaction?

David the Psalmist said of God, *"When you open your hand, you satisfy the hunger and thirst of every living thing." Psalm 145:16 New Living Translation* God's invitation to his people through the prophet Isaiah still stands. *"Is anyone thirsty? Come and drink – even if you have no money! Come, take your choice of wine or milk – it's all free! Why spend your money on food that does not give you strength? Why pay for food that does you no good? Listen, and I will tell you where to get food that is good for the soul!" Isaiah 55:1-2 New Living Translation*

It's pretty hard singing "Can't get no satisfaction" when seated at the Lord's table, enjoying the benefits of being part of his family and finding your soul at peace with his personal companionship!

November 3
Small Groups

It's been a typical week. It began with church on Sunday morning, a bit of fellowship with friends in the afternoon, then spending time in a small prayer group in the evening.

Monday morning found me in another prayer group of eight to twelve people followed by a one-on-one discipling time with another man. As a pastor I spent a good portion of Tuesday morning with eight staff members, then with nine leadership team members that night.

Then last night we hosted a small Bible study in our home. There were thirteen fellow-learners seated around our family room with Bibles and hearts open to God's Word. So it is becoming clear to me that the majority of growing and moving and 'digging in spiritually' and coming to grips with eternal matters … is going on, not with the Sunday morning crowd, but with just one to a handful of people at a time.

It's Thursday morning and I'm at my favorite coffee enclave and the evidence of the 'small group thing' is all around me. I can see two small meeting rooms where men are together studying God's Word and praying with each other. Next to me is a table of three who are going through a study together as they grow in God's knowledge and grace. And right across from me are two men in earnest discussion about spiritual matters.

I once read that God's Kingdom does not grow 'city by city,' or 'church by church' or 'meeting by meeting,' but 'person by person'. And I believe that. I don't minimize what happens when we gather in large groups. (What pastor ever would?) But I believe we put way too much expectation on those events and too little value in what happens when we grow through smaller units.

If you don't already, why not add to what happens Sundays by purposefully seeking out a small group of people with whom you can share spiritual life. Don't be a Lone Ranger, and don't get lost in the crowd either!

"How wonderful, how beautiful, when brothers and sisters get along! It's like costly anointing oil flowing down head and beard, Flowing down Aaron's beard, flowing down the collar of his priestly robes. It's like the dew on Mount Hermon flowing down the slopes of Zion. Yes, that's where God commands the blessing, ordains eternal life." Psalm 133:1-3 The Message

November 4
Be Reasonable

> *"Come now, let's settle this," says the Lord. ("Let us reason together ... " KJV) "Though your sins are like scarlet, I will make them as white as snow. Though they are red like crimson, I will make them as white as wool. 19 If you will only obey me, you will have plenty to eat. 20 But if you turn away and refuse to listen, you will be devoured by the sword of your enemies. I, the Lord, have spoken!" Isaiah 1:18-20 New Living Translation*

We can be so unreasonable!

We all have it in us to defy authority and push as hard as we can against the rules. But since God made the rules that give life meaning and direction, we'd best listen to Him and follow the rules.

God gathers us for the game of life and says, "Here's is the way the game is to be played. Here are the boundaries and here are the rules."

We respond, "But in our neighborhood the boundaries are a lot farther out. And we get unlimited strikes. And if we don't feel like playing we sit out and if we're having a really good time we never have to take a break. And we play that you can do anything you want to win."

And God responds, "Oh, really?"

Most of us have laid the two 'life-living-methods' side by side and compared them. We know from our own experiences and from the real life examples of others around us that playing by our own rules ultimately results in disastrous living and a really lousy time.

However, those obeying the Rule Giver get to eat of the fat of the land with plenty to eat ... and that sure beats being devoured by the sword of the enemy!

Let's be reasonable. Play by God's rules.

November 5

Drifting

> *"We must pay more careful attention, therefore, to what we have heard, so that we do not drift away." Hebrews 2:1 NIV*

> 'Drift' = to move in a slow, smooth, gentle and unforced way, usually without any direction or purpose

Drifting doesn't sound at all dangerous.

Yet it's the very presumption of safety that infuses it with so much peril.

It's not purposefully setting off in a wrong direction. It's not willfully moving into a hazardous situation. There is not a deliberate determination to strike off from the safe and plunge into the irrational and unexplored.

All it takes is a lack of attention. A lapse in judgment. A neglect to stay diligent. Drifting places a person on "a way that seems right" but can end in disaster. (Proverbs 14:12)

A Maryland highway engineer back in the early 1920s discovered that more accidents occurred on straight stretches of highway than on the curves. That's because we pay more attention in a curve. It's on the straight stretches that we tend to drift.

Pay attention to little signs of drifting in your life. Is your personal time with God diminished? Are you spending less time with spouse and family? Is God's Word fighting a losing battle with the entertainment in your life? Has it been awhile since you fellowshipped with other believers?

There is a way that only seems right, but there is a way that is right. Don't drift … aim!

*"Do you not know that in a race all the runners run,
but only one gets the prize? Run in such a way as to get
the prize … Therefore I do not run like a man running
aimlessly;" I Corinthians 9:24, 26 NIV*

November 6
Faith's Flourishing Finish

They both laughed at God's promise.

It was a promise easy to laugh off for both of them… fathering a child at 99 years of age and giving birth to a child in your ninth decade! But God said it would happen and now they had to respond to His promise.

We watch as Abraham falls to the ground and laughs. And later as his wife Sarah manages to stifle her laugh, but laughs nevertheless. Not just a giggling, embarrassed laughter; the Hebrew word for what they did is also translated as 'mocked.'

So much for great faith!

But this isn't a devotional about faith or doubt or laughing in God's face. It's about recovery; about starting poorly and ending with a flourish. It's about doing a 180 in attitude or direction; about getting it right while there's still a chance.

For the story of Abraham and Sarah and the preposterous promise they were given doesn't end with the birth of Isaac, even though his birth confirmed God's integrity. Their rather rocky start in Genesis comes to a startling conclusion in the book of Hebrews. As we walk along the Wall of Faith … we take note of God's commendation to those who possessed unusual and exemplary faith.

We stare in astonishment at two plaques on that wall. There, under the picture of a rather ancient looking woman with a knowing smile on her face are these words: *"It was by faith that even Sarah was able to have a child, though she was barren and was too old. She believed that God would keep his promise." Hebrews 11:11 New Living Translation*

And next to her the picture of her husband ... this man whose faith took him from the familiar into the unknown, from the land of his birth to a land only promised and imagined. About his life the caption reads: *"And so a whole nation came from this one man who was as good as dead ..." Hebrews 11:12 New Living Translation*

Remember, it's how we finish in God's Kingdom that counts. We can stutter-start, question God's promises, struggle at times with our relationship with this God who makes preposterous promises. But we can get it right. We can finish the course with high grades, living in the promises made to us. Don't look back. Consider the One who promised faithful to the end, and joyfully make your way there.

November 7

Extravagant Kindness

The question wasn't asked ... just thought: "If I ask you for a drink, will you water my camels, too?"

That mental question was posed by Old Testament patriarch Abraham's servant ... on a mission to find a wife for his master's son Isaac. With little experience in the 'match-making' arena, he had devised his own spiritual fleece. "If she not only gives me, a stranger, a drink from the well, but offers to water my ten camels as well ... that will be my sign that she is the one God has chosen." (Genesis 24)

Enter Rebekah.

This Mesopotamian beauty is about to step into not only world history, but the very lineage of Jesus Himself at this moment. So her entrance is to be noted with great interest. What will she do?

Abraham's servant watches Rebekah approach. She descends to the spring, fills her water jug and comes back up preparing to take the water home. "Please," asks the servant, "may I have a drink of water?"

The tension he feels after his month long trip to be at this place at this precise time is palpable. The butterflies in his stomach are not even attempting to fly in formation. The focal point of his assignment is being viewed with breathtaking intensity.

Rebekah eyes the stranger … then the caravan of camels behind him. "Yes, of course you may have a drink," she replies. Then adds: "And I'll draw water for your camels as well!"

A minor act of kindness on her part? Absolutely not. Here was a lady willing to go way above and decidedly beyond mere kindness. Ten camels would easily drink 300 gallons of water … each jug carried up from the spring and poured into a trough.

And in this one extraordinary act of kindness Rebekah is propelled into one of the most lush, spectacular and spiritually defining stories in all of recorded history.

God still does some amazing work through human kindnesses … let Him do some of it through you.

> *"'Master, what are you talking about? When did we ever see you hungry and feed you, thirsty and give you a drink? And when did we ever see you sick or in prison and come to you?' Then the King will say, 'I'm telling the solemn truth: Whenever you did one of these things to someone overlooked or ignored, that was me—you did it to me.'" Matthew 25:37-40 The Message*

November 8
Going Up Or Down

> *"Praise be to the God and Father of our Lord Jesus Christ, the Father of compassion and the God of all comfort, who comforts us in all our troubles, so that we can comfort those in any trouble with the comfort we ourselves have received from God." II Corinthians 1:3,4 NIV*

It's amazing to watch it work. About the time I'm heading down emotionally, financially, physically or spiritually … someone nearby is on their way up. They reach out their hand and in the span of a word, a phone call, a hand on the shoulder or a prayer, there is renewed buoyancy in my life. In another time the roles are reversed. My previous comforter is in need of some of it himself. This time it's my hand, my prayer, my checkbook that provides some traction on the slippery slope of living.

Immaturity reads the above passage like this: "…the God of all comfort, who comforts us in all our troubles, so that we can be comforted and become comfortable." Even baby Christians know that that isn't how it's to work. That's putting all the emphasis on me. That's assuming that God's grace and blessing are to screech to a halt in the cul de sac where I live. And it takes the heart out of the Gospel … the Good News of God's love extended.

This week we need to take stock of our present condition. For some the tide is in, the sky is blue, the bank made a $250 error in your favor and you can almost hear angels singing. For others, the tide is out. There's nothing but debris left on the beach and the IRS has made an error not in your favor! But remember …we're all in this adventure called life together. And as believers, our hands are either reaching out for help from someone momentarily stronger, richer, smarter or we're reaching out to touch someone who needs something that we presently possess.

It's a great system.

Passing The Faith Along

"God places the lonely in families;" Psalm 68:6 New Living Translation

I was immersed in the words of an old hymn ... *In shady green pastures so rich and so sweet, God leads his dear children along ...*

It describes times of cool water bathing weary feet ... of going through waters and floods ... experiencing great sorrow, yet being able to sing a God song. Additional verses speak of both being on the mountain in sunshine and walking through the darkest of valleys. The common theme is that God is continually leading and eventually will direct us away from the mire and clay and settle us in eternity's day.

As the words were being sung I felt myself drawn into this procession of the ages. Nearby and in front of me was my father who has made it safely into that eternal day. But I sensed others ahead as well. My grandparents were a part of this eternal convoy as were D.L Moody, Charles Spurgeon and the Wesley brothers, John and Charles. Further toward the front were Augustine, Martin Luther and the early church fathers. And beyond sight, but part of the procession nonetheless, were the Biblical patriarchs of the Old Testament.

Never had I experienced such an attachment to so many believers who lived and died prior to my time on earth. It was both awesome and sobering. It was moving out from life far enough to catch the macro view of the spiritual journey we all are on. What do I owe these legions of faithful? Does their dedication and walk with God give me an addendum to my life's agenda? My responsibility to those who have gone before me didn't really dawn on me until I looked behind me.

There were my two sons, their wives and eight who call me Papa. In this grand pilgrimage, I serve as a link between those ahead and those following. I owe my spiritual predecessors the debt of passing my faith along. It's what makes praying for my family such a joyful and urgent part of every day of my life. My prayer is simply, "Lord, may all who come behind me find me faithful. And allow me to make their journey a little easier and a little more joyful."

That's a pretty hefty goal for this week.

November 10

Clean Hands and Feet

After an extremely dirty journey in an open-windowed bus coming down from a mountain retreat in China, dust covered everything. The shower was a welcomed sight. But as I washed the red dust of China out of my hair, I realized that I could never wash the memories and impact of this great nation out of my heart and soul.

In much the same way, here in China it is culturally expected that when entering a home, you remove your shoes and either 'sock it' or use slippers provided by your host. The dirt of the sidewalk and the effects of walking through environments you would not want in your home can be eliminated simply by leaving your shoes at the door.

But simply taking a shower or removing shoes cannot remove some of what we come in contact with while journeying through life. And so we must be very careful. What we 'step in' spiritually may have a long-lasting effect in our lives. It's imperative that we guard ourselves from the 'red dust' of our culture's perversions … its life-sapping cynicisms … from those deadly agents that stay with us after our showers and cosmetic clean-up.

Just as the amazing effects of this time in China will remain with me for the rest of my life, so there are actions, sights and thought patterns that will effect every day of the remainder of my life.

This week, God and I are going to be selective. There are things that the two of us will reject outright. They are dangerous to my soul and to my usefulness as a child of God. Instead, I will take the Apostle Paul's admonition from Philippians 4:8 where he tasks us thusly: " … *you'll do best by filling your minds and meditating on things true, noble, reputable, authentic, compelling, gracious – the best, not the worst; the beautiful, not the ugly: things to praise, not things to curse."* The Message

Keep more than your feet and hair clean.

Is Anything Happening?

Waiting ... we do an inordinate amount of it but never seem to get better at it.

But what about waiting on God? Does the fact that He's the One we're waiting on make it any easier? Not necessarily.

Let's say that God has given you a promise, a dream ... has etched a vision of your future on your heart. But it hasn't happened yet. It's still an unfulfilled promise, a dream not come true, a vision getting blurry with the passing of the days. What do we do in that scenario?

God's word through the prophet Habakkuk instructed: *"... these things I plan won't happen right away. Slowly, steadily, surely, the time approaches when the vision will be fulfilled. If it seems slow, wait patiently, for it will surely take place."* Habakkuk 2:3 New Living Translation

Faith is not simply waiting for something to happen. It is waiting ... knowing that while you wait something is happening!

♦ While Moses waited in the desert, God got an entire nation ready to relocate.
♦ While David hid in caves and waited, God was preparing his throne.
♦ While Job waited and worked through the darkest days of his life, God was multiplying every one of his resources.
♦ While the shepherd boy waited, Goliath foolishly moved within a stone's throw of the slingshot's range.

♦ While Elijah waited Israel worked their way through every false prophet until only Jehovah was left.

♦ While Jesus apparently waited too long, behind the scenes God was making the final arrangement for a spectacular 'resurrection' service.

Don't ever make the mistake of assuming that what you are seeing and hearing is the end of the story. God's most astounding work is done in a place quite unfamiliar and hidden from our eyes and ears, but in the fullness of time (His, seldom ours) will be revealed for all to see.

November 12

Tides In / Tides Out

I'm looking out the window at grey skies. The wind is moving through the bushes and there is snow within eyesight. The white stuff is high on a nearby hill, but even so it's not supposed to be there. This is Southern California. And the sunshine I came looking for down here they are enjoying back in Seattle in abundance.

Life.

There is variety and surprises around most corners. Life seldom comes at us straight, slow and predictable. Uphill, downhill, curves, trials, ecstasy, boredom and thrills … live through a normal month and you're likely to encounter some or all of the above.

There are times when the 'tide is out.' And with it goes strength, resources and the completion of plans. And then the 'tide comes in' and the sun breaks out, testimonies of praise pour from our lips and we're sure that God is certainly on his throne. All is well in our world.

But faith needs both environments to flourish. Important lessons come to us both at high tide and low tide. School is always in session. The Apostle Paul responded to the variables in this way: *"I've learned by now to be quite content whatever my circumstances. I'm just as happy with little as with much, with much as with little. I've found the recipe for being happy whether full or hungry, hands full or hands empty. Whatever I have, wherever I am, I can make it through anything in the One who makes me who I am."* *Philippians 4:11-13 The Message*

 It was a wise man who once penned the words "This Too Will Pass." It's not fatalism; it's not lack of faith. It's simply the understanding that life contains more than just the ingredients we want ... but in every situation there is One who maintains complete control. And He's my personal Friend.

November 13

I'll Go – Send Me

> *"We have different gifts, according to the grace given us. If a man's gift is prophesying, let him use it in proportion to his faith. If it is serving, let him serve; if it is teaching, let him teach; if it is encouraging, let him encourage; if it is contributing to the needs of others, let him give generously; if it is leadership, let him govern diligently; if it is showing mercy, let him do it cheerfully." Romans 12:6-8 (NIV):*

The Apostle Paul lists the 'equipment' God has placed within his body and expects to see used on a regular, daily basis. If you're prophetic and have a good grasp of right and wrong, then use that gift. If you're a server, then serve. If you can teach, then do it!

 If you're an encourager, don't keep it to yourself ... it defeats God's plan for your life. If you're a giver, start giving, regularly and carefully. If you have leadership qualities, then, for the Kingdom's sake, start leading. If you are compassionate, step forward in your mercy gifting.

You are not a 'lay-away' Christian … your time is now! You haven't been shelved in a back room for a season to come. The season's here.

When Isaiah had his unique encounter with this 'gift-giving God' and realized he had been made a clean person in a very dirty world, God asked, "Who should I send?" Isaiah's response? *"I'll go. Send me." Isaiah 6:1-8 The Message*

Today, the competition for our time and energies are vast, so we give God's question a different answer.

♦ "My Sunday School teacher knows more than me. Send her!"
♦ "My spouse is far more compassionate than I am. Send her!"
♦ "Hey, my pastor gets paid to do it. Send him!"
♦ "The professionals seldom make mistakes. Send them!"
♦ "He's seminary trained. Why not send him?"

But God overwork some while letting others slide. He is looking for you. There is a task with your name on it, requiring just the gifts He has put in your life. The good news? It really isn't work when you partner with Him. It's satisfying, always productive and at times hilariously joyful.

With "I'll go; send me" on your lips, obedience in your mind and anticipation in your heart, step out onto the playing field. It's game time and our Coach needs and wants you!

November 14
Big Rocks

"Seek the Kingdom of God above all else, and live righteously, and he will give you everything you need." Matthew 6:33 New Living Translation

A professor stood before a roomful of the brightest and best. All were high intensity, success-at-any-cost, go full out until you get what you are going after kinds of students. He held up a large glass jar and proceeded to fill it to the top with large rocks.

"Is this jar filled?" he asked. The general consensus was yes.

He then took a container of gravel and poured it in among the rocks until the vacant places were filled. "Is it full now?" he asked. This time most of them saw where this experiment was going. "Probably not" was their response.

"You're correct" he said as he poured almost a cup of sand into the mixture. And finally a cup and a half of water completed the filling of the jar.

"And what does this tell us?" he inquired of his now intrigued students.

"That there's always room for more when you think there isn't" came a quick reply.

"No," he said. "The truth of this illustration is that unless you put the big rocks in first, you'll never get them into the jar."

Point made.

In a day in which the 'big rocks' of relationship with God, our family and friends lay on the counter while our lives are filled with the gravel and sand of lesser things … this is an important lesson.

A Netflix download takes precedence over quiet time with God. A morning newspaper is deemed more important than conversation with a spouse. A Nascar race is valued over fellowship with a local congregation.

We 'sand and gravel' ourselves right out of the relationships that should and could mean more to us than anything else in life. At the end of our lives, we will not ask to be surrounded by our bowling trophies, reruns of favorite TV shows or a record of the games of Trivial Pursuit that we won.

This week, contemplate the important things that will make your life complete when it is completed. And get those into the jar first!

May you find joy (and proper priorities) on your journey!

November 15

Should We? Can We? Will We?

"Everyone has heard about your obedience, so I rejoice because of you; but I want you to be wise about what is good, and innocent about what is evil." Romans 16:19 NIV

There is a fascinating series of questions that confront us when challenged by a truth or command in God's Word. Let's say we've just come upon Luke 9:23 where we are told by Jesus to 'deny ourselves.' We find it just as we are about to cross the narcissistic bridge into the land of 'go-into-debt-because-you-deserve-it.'

We've all been there.

So now the first question … *should we?* Should we deny this strong pull toward self-gratification? Apparently so, since Jesus told us to. But, *can we?* Of course we can. We can turn away from the lure, say "No" to the salesman, figure out a more altruistic use of our resources.

At this point the winner is yet to be determined. The choice between egoist and humanitarian lies before us. Will I be selfish or noble? The outcome always comes down to our answer to the final question: *will we?*

This challenge to obedience is a constant companion in the life of anyone wishing to please his Master. Settling it today doesn't mean I won't be confronted by it tomorrow. But answering it correctly today will make wiser choices tomorrow a bit easier.

Also found in our 'believer's operating manual' is the call to love our enemies (Matthew 5:44) Again, once exposed to truth, the first question is answered: yes I should. But can I? Can I forgive that one who has caused such penetrating pain in my life? Can I love someone who will most likely never reciprocate … who only and always expresses disrespect and loathing to me?

That answer is more difficult to breech, but with soul searching and a gritty determination to please Jesus we admit ... yes I can.

And here comes that final interrogation of the Spirit ... will I?

In the successful navigation of these three questions and answering "Yes I will" we always move toward the Father. We become more and more like his Son. We quit living for ourselves and gladly leave behind the empty feeling that accompanies selfishness. Our obedience begins taking the 'self' out of 'myself' and turns the 'my' into an obedient lifestyle that allows room in our lives for all that God has been wanting to give us.

Is it worth it? I'll let you answer that question yourself!

November 16
Questions

When God asks you questions, He's not looking for information.

When God asked Adam and Eve where they were and what they had done, it wasn't because He didn't know. He wanted them to acknowledge the answers.

When God asked Job where he was when the heavens were set in place, He knew full well that Job hadn't been anywhere close to the action. He wanted Job to admit his limitations and have his pride dealt with.

When Jesus asked the disciples who people thought He was, He already knew the talk going around. He wanted them to analyze their own perception and confidence in who He really was.

When God asked both Moses and teenager David what was in their hands, He could see the staff and the slingshot quite clearly. He was fishing for an awareness that with His help the meager utensils they possessed would be more than enough for the job He was giving them.

When God asks questions it's always for our benefit. We are the ones who need the enlightenment, the encouragement, the change of perspective. Questions serve the purposes of God very well. They get us involved and thinking. We begin to see what previously was obscure. His job is to ask the questions ... ours to grapple with the answers and the implications of those answers.

This week what questions might God ask you? Perhaps, "What's that in your hand? Can I use it?" Or "Do you know where you're going?" Maybe you'll hear Him ask "How much do you love Me?" The one I get asked more than any other seems to be "Do you really trust Me?"

Knowing that He already knows all the answers makes me more aware of how seriously I need to take the inquiries. My correct and honest answer is important to God, but I'm the one who benefits the most, because my response to Him assures me of ongoing guidance and unbroken fellowship and I want those things desperately.

"Test me, Lord, and try me, examine my heart and my mind;"
Psalm 26:2 NIV

November 17
Happily Ever After

"A crowd soon gathered around Jesus, and they saw the man who had been possessed by the legion of demons. He was sitting there fully clothed and perfectly sane, and they were all afraid. [16] Then those who had seen what happened told the others about the demon-possessed man

and the pigs. ¹⁷ *And the crowd began pleading with Jesus to go away and leave them alone." Mark 5:15-17 New Living Translation*

What is there about the absurdities of life, that when fixed, scares us so much?

Why, when the grotesque becomes normal does it shake our world up?

The verses above should fall under the category "and they all lived happily ever after." It's the perfect ending to a truly disastrous life. Jesus comes upon a man whose life had been controlled by demons. The possession was so complete that this naked wild man lived in the cemetery and roamed the wild countryside. Even chains could not hold this man and his terrorizing behavior in check.

Until Jesus crossed his path.

In short order the man was released from the demons, was fully clothed, in his right mind and sitting quietly at Jesus' feet. And that scared the townspeople more than the demoniac's previous conduct. What's wrong with this picture? Someone has said that when the subnormal becomes normal, then normal is seen as abnormal. And we live in such a cultural miasma.

These are times that our parents and grandparents could never have seen coming. Destroy an eagle's egg and you're in trouble with the law; but destroy the life of your unborn baby and that's fine with the law...even protected by the law. In a culture that glorifies greed, lust and an 'every-man-for-himself' attitude, Godliness with contentment has become an abnormality.

Today you will have opportunities to lay the real alongside the fake. You can make decisions based on love and care and integrity that will help those around you realize that they have been riding a bicycle with crooked handlebars. You can establish patterns and strengthen habits that prove the abiding effects of living for something bigger than anything in this world.

Because, after all, God does want us all to live happily ever after.

Leaving An Inheritance

It's funny what being seventy years old does to a person.

You pay special attention to things that previously never crossed your mind. And you forget about lots of stuff that used to be very important to you. I've come to the conclusion that God planned for that to happen.

Even Scriptures contains truths that, while always there, somehow stayed concealed… until we're ready to deal with them with a bit more objectivity than we had when we were younger.

And so, it came to pass, that as I was reading in the book of Proverbs, chapter thirteen and from the Living Bible paraphrase, this caught my attention: *"When a good man dies, he leaves an inheritance to his grand-children;"* Since I think of myself as a fairly good man (with gobs of help from all three members of the Trinity!) and since at my age you might say that I've been back inside for quite a while after the last recess of the day, it seemed good to ponder this verse.

Having spent almost fifty years in the ministry, the likelihood of leaving anything financially extravagant is about as likely as me being able to understand Pokemon before I die. So I've looked at other things of value to leave behind. Those would include: a good name, a history of obedience to God's will for my life, the example of the growing love I've had for their mother for almost fifty-one years and a model of never taking yourself so seriously that you can't laugh…even at yourself.

But now I've got eight grandchildren to think about! What do I leave behind for them? They probably don't need a lot more stuff. And their young expectations of Grandma and

Grandpa aren't all that complicated...just be willing to hang out with them, love them and occasionally cut them a bit more slack than their parents would. So what else do we leave them?

Here's my plan: I will love them so completely that even across the country, they can lie in their beds at night and feel my love. I will diligently look for their strengths and promote those and will take note of their weaknesses and struggles and come alongside them in prayer and counsel to see each of those minimized, for God's sake and theirs.

So what about you? What kind of gifts will the work of your hands and the work of your heart be in the lives of those who follow you?

> *"We have a priceless inheritance—an inheritance that is kept in heaven for you, pure and undefiled, beyond the reach of change and decay." I Peter 1:4 New Living Translation*

November 19
The Crosses

They're imbedded in the sand on the side of a seldom-used two lane blacktop here in the desert. Two simple crosses serving as memorials to two friends who both lost their lives on April 25, 2003. The shadow of a power pole and the occasional tribute of an unopened can of beer left beneath the crosses, give some hint at what may have contributed to their deaths.

For Kris Folsom and Clifford Drew, their road ended at the side of this one.

What had they been told about the Life Giver? Had they ever been formally or informally introduced to the One who conquered death so that they wouldn't have to be defeated by it? During slightly more than two decades of living had Jesus ever been made to come alive in their hearts and imaginations?

Were they ever given the opportunity to sample the abundance of life that only comes from knowing Life?

Walking past those crosses reminds me that there are many crosses that have been planted by people who at one time or another came into my life. Some left this world alongside a highway. Others left their cross on a battlefield half a world away. Some planted their cross in an Intensive Care unit at the hospital.

Pay attention to the crosses serving as memorials for the lives of those no longer with us and remember, in God's Kingdom there are seldom just 'chance encounters.' Be willing to share the Good News with those you have an opportunity to interact with.

Today I just may spend some time with another Kris or Clifford who are about to plant their own cross. They deserve to hear about the goodness of God ... of his Son's amazing trip to his own cross to bear the weight and penalty of their iniquities.

In sharing this good news I realize that no action may be taken by the one I share it with. Nevertheless, no one should plant their cross without coming face to face with the redemption found in God's cross.

"He that winneth souls is wise." Proverbs 11:30 KJV

November 20
Steps

We recently attended the graduation of our grandson Weston. He comes in number 7 in our grandkids and appears to be the last. He was graduating from pre-school with about as much pomp and grandeur as my high school graduation had!

Tomorrow we celebrate yet another grandson's graduation from the eighth grade. Each event marks a serious step forward in life. So much of life is calculated and marked by the steps we take.

* first faltering baby steps into Dad or Mom's outstretched arms
* the steps across the stage to receive diplomas from pre-school through college
* those exciting steps down the aisle to be joined to the love of your life
* steps pacing hospital waiting rooms awaiting the arrival of a new family member
* the steps along a career choice, including stops, steps backward and steady movement forward
* steps that slow a bit as time goes by and strength weakens

We refer to 'the first step' … 'a step in the right direction' … are encouraged to 'step up to the plate'. To the casual observer, our steps appear random, haphazard and even accidental. And to us they may often be just that.

But there is Someone to whom the steps of our lives are anything but chance. There is a Heavenly Father who charts the path of our steps while we still dwell in our mother's womb. As the Psalmist said in Psalm 37:27: *"The Lord directs the steps of the godly. He delights in every detail of their lives." New Living Translation*

This may be a good time to 'watch your step' … to 'step out' in faith … or to 'step over' some obstacle in your life. But it's a really good time to reflect on the intimate care of the Step Watcher who is delighting in every detail in your life!

May there be joy for your journey!

November 21

Miracles From Unexpected Directions

Miracles often don't come from the direction we are looking.

In II Kings 5 we are introduced to Naaman, a decorated soldier who had brought great victory to his Commander in Chief, the king of Aram. Naaman is valiant, trusted and apparently indispensible ... and he has leprosy.

His wife's servant girl suggested that he go to Israel and be prayed for by the prophet who lived there. Desperate to be cured, he took gifts of silver, gold and fine clothing and with his entourage found the home of Elisha. With all the markings of a 'state visit' Naaman expects certain protocol to be followed for him to receive his healing.

His servant knocks on the door and a servant, not the prophet greets them and says, "My master told me to tell you to go and dip yourself seven times in the Jordan River and you will be cured."

Naaman was disappointed and angry. "I expected him to come out, greet me and wave his hand over me as he appealed to his god ... but, dip seven times in a muddy river? It's absurd. It's illogical. It's demeaning. At least he could have had me dip in our own rivers; they're cleaner than any of the water around here!"

Naaman almost walked away from his miracle. And if it weren't for the urging of his men, he would have returned to his own land still leprous and dying.

We, like him, sometimes look for 'rational miracles' which by definition is an oxymoron. There's nothing rational about God's supernatural dealings in our lives. But because we attempt to understand the incomprehensible we are often caught by surprise with not only the miracle, but how it arrives.

We're at the dock, waiting for our 'ship to come in' when God is arriving at the airport with our miracle. We're looking to the east, when it approaches from the west. We assume it will come via angels when it's coming through a friend. We listen for something loud when it comes softly.

Remember, God has many ways of meeting the needs in our lives. We sometimes ask for only a pain reliever when He wants us to have the cure. What is 'mind blowing miraculous' to us is simply ordinary to Him.

Give God the latitude to come into your life according to His expectations and plans for you … not just your expectations from Him.

> *"You are the God of great wonders! You demonstrate your awesome power among the nations." Psalm 77:14 New Living Translation*

November 22
When Belief Becomes Faith

Mike was babysitting his five year old daughter Melissa while he was repairing the roof. Not a good combination in the best of times.

As Mike returned to his ladder after a visit to the garage to get a tool, he found Melissa on the roof, grinning widely. As he began ascending the ladder, she began running from his advance, further endangering herself. He backed down and asked her to sit down, but she had a growing fascination with 'edges.'

Realizing that he couldn't get to her fast enough by climbing the ladder, he positioned himself under her and told her to jump. She looked down, saw her dad below and at even her young age, believed that her dad could catch her.

But it was at the moment her feet left the roof that her belief because true faith!

♦ Abraham's belief in God's promise of his becoming the father of a nation … became faith when he raised the knife over his son (his only son!) *Genesis 22*

♦ Gideon's belief that God would use him to free his people from the Mideonites … became faith when he set out at night with just 300 men to face 135,000 tested enemy soldiers. *Joshua 7*

♦ Peter's belief that Jesus' invitation to water-walk was do-able ... became faith when with feet in/on the water he let go of the side of the boat. Matthew 14

♦ Moses' belief that God's rescue could get Israel to the Promised Land ... became faith when he stretched out his walking stick over the Red Sea as a vast multitude of his disbelieving fellow-countrymen looked on skeptically. Exodus 14

♦ And Israel's fledgling belief in Moses and his God ... be-came faith as they stepped between the towering walls of water and made their way across the Red Sea

There is no question but that our belief systems need testing. Otherwise it's just so many words coming out of our mouths. As some point we will be required to act on our confes-sion. God is wanting the words of our mouths to be backed up by an assurance in our hearts.

It's possible to speak positively about things we aren't posi-tive about. But when faith's been tested, then the mouth begins speaking out of the abundance of those convictions. Those words are powerful and priceless.

Be ready for your beliefs to be challenged until they turn into faith. Our world needs to see the reality behind what we've been saying!

November 23

Bark At Your Own Stuff

"Summing it all up, friends, I'd say you'll do best by filling your minds and meditating on things true, noble, reputable, authentic, compelling, gracious—the best, not the worst; the beautiful, not the ugly; things to praise, not things to curse." Philippians 4:8 The Message

We have a 'grand dog' living with us on our acreage in the desert. She belongs to our son David whose temporary backyard cramps the style of an 80 pound lab. DD (David's Dog) has a habit shared by many of her canine relatives.

She barks at what other dogs bark at.

She can be laying near me as I work in the yard ... hear a dog bark in the distance ... and immediately take up their excitement over whatever it is that has excited them. She's clueless as to whether they've seen something, smelled something or heard something. If they're barking, she's barking.

Kind of like many of us in this 'share-everything-with-everybody' culture we're wrapped in. We applaud people and events that don't deserve our ovation. We gush because someone around us gushed.

We've lost that spiritual discernment over what is important and what isn't ... over what is acceptable and what isn't. There are people who bark over things that if we admitted it, don't even deserve a glance, let alone a bark.

If we are people of the Word, then we have a really good idea of things worthy of our accolades. In the Scripture above we are told that if something is true, noble, right, pure, lovely or admirable ... it then qualifies as excellent and we are to bark at those kinds of things. Run those attributes through your 'bark filter.'

Decide to write your own life story and write it in the first person. Don't indiscriminately begin to bark just because someone is holding up the "Applause" sign.

There are people doing the noble thing, there are lofty ideas and concepts far removed from 'gutter culture,' there are sacrifices being made for the good of others, there are pure, lovely and admirable deeds being done all around us.

Cheer for them! Encourage them with your support. Never applaud something that Jesus died to redeem us from.

November 24

Ingredients

I don't like mustard. Never have and probably never will.

However, yesterday while thoroughly enjoying my daughter-in-law's exceptional meatloaf I discovered that part of her 'secret sauce' coating the outside and leaving it with a fabulous crust ... was mustard.

Now at 69 years of age I can no longer categorically say that I don't like mustard, because in that sauce and with those other two ingredients, mustard played an important and tasty part.

Ingredients.

Romans chapter eight talks about the ingredients of life. If given the choice we'd leave some of them out of God's recipe for our lives. Note: *"And we know that all things work together for good to those who love God, to those who are the called according to His purpose." Romans 8:28 New King James Version*

I'm pretty sure that the Greek rendering of 'all things' should read 'all things.' And that's where the rub comes. For included in those 'things' are things we don't like. Never have and probably never will. Things like disappointments, broken hearts, hurting bodies, betrayals and bewildering trials that at times come from all points on the compass.

Although we don't like them or the flavor they leave in our mouths, they are part of the mixture of life. And we can be sure of this: Regardless of their origin (some from the beneficent hand of God, others come as byproducts of living in a fallen world) God is combining them into a winning recipe that will both bless us and accomplish his purpose for our lives.

So don't panic if something distasteful to you is being added to the mix. Trust the Chef on this one. Somewhere down the line your life will be put on the buffet table and in front will be a sign that reads: "Taste and see that the Lord is good."

Your life will bring glory to God and satisfy the hunger of those around you.

Ingratitude

"After that generation died, another generation grew up who did not acknowledge the LORD or remember the mighty things he had done ... " Judges 2:10 New Living Translation

Ingratitude ... the culprit behind so much bad behavior.

It ignores blessings ... it assumes entitlement ... it breeds jealousy ... it refuses to be content ... it drives life unmercifully ... it ends up the cruelest taskmaster.

When King Solomon gave Hiram the king of Tyre twenty Galilean towns to thank him for the wood he supplied for building the temple, Hiram glanced at the gift and sneered, "Worthless!" (I Kings 9) INGRATITUTDE

As soon as Israel settled in to the Promised Land with all the perks associated with that astounding gift, they looked around for another god to worship. (Judges 10) INGRATITUDE

When Joseph interpreted the cup-bearer's dream and told him he would be freed in just three days, he asked simply to be mentioned to the king when the cup-bearer stood before him again. The man promptly forgot Joseph and his request. (Genesis 40) INGRATITUDE

Jesus changed the lives of ten lepers forever when He healed them and restored them to full citizenship. One returned to thank him while the others felt they were owed the miracle and their sense of entitlement eliminated the need to say "Thanks." (Luke 17) INGRATITUDE

Just as God through Joseph foretold the cup-bearer's future, He told us what life would be like in our day: *"You should know this ...that in the last days there will be very difficult times. 2 For people will love only themselves and their money. They will be boastful and proud ...and ungrateful. They will consider nothing sacred." II Timothy 3:1,2 New Living Translation*

And ungratefulness does that. It considers nothing sacred. In other words, it fails to comprehend that behind every good gift in our lives; behind every material blessing; behind each fulfilled dream stands an incredible God. It fails to see the many links connecting Him to our lives in a myriad of ways.

When blessed in any way, I want to be quick to connect the dots. I want to acknowledge God not only for who He is, but also for what He does in my life. Ungratefulness may be at epidemic proportions around me, but in me God will find a truly thankful heart.

November 26
Inclusive Thanks

"Be joyful always; pray continually; give thanks in all circumstances, for this is God's will for you in Christ Jesus." 1 Thessalonians 5:16-18 NIV

How very much like God's Word ... to challenge the conventional thinking that often goes on between my two ears. That verse could easily have encouraged us to give thank 'for good circumstances' or for 'anything that has blessed you.' But the word 'circumstance' for which we are to be thankful is preceded by a word that expands the instructions until they include 'all' circumstances.

I'm sitting at my computer in this Thanksgiving season, working on my 'list.' You know 'the list.' It's that selective sampling of the past year, drawing from it those people, events, gifts and blessings that brought me joy and happiness. It typically excludes bummers, disappointments, let downs, trials, illnesses, deaths of friends or family members, tight budgets, doing without, etc.

But God tells us through the Apostle Paul to make these trips down memory lane inclusive … not exclusive. Our list of things to be thankful for must include 'all circumstances.' Maturity calls for seeing God's hand and his provision in all things, not just those which brought a smile to our face or money into our bank account.

Can you thank God for the period of trial that raised your awareness of God's comfort? Can you appreciate the financially tight times that proved that God doesn't walk away from his kids? Can you find any satisfaction in that illness that brought friends close and gave you an opportunity to rework some priorities in your life?

Did the betrayal of a close friend help you understand what Jesus went through for you, without a whimper or complaint? Did that devastating death give you a closer view of heaven and a deeper desire to get there someday?

This week, can you give thanks in all things and find joy in your journey … all of it?

November 27
Thanksgiving: Ponder This

WARNING: THIS MESSAGE MAY MESS WITH YOUR PLANS FOR THE WEEKEND!

"So, how was your Thanksgiving?"

"Tiring, but so worth it. Watched a couple of games on TV before we grabbed a chicken salad sandwich and then headed to BestMart to get in line. I wanted one of the $25 50 inch plasma TVs, but there were already 150 people in line who got there on Tuesday. But, hey, came away with a new HDMI cord, several movies that I had wanted and a $35 printer as a backup in case either of my present ones give out."

"Wow … I'm tired on your behalf. Bet you were glad for a quiet Saturday."

"Oh no, Saturday was just as busy. Black Saturday/Small Business Shopping Day. Probably spent as much time driving around as we did shopping, but you should see the stuff in the trunk. It was pretty awesome. But I will be glad to get to stay home Monday and shop. Cyber Monday you know."

"Well, at least you probably got your Christmas shopping done, right? That's got to be worth some of what you went through."

"Actually, I doubt we got any Christmas shopping accomplished. Mostly things we saw and needed ourselves … maybe not necessarily needed, but saw and wanted. Anyway, it was pretty awesome. What did you do?"

"Had the whole family over … turkey came out about one and somehow got all of us around the table. Can't remember when I ate more, laughed more or enjoyed more. Couldn't help but stare at each of the grandkids and ponder where time has gone. It's hard to believe we could eat anymore that day, but around six we made turkey sandwiches, brought out the pies again and laughed and cried our way through our favorite Christmas movie. Pretty special day, really."

"Bummer … you missed all the sales, didn't you?"

"Actually? I don't think I missed them at all."

Remember – Thanksgiving is a time to be thankful for what you have; not a day to covet everything you don't have.

" … true godliness with contentment is itself great wealth."
I Timothy 6:6 New Living Translation

May you have joy and plenty of family on your journey!

November 28
Fooling Ourselves

Do not be deceived: God cannot be mocked. A man reaps what he sows. The one who sows to please his sinful nature, from that nature will reap destruction; the one who sows to please the Spirit, from the Spirit will reap eternal life. Let us not become weary in doing good, for at the proper time we will reap a harvest if we do not give up. Therefore, as we have opportunity, let us do good to all people, especially to those who belong to the family of believers. Galaians 6:7-10 NIV

No one is going to make a fool of God … no one.

Nobody standing on a corner with fist in the air yelling, "Neener, neener, neener" ever makes God appear to be stupid. The sneering, curled-lipped proclamation "God? Why there's nothing to the myth" doesn't shake up the throne room of the Almighty. But the most obvious form of God-bashing comes from ignoring the simple truth that we reap exactly what we sow.

It would indeed be a mockery of God and his power if we could flaunt his commands with impunity … head to Tarsus instead of Ninevah and somehow get by with it. But that's the faulty thinking of many today, including, sorrowfully, many who claim to be believers.

A man sowing abuse, neglect and harshness in his family is not rewarded with loving, trusting relationships. He harvests brokenness, anger and disunity.

A woman sowing only to her career with little thought to the needs of her small and dependent children does not usually end up with appreciation from them later in life. Instead, she finds built up resentment and a relational distance that she can't cover.

A teen sowing rebellion and distrust of any form of authority never finds security or freedom, but rather gathers up the
husks of isolation, uncertainty and a growing list of regrets.

And the list goes on ... the business man who violates ethics,
the newly married who sneers at faithfulness, the student who
flaunts truth, the pastor who dismisses servanthood as unnecessary ... none will mock God's life-transforming commands. All
will reap what they have sown.

Look carefully at the words you speak, the activities you engage in, the attitudes behind both words and deeds, and see them
as seed that you are putting into the soil of your life. Then lift your
eyes and gaze into the future and contemplate the kind of harvest
you really want. If necessary, make some important corrections.

November 29

Now Faith Is ...

"Now faith is..." Hebrews. 11:1 NIV

I get a bit frustrated by people who continue to claim that faith
will get you what you want ... when you want it. To them the
bottom line is: did you get what you wanted?

To hear them talk, wanting something bad enough (faith) is
all you need. Didn't get it? Obviously you lack faith.

But when I stand that faulty theology up against what is
found in Hebrews chapter eleven, some glaring inconsisten-
cies show up. After commending the incredible faith of Abel,
Enoch, Noah and Abraham we read this: *"All these people were
still living by faith when they died.* They did not receive the things
promised, they only saw them and welcomed them from a distance. And they admitted that they were aliens and strangers on
earth." *Hebrews 11:13 NIV*

Faith to these fine folks centered on promises from God, not
desires of the heart ... faith that looks further into the future than

our immediate circumstances. Faith says, "I may not be getting everything I want or even feel I need here, but God has something far better awaiting me down the road." This is the kind of faith that can go to the grave with stuff undone and with longings unfulfilled.

It's true that through faith some walked through the sea on dry land … conquered nations, administered justice and gained what was promised. Others through faith shut the mouth of lions, quenched the fury of the flames and escaped the edge of the sword … people had weakness turned to strength and became powerful in battle. Some even received their dead raised to life!

But others, through faith, were tortured refusing to be released just to gain a better resurrection. Some, through faith, faced jeers and flogging while others were chained and put in prison. To some came stoning … to others came death by the sword. The writer of Hebrews sums it up this way: *"These were all commended for their faith, yet none of them received what had been promised. God had planned something better for us…" Hebrews 11 39,40 NIV*

And that is what faith clings to … not necessarily a better life now, free from hassles, bills and occasional physical difficulties … but to the fact that God has something better in store for all of us who week by week and day by day keep believing regardless of life's circumstances! So go ahead and believe for today, but if the answer is delayed or denied just remember that God saves some of his best gifts for later!

November 30
The Contents of Your Heart

We turn on the faucet and pure, cool water comes out … in abundance. How would we have responded in the Sinai Desert to being thirsty?

Our pantries and refrigerators have food enough for the foreseeable future. Could we have handled being hungry before the manna showed up?

With alarm systems tied into security offices, double locks on the doors and barred windows, would we have screamed in fright at Jesus walking through the storm using waves as stepping stones?

The medical community can almost do miracles and most of us are just minutes from the nearest emergency room. So what condition would our hearts have been in while walking our son, our only son to his gravesite?

Tough questions. And they're not meant to be answered by you or me right now.

Because we don't know! Our hearts are often a mystery to us.

We are often critical of the characters in Scripture who murmured, showed overpowering fear, who balked at the possibility of the supernatural and managed to work God right out of the equation. But are we any different?

In Deuteronomy chapter eight, God is replaying a bit of Israel's history. He says this:

> "Remember how the Lord your God led you through the wilderness for forty years, humbling you and testing you to prove your character, and to find out whether or not you would really obey his commands. Yes, he humbled you by letting you go hungry and then feeding you with manna, a food previously unknown to you and your ancestors. He did it to teach you that people need more than bread for their life: real life comes by feeding on every word of the Lord. For all these forty years your clothes didn't wear out, and your feet didn't blister or swell. So you should realize that just as a parent disciplines a child, the Lord your God disciplines you to help you." Deuteronomy 8:2-5 New Living Translation

Since God knows the future, this rite of discovery is not for his benefit, but ours. I desperately need to know the condition of my own heart. Is it soft? Is it hard? Does it believe easily? Is it stubborn? Can faith survive there? Can it trust God through everything?

Allow God to probe your heart. He will orchestrate your life in such a way that you will learn about it. He does it because he loves you and wants maturity in your life. And He's not afraid of disclosure! When his next test hits your desk, pick up your pencil and take it, knowing that whether you know the answers or not, you have a Teacher who wants you to pass.

December 1

As For Me

> *"But if serving the LORD seems undesirable to you, then choose for yourselves this day whom you will serve, whether the gods your forefathers served beyond the River, or the gods of the Amorites, in whose land you are living. But as for me and my household, we will serve the LORD." Joshua 24:15*

In an age of convoluted communication where "Yes" can mean yes, no, maybe or many other things… where grand-sounding speeches convey little of substance … where personal beliefs have been stripped of conviction by our culture's insistence on 'political correctness' until our words are void of meaning, let alone conviction … it's refreshing to hear someone 'tell it like it is.'

Israel is being called by Joshua to a renewed covenant with God. The climate of the day would make a slipshod response an easy one to make. Their flirtatious affairs with the gods of the surrounding nations would require a major u-turn to correct.

Joshua's challenge puts it on the line. "If you think these foreign gods can take better care of you than the God who brought you out of Egypt, destroyed your enemies, kept you safe through decades of wilderness travel and opened up the promised land to you and your children … fine. Go ahead and waste your faith on worthless deities. But as for me and my house, we're going with the God of Abraham, Isaac and Jacob!"

The force of that simple declaration has an immediate effect on the people. Their instant reply was a promise to serve the true and living God. Straight speech not only draws a crowd … it produces followers.

This week you will meet people who want to believe in something but they want to hear it from someone who actually believes it. So take your faith to the market place with confidence and conviction … it's worth more than you think!

December 2
Circadian Rhythm

It's called Circadian Rhythm and you may not be able to clap on beat, but you've got this rhythm. It's the typical biological response we have during each twenty-four hour period. Scientists can tell us that our lowest body temperature will occur at about 4:30 a.m. … that our sharpest rise in blood pressure takes place around 6:45 each morning.

Will you be tackling something that will require your maximum alertness? Do it about mid-morning. And at somewhere close to 2:30 in the afternoon you will be at your most coordinated state. Want to react quickly to avoid an accident? Just be driving at 3:30. One last hint … planning to move that heavy couch? Wait until dinner time and do it just before sitting down to eat.

Of course, this is a generalization and is only typical. However, it seems to be how most of us are wired. This explains our difficulty with work schedules that shift and why it's so hard to get off an airplane and attempt to interact with people whose circadian rhythm is fifteen hours ahead of yours!

That's what makes the words of Psalm 121 so meaningful to me this week. We're told that *"… the One who watches over you will not sleep. Indeed, He who watches over Israel never tires and never sleeps." Psalm 121:3,4 New Living Translation*

It's not that God has insomnia or that an anchovy-laden pizza has messed up his timing. The reality is that He operates on 'eternal rhythm.' So when our strength is at its weakest, He's still incredibly strong. At those times that our timing is totally off, He's as coordinated as ever. He's as alert in the middle of our nights as He is at 10 a.m. when we finally hit our 'alertness stride.'

In other words, as you move in and out, up and down, going from up to down … there is constancy available to you and to me. He never tires and never sleeps. And that's good news.

December 3

Disrupting Despair

"Let your compassion quickly meet our needs, for we are on the brink of despair." Psalm 79:8 New Living Translation

It's easy to spot.

The step slows, the eyes shift downward, shoulders slump, the future dims and the world seems a futile place. Hopelessness casts its pessimistic shadow over the landscape. Despair has arrived!

It settles in as if invited and desired. And as it blots the sun from the soul it whispers, "This is your new existence. Learn to live with it. We're going to be hanging around together for a long, long time."

But there is a powerful Disrupter of Despair … his name is Jesus.

- ◆ To the soon-to-drown, terrified disciples, He comes walking on that which terrifies them … steps into their boat and commands peace to return to their lives. (Matthew 8)
- ◆ To the disheartened sisters whose brother left them way too soon, He shouts to a recently filled tomb, "Lazarus, come on out here!" (John 11)
- ◆ To a man host to a legion of demons, living in chains in the local cemetery, He comes with freedom and a call to ministry! (Mark 5)
- ◆ To the woman whose hemorrhaging as lasted years and cost her everything He offers a simple touch that gives her back her future. (Matthew 9)
- ◆ To a blind man who despaired of ever seeing what others saw … seeing the faces of family and friends, He comes with the gift of seeing eyes. (Matthew 20)

And the list could go on and on. People's despair being permanently disrupted and turned into joy and hope and healing. Where the Despairer whispers "Quit hoping; it's hopeless. Your future is all behind you now," the Disrupter says,

> *"To all who mourn in Israel, (I) will give a crown of beauty for ashes, a joyous blessing instead of mourning, festive praise instead of despair." Isaiah 61:3 New Living Translation*

Today don't buy anything from the one who has nothing to sell but despair. His lies will keep the lid on your life, the joy from your soul and the future God has ordained from you just out of reach.

Instead, invite the Great Disrupter to do for you what He's done for so many others. He has a shipment of hope, relief and "Whew" with your name on it. He knows your address, so let him deliver it.

December 4
Taken For Granted

It was Ralph Waldo Emerson who pondered what we'd do if the stars only came out every thousand years. His response? *"No one would sleep that night, of course. The world would become religious overnight. We would be ecstatic, delirious, made rapturous by the glory of God."*

But alas, someone has observed, stars come out every night and we stay inside and watch television! So while heavens are declaring the power and majesty and creativity of God we yawn and watch a rerun of a sitcom accompanied by a fake laugh track!

It's disconcerting how we take significant things for granted just because they are routine.

♦ the kiss of a spouse at bedtime
♦ the dependability of a car over years of driving
♦ the camaraderie of a friend through decades
♦ the tight grasp of our hand by our child in a crowd
♦ and the astounding faithfulness of God

Consider:

♦ He promised to never leave us (Hebrews 13:5) ... and He hasn't - not once.
♦ He said we could count on Him to bear our burdens (Psalm 68:19)... and He has - faithfully.
♦ He said He'd accompany us through deep sorrows (Psalm 34:18)... and He's done just that.
♦ He said the waters wouldn't overflow us (Isaiah 43:2) ... and they haven't.
♦ He told us that our foundation would be his everlasting arms beneath us (Deuteronomy 33:27) ... and they've been there for us.

♦ He promised us rest in troubling times (Hebrews 4:1) …
and it's always been available.
♦ He has given us 'great and precious promises' (II Peter
1:4) to sustain us in life's storms … and they haven't been
rescinded.
♦ He said He'd take care us, drawing from his great riches
(Philippians 4:19) … and they're still available to us.
♦ He has plans for our future that are good, giving us a future and a hope (Jeremiah 29:11) … and those plans are
still in place!

Wouldn't this be a good day to reflect on the faithfulness
of God in your life? And maybe start by turning off the TV and
sitting outside tonight gazing at God's exquisite handiwork as it
silently, yet powerfully testifies of his greatness.

He's the last One you ever want to take for granted.

December 5
Green Grass

Speaking of seasons …

We're now just a couple of weeks from the official changing
of the season. On December 21st winter arrives and yet within
twenty-four hours we begin getting more sunlight each day. It's
like the promise of spring arriving on the darkest day of the
year.

And here's something else living has taught me. When
spring comes, the grass grows by itself!

That may appear to be a 'duh' observation, but there are a lot
of us who need reminding of that fact. For trying to get grass to
grow in the dead of winter is ludicrous, frustrating and futile (unless you live someplace that never freezes). However, come spring,
the grass does it on its own.

Pushing your agenda into God's established time table doesn't often work. You can plant your garden when it fits into your schedule, but the seeds may not survive. You can dance anytime you feel like it, but if everyone around you is mourning, you'll be 'odd man out.' You can attempt to explain the value of balanced and nutritional meals to your two year old, but it will fall on deaf ears ... a candy bar at dinner time makes perfect sense to her.

It's important not to fight against the seasons in our lives. I've known people who pushed their way through sheer exhaustion only to gain sheer sickness and mandated bed rest. There have been others who have kept battling long after the other side called for a truce and reconciliation. And there are far too many who are at the airport when 'their ship comes in.'

Work to fit into God's ebb and flow. Be conscious of the grander scheme of things going on in your life and the lives of those around you.

"God has made everything beautiful for its own time."
Ecclesiastes 3:11 New Living Translation

December 6
It Has To Be 'All Him'

As humans we love to celebrate our potential. There are no limits, we're told, except what your mind tells you. "If you can conceive it, you can achieve it" is another credo of the human optimists.

And a look at some of the accomplishments of our fellow earthlings would seem to indicate it.

♦ Benoit Lecomte who in 1998 swam across the Atlantic Ocean (3716 miles) in 73 days

- ◆ Dean Karnazes who recently ran 350 miles non-stop in 80 hours
- ◆ A German free diver who stayed submerged for 17 minutes and 19 seconds
- ◆ Fu Bingli, a Chinese man, who did 12 push-ups using only the index finger of one hand!
- ◆ And Mike Powell who broke a 23 year old record by long-jumping 29'4 ½:

But as much as it frustrates the 'human potential fanatics' there are some things that we will never see happen … ever.

Like someone running a mile in under one minutes … regardless of training and athleticism. Or being able to jump over a three story block wall. Or eating 4 twenty pound turkeys with all the trimmings. Or jumping off the Santa Monica pier and landing in Hawaii. Or pleasing God and making yourself fit for heaven all by yourself

And as much as it pains some athletes to come to grips with their limitations, it frustrates and chagrins mankind to admit their inability to produce righteousness. But the formula has never changed. It's by grace that we are saved, and not the result of anything else we do. There's no training program adequate … no self-induced lifestyle change that can bring it about … no amount of determination and guts that can get God to see us in a positive light.

We need Jesus! Notice the Apostle Paul's analysis: *"If you're a hard worker and do a good job, you deserve your pay; we don't call your wages a gift. But if you see that the job is too big for you, that it's something only God can do, and you trust him to do it—you could never do it for yourself no matter how hard and long you worked—well, that trusting-him-to-do-it is what gets you set right with God, by God. Sheer gift." Romans 4:4,5 The Message*

This week come to grips with grace.

December 7
Becoming Like Them

> *"They rejected his (God's) decrees and the covenant he had made with their ancestors, and they despised all his warnings. They worshiped worthless idols, so they became worthless themselves." II Kings 17:15 New Living Translation*

It's a simple biographical statement about a people who lived long ago, but oh, how it speaks of so many today. For we still become what we worship.

There are many altars before which we can bow in worship and submission. Tens of millions prostrate themselves before consumerism. Its high priests ply the airwaves with catchy phrases, using greed and fear to hawk their wares. The emptiness of accumulation soon defines those who worship there.

Others bow before the 'god of the good times' and fill their lives and week-ends with an endless array of activities which seldom satisfy completely, but extract heavy contributions that requires more and more ... more time, more investments in more stuff and ultimately, total allegiance. Again, emptiness wins.

Lest I be misunderstood ... neither good times nor nice things are forbidden in God's Kingdom. They're just not worthy of worship. In their place they are legal and a blessing to us. But never in His place. Anything that displaces the King in our lives hollows us out in the process. We were made to be far more than caretakers of junk ... custodians of full and fuller schedules. We were made to reflect the King's glory in our lives.

Israel was contemptuous of God's call, covenant and desired relationship with them. As Eugene Peterson says, *"They lived a 'nothing' life and became 'nothings' – just like the pagan people all around them." II Kings 17:15 The Message*

We have a choice to make. We must actively work to tear down the altars of gods who do not satisfy and find ourselves daily bowing at the feet of the One who came to bring abundant and truly satisfying life.

December 8

Beyond A Testimony

We're hungry for more than comforting words and good intentions ... from our politicians to our contractors ... from our children to our spouses.

We beg those who lead and represent us, "Don't say it unless you are committed to carrying through on your promises!"

But before you jump to the conclusion that this is about the people who live and work in Washington, DC ... let me inform you that this devotional is about us. This is a challenge to any of us who name the Name of Jesus as Lord and Savior.

There's never been a more strategic and critically vital time for Christians to follow up testimony with conviction. No more hiding behind comfortable clichés. No more cheap talk that's backed up with nothing but hot air.

When the king threatened the three Hebrew young men (Daniel 3:16-18) with death if they did not succumb to the cultural expectations of their day, they were ready with their testimony. *"O Nebuchadnezzar, we do not need to defend ourselves before you in this matter. If we are thrown into the blazing furnace, the God we serve is able to save us from it, and he will rescue us from your hand, O king."*

Quite a testimony. Now notice the conviction that backed up their further words: *"But even if he does not, we want you to know, O king, that we will not serve your gods or worship the image of gold you have set up."* There is something powerfully compelling about people who are willing to go to the mat over their beliefs ... who not only have the words but the conviction to carry the words through to actions.

Search your heart to see if you have the strength to back up your words with conduct. If not, keep your testimony to yourself.

The Blessiness of Messiness

For those of you who prefer your religious life to be neat, tidy, predictable and controlled ... I may have disturbing news for you. You just may have been pursuing a counterfeit experience.

A quick look at the beginnings of the early church will reveal some exciting happenings. Consider: there was the strange phenomenon of tongues of fire, unlearned languages and a mighty wind ...there were huge, unexpected crowds ... suddenly the 'cop-out Kid himself (Peter) becomes a serious and dynamic speaker ...a crippled man is healed in front of everybody ... there is a prison break ... there is a prayer meeting so powerful it almost shakes the building off its foundation ...Peter and John get the pudding knocked out of them by the religious community leaders ... a deacon gets martyred ... two congregants attempt to lie to the Holy Spirit and get permanently zapped ... the number of believers doubles every little while ... there isn't enough room in homes for everybody to live comfortably ... another deacon experienced 'time travel' ... the Church's chief antagonist becomes its most dedicated spokesman ... and the Jews lose their exclusive rights to the Messiah.

All this in just the first ten chapters of the Book of Acts!

If we wish to experience the fervor, the dynamism, the cutting edge of God's interruption in human affairs, then with the excitement will come some of the messiness that goes with it. Every event listed above brought with it a mess of some sort. But it was worth it!

Today you may get to choose between boring and exciting ... between predictability and 'what's-going-to-happen-next?' ... between your control and the force of God's movement.

When the early church finally 'got it all together' and had a place for everything and everything in those places ... it lost something marvelous: The blessiness of messiness!

But even in the mess, there is a promise:

> *"And we know that God causes everything to work together for the good of those who love God and are called according to his purpose for them." Romans 8:28 New Living Translation*

May there be joy (and a bit of messiness) on your journey!

December 10
Recalculating

I don't make it a habit of talking to inanimate objects. You won't find me conversing with fire hydrants, lamp shades or running shoes. I have nothing to say to swinging doors, stop signs or the tires on my car.

But in the summer, I do occasionally tell my tomato bush that it's doing a great job.

However ... the synthesized lady who lives in my car's navigation system and I often communicate. It happens when I take a short cut that isn't on her 'approved' routes and for twenty minutes she insists that I make a safe u-turn to get back to the route she has chosen for me.

There are times, however, when I have nothing but praise for her artificial intelligence. I will take a wrong turn or miss an intersection or get myself totally lost and far off the prescribed course. And then I see the word 'recalculating' appear and I know it's going to be all right.

She finds another route to the same destination.

Kind of like God does for us on our journeys. We run through a spiritual 'stop sign' or turn the wrong way at the right corner or fail to follow the given directions. We find ourselves lost and wonder "Can He still get me there from here?"

The answer? Of course He can. He got Jonah to Nineveh after a stubborn rejection of his instructions. He got Peter out of the slums of betrayal and back on the road of obedience. He redirected King David from adultery to righteous living.

Be assured that God can get you to where you need to be, no matter how far off the map you may have gotten. If you quit arguing and let Him recalculate, He'll have you back where you belong in no time.

> *God, my God, I yelled for help and you put me together. God, you ... gave me another chance at life when I was down-and-out." Psalm 30:2 " (The Message)*

December 11

The Beat Goes On ...

It's scary what a 'list person' can find important enough to chronicle. I've made lists of people to pray for (good list), airline flights taken over six decades (dubious value) and even restaurants that I've eaten at (even I can't see value in this one!)

My curiosity also causes some intellectual hopscotch at times. I will Google for an answer to a legitimate question and then follow rabbit trails that end up in empty rabbit holes. For instance, my search for the political climate of an area where some of my favorite missionaries serve can eventually lead me to Thrifty ice cream's most popular flavor during the winter months!

I find myself asking myself, "How did I get here?" But occasionally trivia leads me to a reflective moment with spiritual implications.

Like today.

I was taking my blood pressure and wondered how many times my heart beat in a day. (115,200) How about in a year? (42,048,000). And up to this point in my life? (an amazing 2,932,317,000 give or take several million!)

My heart beat for the first time twenty two days after my mother became pregnant with me. At its first beat it was the size of a poppy seed and has since grown into the first sized organ that has literally never stopped for almost 3 billions beats!

My amazement at this astounding creation residing in my chest had to give way to the Creator who put it there and superintends and services it daily. For my heart gets to rest between every beat, but the God who also dwells in me never has that luxury.

The Psalmist reminded Israel that their Guardian God never slumbers or sleeps. (Psalm 121:4) So from the time God nudged that seed-sized cell into motion sometime in mid-September 1942, He has been on duty watching over it and the body it lives in. It's beat incredibly fast like when I met the twelve year old girl who would one day be my wife, to slow and leisurely as I've reclined on the beaches of Maui.

But I owe it to the Creator to be more impressed by his constant care than by the equipment He placed within me that reveals his thoughtful attention.

"The Lord himself watches over you!" Psalm 121:5 New Living Translation

December 12
Why Tomorrow Is Important

"Look, I'm dying of starvation!" said Esau. "What good is my birthright to me now?" Genesis 25:32 New Living Translation

'*Now*' is often part of a fool's philosophy ... trading a future treasure for immediate fulfillment. It's saying "No" to tomorrow by saying "Yes" to now. It's thinking about the future only when it arrives.

Almost everyone is guilty of this kind of thinking at some time or another, but this concept of dealing with life is epidemic today. Tens of millions of Americans blithely squander the possibility of future security by satisfying today's hunger. They see, they want, they obtain ... without so much as a thought as to what the real cost might be a year down the road.

But consider: *There are decisions and choices in life which do not seem to have an immediate value to us, but which at a later time will have an incalculable worth to us!* I'm reasonably sure that as Esau watched his father Isaac bestowing the valued birthright on his younger brother he couldn't even remember what the stew he bartered for tasted like!

It's a politician choosing a brief illicit affair in exchange for the crashing and burning of a distinguished career, the respect of his family and the disillusionment of all who knew him.

It's the satisfaction of lighting up the first cigarette to fit into peers' expectations at the cost of years of health difficulties later in life.

It's the temptation to immerse yourself in your job at the expense of losing your family in the process.

It's the insistence of having the finest car, the biggest flatscreen, the most toys in the garage and having to live with the sound of the wolf's banging on the front door for decades to come.

And it's why God in his ultimate wisdom reminds us that we do reap what we sow. Look at Galatians 6:7 in the New Living Translation: *"Don't be misled--you cannot mock the justice of God. You will always harvest what you plant."*

This would be a great day to look as far forward in your life as you can. Decide who you really want to be ... what integrity, peace and relationships you will want to have at that point. Then travel back to today and begin making decisions that will get you there.

The advertiser was right ... you only go around once, so ask God to help you do it right!

May there be joy and wise decisions on your journey!

December 13
Enough Is Enough ... Or Is It?

"We are far too easily pleased." C.S. Lewis

In the litany of Israel's kings, Johoash fits right in. Not the worst, but not the best either. With their enemies wanting to do what Israel's neighbors are still attempting to do ... destroy them, Johoash turns to the aging prophet Elisha.

He honors this man of God who has impacted the nation so much over the years, even referring to him as "My father." With the Syrians lurking just over the horizon, Elisha instructs the king to take a bow, open the window and send an arrow in the Syrian's direction. as a symbol of God's help. The prophet places his trembling hands over the king's as the shot is made – a visual reminder that the victory will not be at the hands of the king alone!

Then something unusual happens. Elisha instructs the king to take the remaining arrows and strike the ground with them.

It's apparently a test to see the resolve of Johoash and how strong his intentions to win a complete and lasting victory.

He strikes the ground three times.

It's enough, right? No, says an angry prophet. "You should have struck the ground four or five times. Now, Israel will have limited victory, not complete." Enough was not enough.

The lesson for us is obvious. We are too easily pleased with our progress, with our devotion, with our disciplines. It's good enough to get by and it's often better than that of our peers. We are so quick to lower our expectations of what we want God to accomplish in our lives. We are prone to lower the standards by which we live.

We are satisfied with enough long before we've had enough.

To those who tell us we're doing fine and should chill out, we reply, "No, not when there's more God has for us. We will strike the ground as many times as necessary to gain the complete victory, to overcome all obstacles, to rid ourselves of any vestige of bondage in our lives."

'Just enough' is not enough as long as God has more for us.

"Not that I have already obtained all this, or have already been made perfect, but I press on to take hold of that for which Christ Jesus took hold of me. Brothers, I do not consider myself yet to have taken hold of it. But one thing I do: Forgetting what is behind and straining toward what is ahead, I press on toward the goal to win the prize for which God has called me heavenward in Christ Jesus." Philippians 3:12-14 NIV

December 14

No Time For Time

"Teach us to realize the brevity of life, so that we may grow in wisdom." Psalm 90:12 New Living Translation

I'd love more time to visit family. I'd love more time alone with Joanie, my wife. I'd love more time to travel to places I've never been ... or been to and want to return. I'd love more time to be able to stop and smell roses, find bargains or attend concerts.

But I have not been given 'more time.' Just time. When I was young, my "Time Awareness Meter" read "ALL THE TIME IN THE WORLD." It now records that I may be running out of time. But while still here, my days each contain 24 hours; my week 168 hours ... the same as you and every other living person around me.

Moses asked God to help us realize the brevity of life, "... so that we may grow in wisdom." Psalm 90:12 That wisdom becomes our life-long coach to help us manage the time issues of our lives. But I must cooperate with the coaching.

The wisest man to ever live said (Ecclesiastes 3) that there is a time for everything ... for planting, building, dancing, laughing, embracing, mending, speaking and loving. However, just because there is **a time** doesn't mean that I will use **my time** to accomplish them.

Having time for what is truly important and satisfying will require making time, taking time or finding time. No one can come up with 'more time' to replace my 'squandered time.' Time management skills or lack thereof are my responsibility.

In a football game, the 2 Minute Warning signals the need for making every play count. It's no longer hours that count ... it's seconds. No daydreaming. No wasted effort. No time to redo what was done poorly. No empty distractions. There's a goal line to get to.

And I want to live that way!

December 15
Truth In Advertising

"... but a beautiful cedar palace does not make a great king!" Jeremiah 22:15 New Living Translation

We forget that the package is not the product!

Not only can the product be inferior to the packaging, but on occasion the package contains no product whatsoever and we've been scammed and disillusioned.

We hear the pitch and buy the miracle chamois at the fair (you know, the miracle fabric the size of a handkerchief that can absorb twelve gallons of liquid when demonstrated). When we get it home it absorbs nothing; it simply pushes liquid around on the countertop!

We see the carefully prepared trailer for an upcoming 'unforgettable movie experience.' then wish we could forget it after seeing it. There are so many times when delivery on an expectation doesn't even come close to what was advertised.

And we do it with people as well. A slick speech and we're onboard. A couple of sound bites, classy apparel and they've got our vote. A convincing portrayal 'on screen' and we're ready to make them our heroes.

The Old Testament prophet Jeremiah carried a serious message to Judah's King Jehoiakim, whose packaging not only fooled the people, but himself, too. This proud king proclaims, *"I will build a magnificent palace with huge rooms and many windows. I will panel it throughout with fragrant cedar and paint it a lovely red." Jeremiah 22:14 New Living Translation*

But God isn't impressed with impressive exteriors and you can't sidetrack his assessment with fragrant cedar and lots of red paint! God sees the heart.

Keep in mind that God isn't fooled by packaging and He doesn't want us fooled by it either. There are many times a day when we must put value on something we see or something we're told. We're suckers if we don't see and hear with an eternal perspective.

Ask for it and then use it for God's sake.

December 16

He Has Risen

"Why do you look for the living among the dead? He is not here; he has risen!"
Luke 24:5,6 NIV

Jesus is often not where we think He should be...or even where we left him.

♦ The religious world was looking in halls of splendor...He was in the womb of a virgin.
♦ His parents searched among friends and family...He was in the temple.
♦ His disciples expected Him to be on the shore under cover ...He was walking on the storm.
♦ The distraught women thought He'd be in the tomb where they'd laid him...He had risen.

Jesus isn't playing games with us...this is not some cosmic game of 'hide and seek.' The problem often lies with us. We expect him to be some static, stodgy icon safely parked on a ledge in a religious institution when instead, He's vibrantly alive, always on the move with creativity and potential and with power an intrinsic part of who He is.

There are places I expect him to be, but following only my personal expectations or my history of where I've found him before, can keep me from finding him in many new and exciting places.

- ◆ I expect him at church…but am surprised to find him in the smile of a small child.
- ◆ I anticipate his presence in my devotions…but am shocked to find him in the questions of a skeptic
- ◆ I look for him in the beauty of a summer sunrise…but find him also in moments of great despair.

Today I will look for him in the unexpected places. I will not be surprised to find him fully engaged in the lives of the people I meet…not just religious people, but all people. I will not look for him only in quiet halls of religious traditions, but also in the cacophony of voices in the marketplace. And I will definitely not look for him among the dead…for He is fully alive.

I will find him this week because He has promised that if I make the search, I will not come up empty. And this will bring unbounded joy to my journey.

December 17
Grace and Mercy

"But because of his great love for us, God, who is rich in mercy, made us alive with Christ even when we were dead in transgressions—it is by grace you have been saved." Ephesians 2:4 NIV

It's like deserving a spanking and getting an increase in your allowance instead…only infinitely more incomprehensible and beyond description.

God's mercy was responsible for overlooking my sin by allowing Him to see me through his Son's sacrifice and love. My faith in the cross and its consequences made me a candidate for this extraordinary escape. The Bible says that the soul that sins, dies. Mine had and deserved the spiritual penalty, and we're not talking about a 'time out' or even a spoon to the backside. No, the penalty was to have been an eternity separated from God.

But God's mercy rescued me. Mercy is 'not getting what we truly deserve' and its synonym is "Whew! And God is rich in it and passed on his wealth to me.

But then along came grace. Mercy just released me from eternal punishment, but God's grace had something additional to offer in its place. God's grace now makes available and lays out the incredible love of God and the exquisite plan He has always had for my life. It includes the gifts He has placed in my life.

He wants to live with me forever... even constructing a palace fit for a King's kid. Can you believe it? Grace is 'getting what we truly didn't deserve' and the synonym for grace is "Wow!" We should often add this exclamation to our times of worship and reflection.

It was at the cross that both Jesus and I got something we didn't deserve. He got my sin and I got his right standing with the Father.

Thank God for his merciful cancellation of the penalty of your sin, and then get caught up in the future He has in mind for you because of his 'amazing grace.' And what this can add to your journey is beyond describing.

December 18

A Long Obedience

"Not all people who sound religious are really godly. They may refer to me as 'Lord,' but they still won't enter the Kingdom of Heaven. The decisive issue is whether they obey my Father in heaven." Matthew 7:21 New Living Translation

With the passing of my Dad I have reflected on the direction of his life, the impact and legacy of his life, the strengths and, yes, the weaknesses of the man we knew as 'Doc' Walterman. Watching the labored, final breaths helped me realize why the Apostle Paul at the end of his life used the metaphor of having 'fought a good fight.'

Much of life is a battle.

To be sure there are highlights of laughter and hilarity... great exuberance and strength...times when we almost take winning for granted. But for any child of God passing through this world, the alien culture takes its toll. It's a struggle to go out strong with faith intact and the momentum of your spirit still moving you forward. But that was my Dad.

However, my father's legacy was not that he was a religious man but an obedient man. Dad's territory to impact for God's Kingdom was 'the hill country where the giants still lived.' (See Joshua 14:1-10) God's instructions for his life were seldom accomplished with ease, but he followed those directions with the determination of a servant who loved his master deeply and trusted Him completely. The description "a-long-obedience-in-the-same-direction" fit my Dad quite well.

And what about you? Is obedience to the will of God more important to you than the appearance of being religious? Is your 'godliness' based on the assessment of those around you, or on the smile of God's approval? Ultimately none of us will be judged by a panel of our peers. Their expectations and standards of success will mean nothing. It is God's "Well done, good and faithful servant" that will be the final grade that means everything to us. Let joy join you on your journey.

December 19
These Doors To Remain Open

These doors are to remain unlocked during business hours.

Ever sat sipping your latte at Starbucks and glanced at the aluminum sign above the inside of the doorway? Ever wondered what sort of stupid litigation forced a federally mandated sign to be posted in every business in America? What business owner in her right mind would want the doors locked during the business day? Well, the history is tragic, but interesting.

A fire in a 'sweatshop' in New York City in 1911 started the process. In a fifteen minute period 146 underpaid and overworked women lost their lives when a fast moving fire showed the owner's greed and lack of safety measures when the women found exit doors locked and blocked, fire escapes inoperable, and aisles too crowded with sewing machines to make escape possible. The garment union set in motion a federal mandate that would eliminate the chance of another disaster like this from happening again.

But back to the original question…what enterprising person wants the doors to her business locked during the times when commerce could be moving? And moving this discussion into the realm of God's Kingdom, what thoughtful person would ever conceive of the doors of the Church being locked during business hours, knowing that we market what every person in the world is looking for?

What great time to let the Church out of its business box… to get rid of 'normal operating hours'…to give the Body of Christ another address than the corner of First and Main Streets. The Church suddenly has branch offices all over town! You don't need permission to take the Good News outside the box because God's Word makes it clear that indeed you actually ARE THE CHURCH.

That may not be the best news you've heard today, but for those who don't know Jesus Christ personally, the 'church on the street' could be bringing them the best news they've heard today. Be joyful on your journey.

"Then he said, "Go into the world. Go everywhere and announce the Message of God's good news to one and all.

Whoever believes and is baptized is saved;" Mark 16:15
The Message

December 20
Christmas Dreams

I dreamed a dream in time gone by
When hope was high
And life worth living
I dreamed that love would never die
I dreamed that God would be forgiving…

I had a dream my life would be
So different from this hell I'm living
So different now from what it seemed
Now life has killed the dream I dreamed.
Fantine "Les Miserables"

In the stage adaptation to Victor Hugo's morally-rich story "Les Miserables", we meet Fantine. She's a single mom with a daughter living far away under the suspect care of con-like inn keepers. And having recently lost her job she is being pushed into a life of prostitution. Two short passages from her despondent soliloquy are found above. Read them again.

Oh, how she speaks for multitudes around us.

Life begins with dreams intact…there is every reason to hope for the future…the sky looks incredibly blue up ahead. And then life happens! The enemy of the human soul loves to steal dreams and turn them into smoldering piles of foul-smelling ashes. And it's happened to millions of people who populate your world.

Try to see past the glassy-eyed look of the holiday shoppers. Read between the lines in the hyped attempt at levity. Discern what's behind the slumped shoulders and quickly fading smile when people don't think they're being observed. There are a myriad of slaughtered dreams around us...too many are already living in hell.

Is there spiritual work for people of peace living in a land of chaos? Can the forgiven find a job among those living under the heavy yoke of condemnation and guilt? Can we find gainful employment as light-bearers among those who sit in stifling darkness?

To the Fantines of our world, Christmas must contain God's message spoken through Jeremiah the Old Testament prophet: *11'For I know the plans I have for you,' says the Lord . 'They are plans for good and not for disaster, to give you a future and a hope. In those days when you pray, I will listen.'" Jeremiah 29:11,12 New Living Translation*

Let's help the Fantines around us to find God's forgiveness and see their dreams re-ignited.

December 21
Give Some Grace

"So how are you doing pushing back against the cultural crush of Christmas commercialism?"

Having asked that question, you'd think I'm some kind of a religious 'Scrooge' who in his theological purity despises all but the narrowest of celebratory frivolity.

Not so. But a couple of comments may help keep things in perspective.

- ♦ This is a thoroughly religious holiday season. No arguments allowed.
- ♦ It would hold little significant meaning to us if it were otherwise.

♦ As followers of Jesus, we're expected to see through the tinsel to the truth ... through the wrapping paper to the Babe in Mary's arms.
♦ The secular culture, however, does not have this foundational truth to build a celebration around, although it's available to them.
♦ Therefore we should not be offended if they don't see Christmas through our eyes. Our feeling should be one of sorrow ... our hearts pained because the Greatest Gift to humanity is lost under all the 'stuff.'

I believe we hold non-believing people to a higher standard than they have signed up for ... all in our desire to see them become acquainted with the Savior as we have. And sometimes, in our hunger to see them believe and respond we get a little mold on our attitude! There is an edge to our voices. We come across a bit superior and haughty.

Haughty ... not humble. Hardly a winning way to woo!

So what do we do with all this? Celebrate simply, yet with abandonment. As much as possible project the joy promised the shepherds on that first Christmas night. Don't be overly concerned that everyone is getting it right. You get it right and celebrate with a joyous, optimistic heart.

It's fine to push against the surge of commercialism ... just don't begrudge the celebration of people who as yet haven't visited the manger and met the Baby personally!

May there be joy (and humility) for the journey

December 22
The Hopes and Fears

"I have come that they may have life, and have it to the full." John 10:10 NIV

God and man got off to a rather rocky start back in Eden. That's when we came up with our own version of religion called "I Did It My Way."

When the mountain thundered and shook at God's presence and Moses came down with God's expectations carved in rock no less, we assumed He was less than happy with us. The Psalmist picked up our apprehension when he asked God, "Will you be mad at us forever?"

Our paranoia in God's presence reached its low point during the Dark Ages, when thought and art made it painfully clear that none of us was getting a passing grade from our Creator.

As the Old Testament comes to a close we find the silence of God suffocating. For 400 years He doesn't speak. Our apprehension grows while our hopes struggle for survival. We can't help but wonder if God has had just about enough of us and is calling his experiment with mankind a failure.

♦ I had hoped to meet his approval, but feared I hadn't.
♦ I had hoped He'd see me in a good light, but feared the darkness of my life made me all but invisible to Him.
♦ I had hoped that the good things I did would outnumber the bad things … but feared they didn't.

But just when hope was nearly extinguished, I spotted a Light in the darkened streets of Bethlehem. Drawing near I found myself looking down into a tiny face … the very face of God. And in that moment came the realization that I had totally misunderstood God.

He had come to pardon, not to punish! He was here to vindicate me, not victimize me! His plan was to lavish love, not mete out judgment! The hopes and fears of all the years met God face to face … and hope won!

May the joy of Christmas give your journey significance!

December 23
Attempted Robbery

The greatest heist in the history of burglary has to be the attempted stealing of Christmas from our culture. At first it was more of a slight of hand ... a 'pick pocketing' of preferred tradition. It's just a different way of doing what you've always done, we were told. So we reluctantly accepted the changes.

But the 'hand in our pocket' soon became a mugging in the alley and the comforting norms and monumental meanings of the season were stripped away and we were left with something quite cold and sterile ... a winter holiday if you will.

Any thinking person, however, would have to admit that Christmas is certainly more than a cold weather Columbus Day! There's a powerful reason why the entire world feels the seismic disturbance of this celebrated day.

It's not just that we need another day off ... not just because we need another excuse to make an extravagant meal (I've hardly worked off Thanksgiving's turkey!). We don't need Christmas to help the merchants finally realize a profit for the year. And the celebration isn't even about people loving enough to want to give gifts to family, friends and sometimes total strangers.

Oh no. There's only one reason why this holiday deserves every bit of the attention it gets. Because it's our yearly reminder of the thunderous gift of God in the sending of His Only Son to walk among us, and then offer Himself as a sacrifice for our sinful waywardness. The coming of that Babe of Bethlehem is still changing lives, families, communities and entire nations. It's that momentous!

So this week, while the mall plays songs that talk about snow, presents, trees and Old Saint Nick, I'll hype Jesus every chance I get. I'll say less about those who have stolen Christmas and more about its significance to me. I will not let their loss of meaning steal one speck of my joy nor diminish my awe of God coming down the stairway of heaven with a Baby in his arms.

> *"God wasn't attracted to you and didn't choose you because you were big and important—the fact is, there was almost nothing to you. He did it out of sheer love ..."*
> *Deuteronomy 7:7 The Message*

May you find joy and relevant, meaningful celebration this month.

December 24

God's Wish List

I have no gold. Not even a sixteenth of an ounce. I think I'm allergic to frankincense. And I wouldn't recognize myrrh if someone smeared some on the back of my Christmas sweater. So what do I give the Babe of Bethlehem this year? What's on the 'wish list' of the One who appears to have it all?

It's not that we don't offer Him anything. He regularly gets stuff from people ... mostly from religious people. We don't give him old ties or second-hand shoes, but He does get broken promises and half-fulfilled commitments. We don't box our unused, duplicate appliances, but He does get our left-over strength ... our almost depleted energy. (Even at Christmas we give Him second billing to snowmen, red-nosed reindeer and an imaginary fat man who promises the world but in reality has nothing to give!)

We assume that anything that comes from us carries high value to God and is automatically prized by Him. But that isn't true.

A similar 'wrong gift' scenario is found in Psalm 50. God's people were busy presenting gifts that had little meaning to God. Some were even sacrificial in nature. They assumed they were giving things to God that He needed and longed for. But God is not secretive about what He would like from us.

"What I want from you is your true thanks; I want your promises fulfilled. I want you to trust me in your times of trouble, so I can rescue you, and you can give me glory."
Psalm 50:14,15 The Living Bible

There it is ... God's wish list. He wants our thankfulness, not as an afterthought but as a way of life. He wants us to keep our word ... with Him and others. He really prizes integrity and faithfulness. And most astounding of all, He receives great joy when we need Him! He loves it when we throw ourselves on his strength and rely fully on the love He has for us.

These are gifts God always wants. He can never have too many of them. Take an honest look at what you normally give to God. Then look again at the list from Psalm 50 and resolve to give Him what He really wants. May this coming year be one in which you and God both get meaningful gifts.

May you experience wonderful joy for your journey! And from Fresh Heart Ministries comes a prayer for a most joyous Christmas ever!

December 25
Christmas, Not a Grudge

God made Christmas available. Our sins made it necessary.

That's the reality of Christmas that few celebrate. Even Christians don't really get around to acknowledging the 'why' of the Virgin Birth until Good Friday. It's the dark side of the holidays, if you will.

We prefer to wrap ourselves in the lights, the beauty of our nativity crèches and songs about peace on earth and goodwill accessible and abounding. The warmth and potential of the

Christmas season offer us so much! We are more comfortable celebrating the *fact* of the Incarnation rather than the *reason* for it.

And lest I steal your joy, let me hurry to add ... God wants us to concentrate on the thrill of his rescue. Our rescue from sin, from unbreakable habits, from despair ... from ourselves at times! He went to great lengths to steer our festivities in this direction.

He could have conveyed the Christmas story from an entirely different perspective. His conversation with us could have sounded something like this: "I hope you appreciate what I'm doing for you here. Don't ever forget what your selfish, destructive sin cost me. I had no other choice but to come and get you out of the mess you got yourself into. I want you always to see me as the Rescuer you had to have."

But He came to us reading from an entirely different script! From the pen of the Apostle Paul who knew both the fact of and the reason for God sending his Son ... from a man whose theology is quite sound ... comes this treatise on the subject: *"And I am convinced that nothing can ever separate us from God's love. Neither death nor life, neither angels nor demons, neither our fears for today nor our worries about tomorrow--not even the powers of hell can separate us from God's love." Romans 8:28 New Living Translation*

It's God's love, not his grudge that we bask in. In coming for us to establish a permanent relationship, He carries no rancor, bitterness or resentment. Every indication proves repeatedly that his was a liberation of love ... a love so formidable and all encompassing that He was willing to pay any price to make it happen.

God is welcoming you to his extravagant Christmas party with only the purist of intentions. He wants your love, not your fear. He desires that you be filled with hope, not guilt. It's true that our sinfulness necessitated him coming, but he came, not with finger pointing but with arms outstretched.

Enjoy this Season of your journey! It's what He wants!

December 26
Tea Bag Thanks

Our grandsons Jackson (10) and his brother Weston (9) were opening their Christmas presents from us. We had been informed that they would both really appreciate gift cards from Amazon. Not having any legitimate Amazon boxes for the cards, Joanie used a couple of empty tea bag boxes that seemed to fit the purpose nicely.

I didn't catch the exact moment the wrapping paper came off the boxes, but within a minute, both of them came over to us and hugged us … thanking us for giving them boxes of tea bags!

There's no chance that tea bags were on either of their Christmas lists, yet each of them expressed thanks for a gift that hadn't met their expectations. We both laughed as we coached them to look further into the boxes, but inwardly we amazed at their ability and willingness to accept a gift with less value than they probably expected and do it with uncommon grace and maturity.

Let's face it – many today aren't satisfied with even more than they deserve. Enough just isn't for multitudes of ingrates. We're sure we should be getting more, not less. The willingness to be thankful in all circumstances is a decision not many are willing to make.

There's a saying that I've made when talking with friends about money earned during my life. "I've never been paid what I'm worth" I tell them, and then add "And am I glad!" Do I really mean that? The answer isn't quite clear, even to me.

But the truth is, few of us could have earned the kind of favor we have received from God. We're not good enough, smart enough, frugal enough or educated enough to have gotten where we are without some amazing 'outside help.'

And so as I look forward to another year in which I strive to 'get it right' I will endeavor to be thankful for both the gifts that are way over the top, leaving me awed ... and the things that didn't quite fulfill my expectations. God knows the gifts needed in my life and even if they're tea bags, I will receive them with gratitude.

Just like my grandsons!

"Be thankful in all circumstances, for this is God's will for you who belong to Christ Jesus." I Thessalonians 5:18 New Living Translation

December 27

Apparently Is Not The Same As Actually

"It looks dead out there," my wife said, looking into our backyard.

And she was spot on correct. From the brown grass to the lifeless rose bushes, the bare butterfly bush and 'branches only' fruit trees ... it all looked dead. And if I hadn't seen it happen every spring for many decades I would have assumed that we needed to tear everything out and start fresh this year.

But my plants, trees and grass could agree with Mark Twain when he said "the reports of my death have been greatly exaggerated." With the outward veneer indicating "dead!" there is a veritable detonation of life beneath the surface shouting "You'll see!"

♦ Kind of like God-given dreams that lie dormant in the cold winters of waiting for the right season to burst into fulfillment.

♦ And like the Word of God hidden away in a heart, out of sight and thought gone from memory ... when suddenly needed and anointed and thrust into a situation desperately needing God's perspective or assurance.

♦ And like the aging saint who more and more resembles death … yet inside is host to more life than this world knows what to do with.

Don't ever be misled by the outward and obvious. Real life is often camouflaged. Lazarus' life was hidden in a tomb. Daniel's life was tucked away in a 'den of death,' surrounded by hungry lions. The lives of the three Hebrew children were hidden inside a ferocious blast furnace. Elijah's future was temporarily tied to a dried up brook. Hosea's ministry potential was linked to the acute embarrassment of an unfaithful wife. Gideon starts his resume hiding from local thugs.

What you see is not always what you get!

Remember this: Despite what it may look like at the moment, life always wins over death for a believer. Light always conquers the darkest of darks. There is within us the pulsating brilliance of a life given by God that knows no winter and whose entire eternity is as sure as all of God's promises.

"God is not the God of the dead, but of the living."
Matthew 22:32 KJV

December 28
Commit or Omit?

At my age I'm doing fairly well handling the sins of commission. There are fewer and fewer things I shouldn't do that I am doing (committing). Except, possibly, driving over the speed limit!

But, hey, this is California and ten over the speed limit puts you in the pack of aging octogenarians in their fifteen year old Buicks, and gets me passed by blue haired ladies who barely can see over their steering wheels.

No, I'm feeling quite smug over the commission category of sinning. It's the sins of omission that I still struggle with. You know … the things you know you should be doing and conveniently 'omit' from your life.

It's the word of encouragement you know you are to share with someone and you clam up. It's the word of instruction from God's Word that you got last Sunday in the sermon and you choose to ignore it. It's being exposed to a legitimate need and then talking yourself out of involvement.

It's coming face to face with Solomon's words in Proverbs 24:11 (*"Deliver those who are being taken away to death, And those who are staggering to slaughter, Oh hold them back"*) and knowing it easily refers to abortion but then caving to culture's prevailing assessment that what a woman does with her body is a personal decision. So what we know to be truth deep inside is hidden from view lest we be accused of being meddlesome.

One commentary describes the sin of omission as "knowledge without practice." We as Christians have been accused of being 'educated beyond our obedience.' I think I may fit into this sad niche occasionally.

Let's work on this insidious form of disobedience. Let's be people who are not only instructed by God's Spirit, but led by his Spirit as well. That means that if God has something to say, we will say it. If He has someplace that needs us, we will go there. If He cries over sin and its effects in our world, we will cry with Him. If He says something is wrong, we won't manufacture an excuse in our hearts that makes it permissible.

If we are going to omit anything, let's omit a life that doesn't take God seriously!

December 29

Hopeful Waiting

He will not shout or raise his voice in public. He will not crush the weakest reed or put out a flickering candle. He will bring justice to all who have been wronged. He will not falter or lose heart until justice prevails throughout the earth. Isaiah 42:2-4 New Living Translation

For those of us waiting for civility, justice and normalcy to return to our world … waiting to see humanity placed on the endangered species list … waiting for our leaders to use, if not Godly wisdom, at least common sense …

For those of us wondering if things have gotten beyond God's ability to repair, these three verses should come as assurance.

Eschatology is not my strong suit. I can't argue as to whether God will fix things with us here or gone … but fix it He will. As it states above, He will not quit until justice prevails everywhere. There is coming a day, very soon, when He will put the price tags back where they belong. When an unborn baby will be worth more than an eagle's egg. Where integrity will get you more than bullying and scheming will. Where righteousness is applauded, not ridiculed.

That day is coming.

But in the meantime we need to consider this possibility: it may not arrive boisterously. Jesus may have raised his voice in the temple, but mostly his kingdom and his purposes arrived quietly with little fanfare. We assume that spiritual progress must make noise, but the Kingdom often invades stealthily.

And in the process, those of us whose hearts tremble, whose wick is flickering with questions and anxiety … for those of us whose frailty is standing against tornado-like winds, He comes with hope and healing. He will not allow the reed to break or the flame to die.

God is not in a dither … nor should we be. He isn't fraught with anxiety, nor should we be. He doesn't believe for a second that Satan is going to win this one, nor should we.

So grab hold of the hope that He offers. If you feel you are at the end of your rope, tie and knot and hang on … his cavalry is coming. You just may not hear them!

"I will exalt you, Lord, for you rescued me. You refused to let my enemies triumph over me." Psalm 30:1 New Living Translation

December 30
Trust, Then Sleep

Her name was Maria and she occupied a seat between my wife and I on an evening flight from Atlanta to Southern California recently. She was one of the last to board and took her seat slightly out of breath. Joanie asked if she were OK and after a few brief exchanges and a glass of Coke, she put her head back and slept until the last half hour of our journey.

Immersed in my reading, I took little notice of the conversation going on between Maria and my wife. But the story told was of a surprise birthday party for her elderly mother that she had missed because she had been bumped from her scheduled flight the day before. Now she was going to surprise her mother, who by this time did not expect her daughter to get to California.

Joanie asked where her mother lived. "Apple Valley" was the reply.

"Oh really," Joanie responded with growing interest. "How are you getting there once we land?"

Maria simply said, "I have no idea. I prayed as I left Atlanta for God to provide a way up there (about 60 miles over the mountains). I know He will make it possible. I told my mother to wait up pretty late because there would be a package coming to her home from me," she added with a twinkle in her eye.

My ears tuned into their conversation as Joanie said, "Well, it's interesting that God put you between two people who will be driving up to Apple Valley when we land. I guess you have your ride!"

As Maria gave thanks for God's provision I couldn't help but admire this little lady's simple, yet profound faith. She prayed for a ride, then calmly fell asleep confident that while she slept, God would do what she had no way of doing.

Today find true rest as you place your future, your ambitions, your fears, your needs safely in God's hands.

> *"I cried out to the Lord, and he heard me from his Temple in Jerusalem. Then I lay down and slept in peace and woke up safely, for the Lord was watching over me." Psalm 3:4,5 The Living Bible*

May you enjoy confidence and peace on your journey!

December 31
Raise The Bar

With the new year hours away, many are addressing resolutions. They're intended to be revolutions ... against current weaknesses and lapses. "This year it will be different!" becomes their battle cry for change.

But far too many adopt the advice I saw recently on a fortune cookie. It read: IF AT FIRST YOU DON'T SUCCEED, REDEFINE SUCCESS. So the bar is lowered:

♦ *Losing 10 pounds in January is tough ... maybe I'll work toward two pounds by Easter.*

♦ *Cutting out ten hours of TV a week is crazy ... maybe I'll just close my eyes during commercials.*

♦ *Keeping my alcohol consumption under control at parties is unrealistic ... maybe I'll just try to not throw up on my date from now on.*

♦ *Becoming Christ-like is a bit ambitious ... maybe I'll emulate one of the disciples instead.*

Ah, that's where redefining success and dumbing down standards won't work. Jesus didn't show up to lower the bar but to raise it. His call to righteous living drives the 'slouch' out of us and puts backbone back where it belongs. His standards lift us above mediocrity and let us feel good about his grace's work in our lives, lifting us up to the successes He knows we can have.

When He beckons us to follow it's along the high road ... the one going someplace special ... the one many miss on purpose because it can be tough. But it's the one on which He walks beside us every step we take.

The road of compromise may seem the easy way, but it's always a dead end. It goes nowhere and cheats us out of God's best gifts. This week, look ahead to the new year with determination to use God's standard of success, not the one found on a fortune cookie.

"I'm not saying that I have this all together, that I have it made. But I am well on my way, reaching out for Christ, who has so wondrously reached out for me. Friends, don't get me wrong: By no means do I count myself an expert in all of this, but I've got my eye on the goal, where God is beckoning us onward—to Jesus. I'm off and running, and I'm not turning back." Philippians 3:12-14 The Message

May you have great joy and expectation for your journey!

Made in the USA
San Bernardino, CA
17 May 2014